Peace Was In Their Hearts

Peace
Was In Their
Hearts

Conscientious Objectors
in World War II

Richard C. Anderson

HERALD PRESS
Scottdale, Pennsylvania
Waterloo, Ontario

We gratefully acknowledge permission from the following for quotations used in this book: *Boston Herald; Friends Journal; Harper's Magazine; Journal of Psychology;* Pendle Hill; *The Oregonian,* Portland, Oregon; Mitchell Robinson from his doctoral dissertation, Cornell University; *Saturday Evening Post; United Media;* and *The Washington Post.* Specific citations and other identifications are noted in the text.

HERALD PRESS
Copyright © 1994 by Richard C. Anderson
Published by Herald Press, Scottdale, PA 15683
     Released simultaneously in Canada by Herald Press,
     Waterloo, Ont. N2L 6H7. All rights reserved
International Standard Book Number: 0-8361-9053-X
Printed in the United States of America

1 2 3 4 5 6 7 8   00 99 98 97 96

Peace Was In Their Hearts

we are called to life
and our souls know
that killing
is against our hope
and against our belief
that man's simple destiny
is to learn
how to love his fellows
of which
war is not a part

Contents

The nature of life for a rejected minority confined to a "splendid isolation." The impact of separation and rejection. Public reaction to conscientious objectors. Post-war adjustments. Media coverage.

The richness of ideas, beliefs, and faiths from people of diverse backgrounds. The intensity of personal relationships and the growth of individual convictions. Changing beliefs about the nature of conscription.

Experiences encountered by COs in their return to civilian life after World War II. Post-war adjustments and challenges in a new world. The affirmation of beliefs and a lifetime commitment.

The survival and growth of a brotherhood of believers. The bonding and affection that grew with the years. "Friendships without equal."

The lifelong commitment to a peaceful brotherhood. The agonies and the hopes that peace is not an idle dream.

The careers of World War II COs as they practiced their faith in an enormous array of occupations. Meeting the demands of a high ideal. Reflections on personal successes, failures, disappointments, and achievements.

Preface

This story is about a group of men who "refused to go" to the killing fields of World War II—men who were classified by American conscription law as Conscientious Objectors (COs) to military service. The book will explain <u>what</u> they did during that war; but more importantly, <u>why</u> they rejected service in the military.

In the Western world, refusal to join military forces or to fight in war goes back to the pacifist doctrine of the early Christian church. In other parts of the world, pacifism is rooted in religion and social custom before recorded history. In the modern world, the United States and a growing number of other countries recognize the individual's right of conscience in refusing to fight in war. The 1940 United States conscription law exempted religious objectors—Conscientious Objectors—from military duties, requiring instead civilian "work of national importance" under civilian direction. This program became known as Civilian Public Service (CPS). Draftees were sent to forestry camps, mental hospitals, health care agencies, medical and health experiments, farms, and a wide variety of other civilian endeavors. Of the 12,000,000 people drafted by Selective Service during World War II 12,000, served in Civilian Public Service.

Another group of COs who were willing to perform noncombatant duties in the armed forces were assigned to military units as "1-A-O's". There were 25,000 so classified and inducted into the armed forces. There were others who refused to accept the government's right to conscript them for anything. Some of these were never identified by Selective Service because they did not register for the draft, while others who did register were imprisoned for refusing to comply with the draft law. How many people took this course is difficult to determine, but Selective Service reported that there were over 6,000 convictions for violations of the Act involving religious objectors. A total of 72,354 registrants filed for conscientious objection status from 1940 to 1947.[1]

There were also a number who, after first accepting assignment to Civilian Public Service, believed they had compromised themselves by complying with conscription and left their CPS units—"walked out". These "walk-outs" were later prosecuted for violation of the draft law.

This book tells about the lives of men drafted into Civilian Public Service. In 1989 a questionnaire was sent to three thousand ex-CPSers (all the names that could be found), and one thousand (1014) replied. They told about their reasons for being COs, their wartime experiences, and the impact of their beliefs on their later lives. They had vivid remembrances of their CPS years, and the descriptions of their lives after the war are colorful and engaging. Appendix C contains a list of the questions used in the questionnaire and a tabulation of the subjects brought up in the answers. This listing requires several pages, showing the intensity with which these men feel about their beliefs.

The purpose of the questionnaire was to learn what it was like to be a conscientious objector—what it meant to the men during the war and what it meant in their later lives. The focus was on their belief and how it played out in their lives. The comments and opinions expressed throughout the book are in the men's own words. They have not been filtered or interpreted. You will see the story as they told it. First names of respondents are used, but last names have been omitted.

Do the opinions and ideas of the one thousand accurately represent the other eleven thousand who served in CPS? That is difficult to say. Public opinion polls use much smaller samples than we had, but we did not employ their professional sampling techniques. The answers probably are reasonably representative because they came from a cross section of the total assignee population—by age, education, occupation, religious affiliation, and length of CPS service. Also, the same types of comments occur frequently, and they are similar to those found in other accounts. At the same time, the unique individuality of this group makes any claim of accurate representation highly risky. The comments of the one thousand were meticulously recorded and are thoroughly reported, but I make no claim that they accurately reflect the total CPS population.

Throughout this narrative individuals appear to be speaking to each other in the same place at the same time. They are indeed talking with each other—as they did interminably during the War—but this time it is through their questionnaire responses. To understand the texture of these stories, one might imagine that the thousand have gathered in the same place. In the words of a prominent TV interviewer, this was my way of telling the story for you.

You will occasionally see what appear to be repetitions of the same idea or opinion. Indeed, these people did have similar thoughts and feelings about a wide number of things. There are, however, great differences in the way they see their faith playing out in the world and particularly in the way they express themselves. I thought it was important for the reader to hear not only the wide range of opinion but also the unique and varied way in which different individuals speak. Therefore, while you will hear the same ideas more than once, the way they are said will show you the great diversity of people, their values, and their aspirations.

The tale begins on a train carrying a group of newly drafted COs to their first CPS assignment. This episode did occur; but, as mentioned above, not all of the conversations in this account actually took place on that particular train. Similar composite conversations will be found in settings typical of the places where COs lived and worked, but the voices will be from different times and places.

After the war ex-CPSers worked in a great range of occupations and avocations. They were activists in the cause of human brotherhood, tending to the sick, educating the young, defending the rights of the abused, administering to the souls of the forgotten, growing food for the body, healing ruptured emotions, marching in peace parades and protests, or erecting homes for the homeless. The diversity of activity among this little band was truly remarkable.

The selectivity of human recall being what it is, many unpleasantries seem to have been forgotten—but not all. The overwhelming impression is that CPS left an indelible imprint.

These men had opinions and ideas about quite a number of things, and I have tried to present a balanced range of views. Some issues were mentioned a great deal and others were brought up infrequently. One would be hard pressed to find any issue on which everyone would agree. For instance, the men often spoke about the isolation of their work. At the same time, however, some projects were in towns and cities, and men assigned to these jobs had much public contact. Thus, even though some issues may appear to represent the total group, the reader should assume that there was a range of experience and opinion.

The first part of the book describes how the men came to be classified as COs, what they did during the war, and how they viewed their wartime experience fifty years later. CPS was a time of intense self-inquiry, self-interrogation, and introspection. Chapters 7 through 10 deal with the years after the war. COs were found in virtually every trade, business, and profession, and you will come to understand their particular approach to their occupations and avocations. Chapters 11 and 12 explain why people believe in pacifism and how they become conscientious objectors. The Epilogue is a brief outline of the pacifist's critique of warfare.

The pacifist challenges conventional beliefs that humans are forever destined to war with each other, that war has beneficial results, and that there are "good" wars. For the CO the ultimate question is not <u>whether</u> wars will end, but <u>when</u> they will end and <u>how</u>. The pacifist has much to say about the when and how.

* * * * * * * * * * * *

There is no way to know the number of people who contributed to this project. Ideas have come from so many sources, both direct and indirect, known and unknown. First, of course, was that warm outpouring of response from the thousand people who responded to the questionnaire and who followed up with visits, letters, and telephone conversations. Their ideas, suggestions, and encouragements have made the adventure a precious experience. The rewards are in seeing the work translated into what I hope you will find to be an intriguing story.

Several CPS alumni reviewed various portions of the manuscript and gave me marvelous suggestions: Harold Bock, Charles Davis, Lloyd Hall, Rudy Potochnik, Howard Schomer, and Carl Verduin. A number of others reviewed the completed manuscript: Roger Drury, Doris Glick (CPS auxiliary and wife of Lester Glick), Arthur Harris, Morris Keeton, Robert Kreider, Robert Kleinhans, Jesse Mock, and Harry Prochaska. A special word of appreciation to Mitchell Robinson whose doctoral dissertation on CPS at Cornell University was a great source of independent viewpoint. A great friend of longstanding, Judge Richard Tuttle, helped me understand how it all would sound to a sympathetic non-CO.

There are four other people who provided a clear and guiding counsel through the total project. Their meticulous and incisive review of each chapter, however, exceeded my greatest hope. They are: Howard Hamilton, Louis Neumann, Louis' wife Nancy (Foster) who had worked as a dietitian in CPS, and Don Elton Smith. They inspired me to stay the course and to keep the sails trimmed.

My historian son Eric contributed his unique second-generation perspective that encouraged me to reach out to younger readers. My architect son Dennis offered his fine sense of design and layout to the physical arrangement of text and illustration. My poet son Brian contributed the introductory poem which so eloquently expresses the heart of pacifism. The patience and understanding of my wife Loretta removed the sting of those many hours in the "dreariness of labor and loneliness of thought". As a CPS auxiliary herself, she contributed many hours to preparing the final text and distributing literature. I am sure she felt much relief when the manuscript finally went to the printer.

1.   Selective Service System, *Conscientious Objection. Special Mono-graph No. 11, Vol 1.* Washington: U.S. Government Printing Office, 1950. pp. 263, 315.

1
On
the Way

The Southern Pacific train, on its regular run from Los Angeles to Seattle, pulled into the fog-shrouded central California city deep in the night of December 4, 1941. Huddled around families and friends in the ancient wooden station were two bewildered young men about to start a new adventure under orders from their Selective Service draft boards. At the call for "All Aboard", the two men, after tearful goodbyes all around, climbed the stairs to the darkened pullman corridor. Two conscientious objectors were thus off to give one years' service in a Civilian Public Service camp in Oregon. I was one of those men.

In the fall of 1941 the question of U.S. involvement in the European war (it was not yet called World War II) was still unanswered. We were unaware then, of course, that our term of conscription would last for the duration of the coming war. As the train clattered into the night, we found our bunks and settled for the night, with mixtures of curiosity, apprehension, and adventure.

When morning came, we found ourselves in the company of eighty other COs who came aboard the train as it traveled through California to its Oregon destination. We were ushered into the dining car for our morning meal by two men who appeared to be Pinkerton guards. As we surrendered our vouchers for the only meals the government would ever supply us, we were joined by other CPS recruits. Those who had boarded the train in Los Angeles earlier the day before had already become acquainted, and the new arrivals were soon absorbed in conversation. We ranged in age from eighteen to about twenty-six.

Some of us were leaving home for the first time in our lives, others were separating from families who disagreed with their CO beliefs, and some were interrupting educations or careers, even though most of us, still in our early twenties, were not yet established in our business or professional lives. Later in the war, draft calls took married men, even some with children.

Considering the climate of opinion in a country on the verge of going to war, many of us thought our stand would harm our future careers. But on this occasion, conversations were animated and friendly; and some queries were inevitable: How did you come to be a CO? How did you fare with your draft board? What does your family think about your being a CO? And of course there were many questions about the work we would be doing. We did know we were going to an old CCC camp.

Most of the conversation dealt with our beliefs about war and how we came to those beliefs. "As a Christian, this is the way that Jesus expects me to go; so I follow as I am led by conviction, teaching, and study," said Howard. Francis had been forced to defend his position before three army officers, "God said to me, 'Stand by My word as your defense, share what you know, and I will help.'"

"Being a CO," Allen spoke up, "was a result of the deep conviction that it is right to stand for things in a nonviolent manner."

Many said that their families' religious heritage—whether Mennonite, Quaker, Brethren, or other—influenced them. Others came from divided families where brothers had gone into the armed services. They were the "odd men out" in their families, leaving both them and their families puzzled and hurt by the division.

The vivid green Oregon valleys passing by the train windows reminded us that we were leaving our previous lives behind, but being with so many like-minded people gave us a sense of comradeship that few of us had known before. For the first time in our lives we were with kindred spirits. Talk was lively, and deep friendships began to form.

Emphasizing family influences again, Hugh observed, "Being a CO was just a result of my upbringing and having a Dad who challenged my thinking . . . and a Mom who taught me that God is Love."

Harlan's description of his childhood had a familiar ring: "My mother said that I ought to make believe in other ways and not think it was right to point even toy guns at people or pretend to do things to hurt people."

"I grew up in a family," James said, "where military service was regarded as strongly anti-Christian and where military personnel were not so much abhorred as pitied—as victims of an evil and exploitative system."

The pain of having been alone came up over and over again. "I took my stand," Floyd said, ". . . in a small community, alone, and with no support from my church, friends, or family. In effect it was like burning the bridges behind me. I was sustained and strengthened by my faith and convictions and was willing to accept the consequences of my decision."

Floyd's story reminded Arthur of his encounter with the draft board. One member of the board, a Sunday school teacher in the Methodist Church, said he was dismayed that someone reared in a God-fearing family could become a CO. "I told him that until I was twelve years old I went to the Methodist Church Sunday School every Sunday of my life. When I was twelve I realized that my teachers did not believe what they were teaching me. So I stopped going, but I kept believing."

"I appeared before a judge twice," Pete said. "The first time he was not convinced and ordered me back for a second hearing. At the next session he asked me again how I came by these beliefs, and I quoted a number of scriptures from the Bible. He became very irritated at my references to the Bible and told me to stop quoting scriptures. After the next question, I hesitated for a long time until he pressed me for an answer. When I again quoted Biblical passages, he shouted, 'I told you not to quote scriptures to me!' ' Well,' I replied, 'that is the only way I know to explain what I believe.' That ended the hearing, but several days later I received the CO classification."

Our dealings with draft boards were fresh in our minds. Draft boards often prided themselves on being tough with conscientious objectors. Many were galled at having to give any CO classifications. It was reported that some boards simply refused to classify anyone as a CO, forcing review by appeal boards and ultimately by a Presidential Board. In the summation of its World War II activities, Selective Service stated, "More than 1,200 boards reported as at no time having any registrants so classified."[1]

In quizzing COs, draft boards had a few stock questions. One of the most common was, "What would you do if someone broke into your home and was about to rape your sister/wife/mother/grandmother? Would you just stand there and do nothing?" This question was seen as a shrewd way of entrapping the unwary CO. If he would use force in protecting a loved one, he would not be sincere in opposing war! Or, alternatively, if he would do nothing to protect his family, he could be labeled a corrupt deviant.

Many young objectors were intimidated by these types of questions. They would not have the presence of mind to ask their interrogators how such a hypothetical situation compared to a battlefield where men are expected to kill other young people whose only crime is that they live in a different country. Or, to ask how the threatened rape scenario related to the bombing of cities and the killing of civilians.

Why were such questions thought to be "pivotal" in determining the legitimacy of pacifist belief? In civilized societies, self-defense and defending one's family is a right of citizenship. Murder, on the other hand, is a crime. How does the sanction of a government to commit murder on a battlefield convert that killing to heroism? It is this little twist of reasoning that the CO finds so outrageous.

The draft board question apparently elicited some flippant answers, too. "Well," Al told his board, "my sister is going to college next year anyway." Apparently, he thought an absurd question deserved an absurd answer.

But the CO's cause is deeply serious. "Our society claims to be built upon Christian principles," Virgil said, "yet we refuse to follow the way of life taught us by the founder of that faith. . . . the sacredness of human life, a gift from God, rejects the view that anyone has the right or authority to destroy human life."

For one to be classified as a conscientious objector, one must show a "religious training and belief". We learned later that the draft boards had serious problems in applying this phrase because of various meanings of "religious". The Department of Justice ultimately identified twelve types of people who claimed to be COs, and these guidelines were to help the draft boards weed out the fake claimants. Presumably, the first two were genuine and the others were not.

1. *The Religious Objector* sincerely believes in a personal Creator whose immortal laws forbid the killing of human beings, particularly as set forth in the Commandment "Thou shalt not kill." He believes that war is contrary to the spirit and teachings of Christianity and in opposition to God's will, and he cannot participate, without subjecting his soul to eternal perdition.

2. *The moral or ethical objector* considers war inconsistent with his moral philosophy and humanitarianism which is independent of religious beliefs, except as it may be predicated upon a belief in a brotherhood of man. That concept is not based on a belief in the fatherhood of God. His conscience is bound by a moral law, which enjoins him from having to do with so destructive and futile a force as war, which evidences a breakdown of reason by substituting force. In fact, most of this type of objector denies a belief in a deity except insofar as there may be a moral force in the universe. It is his view that mankind is sufficient to itself, that it owes no obligation to any power except humankind, and that it may achieve perfection in and of itself without the interposition of any deity or supernatural power.

3. *The economic objector*, as a student of history, sees all wars as based upon the inequitable distribution of natural resources, complicated and supported by tariff barriers, immigration restrictions and nationalistic control of colonial markets and sees no hope of this war effecting a more equitable distribution of economic opportunity.

4. *The political objector* sees war as a means of exploiting the masses for the few who are politically ambitious, or for the governments and deceiving the people.

5. *The philosophical objector*, generally a student of metaphysics, possesses a personal philosophy which dominates his way of life.

6. *The sociological objector* whose objections are based upon a theory that war has no place in his own particular ordering of society.

7. *The internationalist objector* would destroy or abolish all international boundaries and sovereignty, racial and trade lines, and consider the world one big family of peoples devoid of war.

8. *The personal objector*, who objects to this particular war, because he believes it to be a war of imperialism or that the Allied Nations have brought it on, or that it is not the type of war in which he can participate.

9. *The neurotic objector* has a phobia of war's atrocities, a mental and physical fear and abhorrence of killing or maiming, and who therefore cannot participate in it.

10. *The naturalistic objector's* objection is physiological, and based upon an abhorrence of blood.

11. *The "professional pacifist" objector* would have "peace in our time at any cost." He would tolerate nothing which would inconvenience his mode of living, but would aggressively limit the liberties of others. He wants to enjoy all the protections of the Government, but is unwilling to bear any of the responsibilities of citizenship in this respect.

12. *The Jehovah Witness* objects to all man-made wars and Governments, but says he is not a conscien-

tious objector to all wars, since he would fight and kill in defense of the Theocracy, his property and his brethren.[2]

If these standards were bewildering to us, they must have been completely baffling to draft boards. When we learned of these definitions many years later, we were startled to learn that we were obsessed with our "own particular ordering of society"; "neurotic" because of our abhorrence of killing and maiming; unwilling to "bear any of the responsibilities of citizenship". We were accustomed to the perils of misunderstanding, but these were calculated distortions.

During the discussion of draft board encounters, someone brought up the "absolutist" position in which one of draft age refuses all compliance with conscription laws. Would not the cause of peace be better served by the CO simply refusing to cooperate with the draft? While this approach was not foremost in the minds of these young draftees, it was intensely debated during the war and in the years that followed. As we will see, in later years some men decided they would refuse to sign up for a draft if ever faced with it again. But for these men at the time, CPS was a "way of letting the government know where I stood."

As we moved about the railroad car becoming acquainted with new arrivals, a sense of camaraderie began to develop. We were savoring the unfamiliar luxury of being with so many like-minded people. And we learned that there were many different bases for individual CO beliefs. Because of the "religious training and belief" clause, conscientious objectors were obliged to state their beliefs in religious terms. There were, however, many other political, social, or economic grounds for opposing war.

"I came at it from essentially an ethical viewpoint," Arthur said. Andrew found his beliefs in many places, "Family life, Christian Endeavor . . . taking to heart Emerson, Longfellow, Jefferson, Paine, Lincoln. . . . "

"You know," Bob said, "most people think pacifists are naive. I think war mongers are naive and unrealistic in thinking that military weapons . . . enhance our security."

"I'm not even sure it's that," another added. "Fifty percent of the people are objectors, but they feel it won't work."

We knew our ideas were different, but what made us that way? Was it a new way of looking at things? Did we see things that others did not see? Why did we take religious teachings so literally? Did we really think we could overcome evil with good? Or was it all a matter of "being a little weird", of enjoying loneliness? The answers to these questions will unfold in the pages that follow.

On the question of loneliness, one man explained what being alone really meant. In all his life Jacob had never heard the words pacifism or conscientious objection and knew nothing about "historic peace churches" or "nonviolent direct action". He had, though, heard a lot about war and about "heroism" on the battlefield. He was moved by the stories of men in war who placed their lives in jeopardy to rescue their buddies. He could relate to these courageous acts, but he always wanted to know why they were there in the first place. He never found a satisfactory explanation, and the insanity of it dumbfounded him.

When the order came for him to register for "selective service", he was curious. Would this be his chance to join some humanitarian work? He went to the draft board to find out what it was all about and was told that the country needed soldiers for the army. All young men would sign up; then a lottery would select the ones to be called up. Well, he explained, he could not do that. But, the Board said, the law requires all young men to register. He could be arrested and imprisoned for violating the law. That did not make any difference to him, he said, because he just could not be a soldier. "Why is that?" the board wanted to know. He had studied the Bible, and as a believer in the word of God, he could not kill anybody.

Finally, one of the board members said, "We have a place for people like you." That sounded pretty ominous. But, he was told, the law excluded "conscientious objectors" from military duty and assigned them to civilian jobs instead. This began to sound more reasonable. He still wanted to know, though, just what was a conscientious objector. The board explained that this was the term used in the draft law to classify people whose religious beliefs prevented them from taking part in warfare. "So," Jacob said, "here I am." For the first time in his life he realized that there were other people in the world who believed as he did about war.

Others had learned about war from Fourth of July orations and from men who "served their country" in other wars. When they saw the endless rows of crosses in military cemeteries, they were shattered by the realization that under each of those crosses was the body of a human being. They felt the same emotions of sadness and compassion that all citizens felt about these fallen men; but instead of seeing it as a result of some noble crusade, they saw it as a result of the folly of their fathers. And where was the glory in that?

Everyone in that railroad car knew what it meant to be "strange". We had experienced the side glances and the whispers: "Well, you know Charles was always a little *different.*"

Paul spoke for many: "It was so good to know . . . that it was O.K. to be 'weird'." On this train we were "In a majority community and not a lonely voice in the dark."

Orie knew the loneliness of farm life, but he also knew the isolation of belief. "When you are alone on a farm, you feel, 'what does it matter what I believe'. But to be in THE GREAT COMPANY of fellows who know why they are there. . . is very encouraging."

After a little stretching and walking the train aisles to get out the kinks from long hours of sitting, the conversation continued. Not all talk was "heavy". We were learning about each other's personal lives, too. We talked about our occupations, our education, our brothers and sisters, what we did for fun, and the like. We were learning about the kind of people we would be living with.

As individual "loners" we had often asked ourselves why we "agreed" to be a minority. Is there some "CO personality", some unique temperament? Even though we saw things in a radically different way, we looked very much like any other group of young people. Indeed, sometimes on these "troop" trains the Red Cross girls saw us only as draftees and included us in their coffee and donut offerings. We wore the same types of shirts and pants, had the same types of haircuts, and talked the same way as anybody else. There was nothing unusual about our appearance. (This is not absolutely accurate for those of our gentle brethren who wore the distinctive dress and beards of their faiths.) There were the outgoing and the aggressive, the quiet and retiring, the rugged and athletic, the sensitive and creative, the promoters, and the scholars. Education and family background were fairly representative of the general population. So why, then, this baffling difference about war?

We were as puzzled as anyone else. Given our religious training, the social, political, and economic climate in which we had grown up, and the general revulsion with war, we could not understand why our views were in the

<u>minority</u>. They made profound good sense to us. So what was different? Independence for sure, certainly an element of persistence, and *an insistence that a principle believed is a principle practiced.* Something born in us? One man said he found himself being a pacifist by nature even as a child. Certainly, something about our temperaments and dispositions seemed different, but no one was ever able to define it.

Many spoke about a persistence in what they did, whether it was in demanding high standards of themselves; being straightforward and open in business dealings; or refusing to compromise moral and ethical beliefs. Perhaps also a little perfectionism. But there is nothing particularly unique about any of these things either. People everywhere lives their lives according to these precepts. We were never able to find a satisfactory answer, and we wonder yet why so many people accede to the call to arms.

With a mischievous smile, Bill described himself: "I consider myself the acme of sweet reasonableness, but others tell me I'll insist on one interpretation or one way of doing something. . . . This is perhaps the personality—or mind-set—that also made it likely that I'd be a CO. This tendency to be uncompromising may have influenced my politics, my religion, and my jobs."

Reed agreed that the CO is an independent cuss, "I'm generally a fairly amiable person . . . never been one to 'go with the crowd' . . . a loner to some degree. Instead of sports, I played the piano, did photography. Instead of going to dances, I was active in church groups, did gardening."

As these musings continued, from the train windows we could now see the vivid green of Oregon valleys and the Cascade mountains beyond, enveloped in their misty clouds. For Californians this was inclement weather, and it was a marvel to see the local farmers working in their rain drenched fields. Any level-headed Californian would seek cover in such a calamity. We were to learn that in Oregon you dressed for the weather and ignored the rain. The "tin suits" of heavily waxed canvas kept the rain out—but the perspiration in.

As the train entered the city of Portland, our thoughts turned to what awaited us at the end of the line. We had spent our time getting acquainted; now we began to think about what we would be doing. We were headed for a former Civilian Conservation Corps camp left over from Franklin Roosevelt's New Deal. We would work on projects run by the U.S. government, but we would live in a camp run by the churches. The information we received before leaving was sketchy, and we were told that work projects had not been fully developed.

What had been a group of strangers was becoming a community. There was a mixture of bravado and timidity, apprehension and anticipation, commiseration, vying for attention, and assertions of leadership. Some assumed they would be "in charge" of things, and others were hopelessly homesick with little concern about who was in charge. Some were "men of the world", nonchalant about the whole thing; others were shy and withdrawn; for many it was their first time away from home; and for still others it was a time of excitement and adventure.

We all shared an aversion to war, but on everything else there was a wide range of beliefs and attitudes. A *Saturday Evening Post* article written at the opening of the first CPS camp in May, 1941, commented on the variety of opinion among COs.

> About the only thing these men have in common is their intense conviction that it is wrong to kill a fellow man. And they are building for themselves, in a Chinese Wall of the human spirit, what to most

Americans must seem a never-never land, an impossible mirage of peace and brotherly love in a world of war and hate.[3]

Uppermost in everyone's mind was, how long would the internment last? On the day we arrived, December 5, 1941, the term of service was for one year; although there was some talk that it would be extended to eighteen months. Two days later the rules radically changed.

When the train finally squeaked to a stop in the Portland station, a number of convoy trucks were waiting at the siding to take us to Cascade Locks, fifty miles to the east. Bags, suitcases, and cartons were retrieved from the train's baggage car and stowed in covered Forest Service trucks. We lined up and climbed into the back of other trucks, seating ourselves on wooden benches which later turned out to be the boxes in which project tools were carried. The convoy of several trucks then proceeded in army convoy style through the winding and scenic highway of breathtaking Columbia River Gorge to Gorton Creek and Wyeth. There was the normal nervous chatter of men uncertain about what came next. Someone broke the tension, "What beautiful country; at least we'll be in the mountains." This was not much comfort for the flatlanders of California, but the beauty of the Gorge did inspire us—and would soften many tense hours in the years to come. Two hours from Portland we entered a small valley at the edge of the Columbia River, and the trucks pulled up to a cluster of austere wooden buildings recently abandoned by the Civilian Conservation Corps. We had just seen our new home, Civilian Public Service Camp No. 21, Cascade Locks, Oregon. The CCC camp was open again, this time for the left-overs from military conscription.

1. Selective Service System, *Conscientious Objection, Special Monograph 11, Vol. I.* Washington: U.S. Government Printing Office, 1950. p. 316.
2. Ibid, pp. 3-4.
3. Robert E. S. Thompson, "Onward Christian Soldiers!", in *Saturday Evening Post*, August 16, 1941. pp. 27, 53-56.

2
The
Fragile
Experiment

This chapter examines the origins of military conscription during World War II and the provision in the Selective Service law for conscientious objectors. You will see how the Civilian Public Service program for alternative service came about, how and why the churches became embroiled in the program, and how CPS was viewed in the perspective of fifty years. The adventures of the COs after arriving at Cascade Locks will continue in the next chapter.

The Selective Training and Service Act of 1940 provided that men conscientiously opposed to military service would be assigned to civilian "work of national importance" when their number was called up in the draft lottery. The exemption of "conscientious objection" from military service has evolved through the long history of military conscription. The following is a brief summary of that history. (There are a number of books in the bibliography that deal with the history of military conscription.)

In the early days of the Christian Church (the religious heritage of most American COs), pacifism was at the heart of Christian belief. The Christian emphasis on pacifism changed after the year 313 C.E. when the Roman Emperor Constantine recognized the Christian religion. By the year 392 C.E. Christianity became the religion of Rome and was open to all Romans. It eventually lost its pacifist moorings, and the new Christians freely joined the Roman legions. Indeed, one scholar reported that membership in the Roman army was at one time closed to non-Christians. The fate of Christian pacifists in the Roman Empire after Constantine was not a happy one, with persecution and martyrdom dogging them for centuries just as all Christians had been oppressed before 313 C.E.

When explorations opened up land in the New World after the fifteenth century, many Christians saw a chance for freedom to practice their faith. Several American colonies were settled by people seeking religious liberty, including escape from European military conscription systems.

In colonial America, Declarations of Rights in four colonies exempted religious believers from service in military forces: Delaware (1776), Pennsylvania (1776), New Hampshire (1784), and New York (1777). An early Rhode Island statute had exempted conscientious objectors from military duties.[1] Madison also included such a provision in the first drafts of the United States Constitution. Before the Constitution's final adoption, however, the clause was omitted because it was thought to be unnecessary. A nation founded on the principle of religious freedom and settled by refugees from European military conscription could hardly be expected to invoke such a system in the new world. So thought the framers of the Constitution.

The U.S. government has invoked military conscription on a number of occasions. The original Civil War draft law made no provision for COs, and many objectors were jailed. (The law allowed drafted individuals to hire substitutes, but this "draft dodging" provision was unacceptable to many pacifists.) An amendment to the draft law in 1864 exempted conscientious objectors from service.

The World War I draft exempted members of the "Historic Peace Churches" [Church of the Brethren (Dunkards), Mennonites, and Society of Friends (Quakers)] from combat duty; but when drafted, they were expected to take the military oath and perform noncombatant duties. COs of other religious persuasions were not recognized in this law. Military units sometimes refused to acknowledge the CO's noncombatant status and attempted to coerce them into combat duty. The result was that many COs ended up in military stockades. Treatment was often brutal, as guards and other inmates tested the COs' resolve. Court martials for insubordination were common, and sentences for "sullen" and "defiant" conduct were severe—up to twenty years at hard labor. Other COs who refused induction into the military services or who refused even to register for the draft were prosecuted in civilian courts; when convicted, they also went to prison.

Treatment of World War I COs in prison, whether civilian or military, was often inhuman. Following the death of two Huttterian Brotherhood COs while in the Leavenworth "hole", CO prisoners went on strike in 1918. This nonviolent rebellion led to radical changes in treatment of prisoners and the release of all COs by November, 1920. None of the excessive sentences was carried out.

Raymond Wilson of the American Friends Service Committee in his testimony before Congress on the 1940 draft law told the tragic story of one World War I CO:

"There was one Mennonite who objected to putting on the uniform, and he was put in a cell and kept in his underwear for several days; and he finally died of pneumonia and [his body] was sent back to his home in the military uniform which conscientiously he could not put on in his lifetime.[2]

The Selective Training and Service Act of 1940, passed by the Congress on September 14, 1940, required conscientious objectors to perform alternative nonmilitary service under civilian direction. The act, signed into law by President Franklin D. Roosevelt on September 16, contained the following Section 5(g):

Nothing contained in this act shall be construed to require any person to be subject to combatant training and service in the land or naval forces of the United States who, by reason of religious training and belief, is conscientiously opposed to participation in war in any form. Any such person . . . shall, if he is inducted into the land or naval forces under this Act, be assigned to noncombatant service . . . or shall, if he is found to be conscientiously opposed to participation in such noncombatant service, in lieu of such induction, be assigned to work of national importance under civilian direction.

During the six and one half years of the Act's existence, there were no changes in this Section.

This book deals only with the conscientious objectors assigned to work of national importance under civilian direction, the program that came to be known as Civilian Public Service. The thorny issue of what was meant by "work of national importance under civilian direction" will be discussed in the next chapter.

During Congressional hearings on the Draft law in the summer of 1940, Congressman Charles Faddis (Pennsylvania) probably expressed the prevailing Congressional sentiment on COs.

If I were to go out and command the troops—and I may—I don't want any conscientious objectors in

my regiment at all. . . . They would be more bother
than they would be worth, and a bad example to the
other men. You could not do anything with them . . .
and I am sure no man who would command troops
would want them.[3]

This view was echoed later in the war by General
Lewis B. Hershey, the Director of Selective Service, in
comments before the Senate Military Affairs Committee in
February, 1943.

I would like to deprive the army of having that
problem [of COs assigned to army units].[4]

Lt. Col. W. D. Partlow Jr. expressed the War Department view in that same Senate Committee hearing.

"The type of people who are conscientious objectors would cause a lot of trouble in the army.[5]

For most members of Congress the compelling
argument for acknowledging conscientious objection seemed
to be that COs were a nuisance for the military.

A broader view on the issue of conscience was
expressed by Francis Biddle, U. S. Attorney General.

Freedom of conscience is a foundation stone of
our Democracy. Consequently, we must respect the
attitude of those persons who honestly and sincerely,
on conscientious grounds based on religious training
and belief, object to participation in war. The fact that
such persons form but a small minority of our citizenry
and that we disagree with their position, does not affect
our obligation to recognize and respect their convictions.[6]

General Hershey, commenting on the opening of the
first CPS camp in May, 1941, also had some lofty words
about the way democratic societies recognize individual
conscience:

"It is an experiment," says Gen. Lewis B. Hershey, Acting Director of Selective Service, "an experiment such as no nation has ever made before. Through these camps for conscientious objectors, we are going to find out whether our democracy is big enough to preserve minority rights in a time of national emergency. I don't know whether the experiment will work or not. But I hope and pray that it will."[7]

An ex-CPSer, commenting years later on the government's recognition of conscientious objection, saw a positive side to the draft law: "By forcing society to make provision for conscience," Reed said, "the CPS camps were of tremendous importance. It was a legal, administrative, and judicial recognition of the validity of conscience in the State. This is a central issue of our time: an institutional recognition of conscience."

When the 1940 draft law was being debated in Congress, many pacifist and church organizations, acutely aware of the injustices inflicted on COs in World War I, determined to correct the errors of the earlier law. Their efforts were rewarded when the above Section 5(g), with its emphasis on civilian work, was included in the law. In the rough and tumble of congressional law-making, the peace group negotiators thought this was the best they could get from a Congress whose opinions on conscientious objectors ranged from cold indifference to open hostility. Some people, however, believed that since the military did not want COs on their hands, a more workable provision could have been obtained.

The most chronic complaint about Section 5(g) was its ambiguity about "civilian direction" and "work of national importance". Congress wanted to keep these "troublesome" people out of the military, but there was never any mutual agreement on what these two phrases meant.

After the law was passed, congressional leaders and Selective Service officials took up the question of what to do with these civilian COs. At this stage, several representatives of pacifist organizations presented the government with a courageous—some would say foolhardy—proposal to underwrite the maintenance of COs assigned to civilian work. The offer was made on the assumption that COs would be given socially significant work and would be under the direction of the sponsoring churches. They also wanted to avoid the injustices of World War I and the tensions of government operated camps. In addition, some religious groups were concerned about exposing their young men to non-Christian influences. (In 1940 it was also assumed that draftees would serve only one year. The proponents of this program did not know, of course, that they were writing a blank check.)

At the time of the original negotiations, Frank Olmstead, long associated with the peace movement, saw the alternative service program as an

. . .unprecedented action of the Government in giving this responsibility to the peace churches. That action was a dramatic tribute to an integrity that all men recognize as trustworthy. Such a recognition is not accidental. It is earned. In this case it has been earned in reconstruction programs in France and Germany, in feeding starving Russians [references to the relief work after World War I], in aid to both sides in the Spanish conflict, in work camps and service . . . on the American continent.[8]

(Olmstead later had a change of heart about the program.)

When church representatives began negotiations, they discovered that the government not only intended to retain control over the work program but that the entire operation would be supervised by the military officers of Selective Service. A bitter disappointment! The best face that can be put on these deliberations is that the parties had misunderstood each other. Olmstead's statement expressed the hope of the church administrators that they would select and operate public service programs, with drafted men assigned to their agencies for that purpose. It is apparent that the government had no intention of giving up control over these draftees any more than they did the drafted soldiers. The Civilian Public Service (CPS) program that came out of these deliberations resulted in a government operated work program and a church-supported camp. In short, the churches provided a home for the men so they would be available to work without pay on government projects.

It is reasonable to assume that government negotiators were not much concerned about the significance of the CO's work. Their interest was in keeping COs out of public view, and the fact that someone else would feed and house them was an unbelievable bonanza. One is probably entitled to conclude that the government accepted this very favorable proposition from what they saw as a group of unsophisticated negotiators.

Berle, an ex-CPSer, was able to see some positive elements in the deliberations: "I learned to appreciate the dedicated men who negotiated with the government on behalf of the many diverse people in the camps and projects. They were actually demonstrating conflict resolution in the most difficult circumstances."

The agreement between Selective Service and the church organizations was formalized by Franklin Roosevelt's Executive Order No. 8675 on February 5, 1941. The Director of Selective Service would administer the program, and he could accept voluntary services from private organizations and individuals. Thus began Civilian Public Service.

The draft law provided for a peaceful alternative to military service, but the definition of "alternative service" was placed in the hands of people who were at the least unsympathetic to the idea of conscientious objection. To the dismay of the people who had hoped for a vital work program, the military officers of Selective Service had their own ideas about that.

The law called for "civilian direction", and it was assumed that Selective Service would be under civilian direction. In April, 1941, however, civilian director Clarence Dykstra was replaced by military officer Lewis B. Hershey. Hershey, in turn, staffed his Camp Operations division with fellow military officers. The fiction of civilian direction was maintained by contending that, while Selective Service administrators were military officers on military duty in military uniform, they functioned as civilians when over-seeing CPS. There was a second rationalization: since CPS work projects were directed by civilians from non-military agencies (such as the Soil Conservation Service, Forest Service, and National Park Service), this met the test for "civilian direction".

Men assigned to CPS would receive no compensation and no support for their dependents. In this way, they would demonstrate the sincerity of their beliefs. Presumably, also, this work-without-pay would balance the sacrifice of men drafted into the military. The troublesome issue of compensation will be dealt with in Chapter 4 below.

CHURCH PARTICIPATION

The wisdom of church participation in a conscription system will be argued as long as there is memory of it. The following remarks show how the draftees felt about it fifty year later.

Aware of the pressures faced by church sponsors in 1940, Chester believed, "CPS was not perfect, but a good step in the right way . . . it fit the needs for that hour."

For Arthur, ". . . it was an improvement over World War I and the best that could be done at the time." David concurred, ". . . compared to W.W. I . . . I think CPS was better organized and resulted in few traumatic experiences for the young man." LeRoy also saw it as a better alternative than World War I: "I deeply appreciated the fact that our Church leaders did not want us to face World War II as in W.W. I. Refusal was the one and only thing then. . . . That meant jail. . . "

Even though he was critical of the CPS program for the way it forced people into involuntary servitude, for Henry, ". . . it was a better way than the army."

Even though it may have been a plausible compromise in World War II, it probably would not and could not be repeated. "I doubt that CPS could happen again," Wesley said. "The close marriage of the Church and the State and the many marginal work assignments would be subject to much criticism today."

There was some strong criticism of the churches' participation, but little outright resentment. Even the most bitter opponents admired the effort of individual church members who kept the program going for more than five years. The government's role, however, is seen quite differently.

"The government," Sanford said, "had convinced the traditional pacifist sects that by administering these camps they were helping the men, when in fact, they were making a vicious system work."

Administrative Discord

Conscription is based on the premise that states have a right to demand public service from their citizens. (As we will see later, many pacifists reject this premise.) The church people who negotiated alternative service must have accepted—at least for the purpose of negotiation—this power of the state. The two parties, however, had quite different perceptions of public service. From the government's point of view, if the soldier is called upon to sacrifice, the CO must sacrifice, too. The church groups and the COs did not disagree on the sacrifice, but they wanted their work to amount to something. Although manpower scarcities did ultimately open a number of humanitarian projects, that was not the goal of Selective Service as it had been for the churches. With the possible exception of fire fighting (the government had anticipated forest fires from Japanese incendiary bombs) and some medical experiments, Selective Service had relatively little interest in the actual work.

In spite of serious reservations about the entire program, most of the draftees thought the churches were sincere. There was a consensus, however, that they had received the short end of the bargain. Selective Service used wartime hysteria and the hostility of "super patriot" groups to assert control over the program.

The following statement by Selective Service officer Major McLean was typical of the government's harassing tactics:

From the time an assignee reports to camp until he is finally released he is under the control of the Director of Selective Service.

He ceases to be a free agent and is accountable for all his time, in camp and out, 24 hours a day. His movements, actions, and conduct are subject to control and regulation.

He ceases to have certain rights and is granted privileges instead. These privileges can be restricted or withdrawn without his consent as punishment, during emergencies, or as a matter of policy. He may be told when and how to work, what to wear, and where to sleep. He can be required to submit to medical examinations and treatment, and to practice rules of health and sanitation. He may be moved from place to place and from job to job, even to foreign countries, for the convenience of the government regardless of his personal feeling or desires.[9]

Statements of this type reinforced the CO's already strong reservations about Selective Service management. They could have been ploys to needle the men, or perhaps they were intended to convince the public that COs were being kept in their place. The fact that this letter was issued by a junior officer at the third level was interpreted to mean that it should not be taken too seriously. Indeed, such pronouncements ultimately became objects of amusement rather than serious concern. Their significance was not in their content; it was rather in how they conveyed the military tactics of the "civilian" Selective Service System.

The antagonism of such organizations as the American Legion were played up by Selective Service to reinforce their domination of the program. Their declarations carried weight on Capital Hill, and Selective Service capitalized on this. As will be seen in Chapter 5, public opinion polls showed that the public was quite tolerant of COs, particularly when their work was known.

The National Service Board for Religious Objectors (NSBRO) was set up by the church organizations to coordinate relations with Selective Service. Director Paul Comly French, without any substantial political clout in a city fueled by political power, constantly faced hostile political maneuvers in Congress and in the governmental departments.

These Washington machinations did not escape the attention of CPS men. Karl was critical of the churches because they "gave the public impression that they were running the camps when in essence all they were doing was paying for them."

Many felt that, once the Churches were committed to the program, the government "tightened the noose". As Robert said: "At first . . . I felt CPS was right. Later (1945) I felt that the government was taking advantage of the peace churches and ourselves."

Many others came to distrust the government, usually the Selective Service System. Leland summarized the sentiment, "[there was a] steadily increasing intervention of the military (Selective Service) in the day-to-day running of the camps. . . ."

In CPS we often heard that Mennonite young men were submissive to authority and were conditioned to follow the orders of their "superiors". Richard's remarks, however, certainly do not conform to this image: "I detect [in myself] a strong feeling of opposition to persons in 'authority'. For instance, I rebelled when told that General Hershey was to visit our unit at Akron, PA and that we should have our bunks and living quarters in good order for his inspection."

Church Management

Aside from the wisdom of accepting a managerial role in the first place, how did the men evaluate the churches' administration? For the most part, opinions were favorable.

In the early years, unit directors were drawn from the ranks of ministers and church administrators. As the war went on, directors were selected from the assignees. Financially pressed sponsors could ill afford the cost of supporting outside directors, and the assignees usually liked having one of their own in the job. From the beginning, also, most of the civilian camp staff were assignees—clerks, secretaries, first aid assistants, cooks, laundry workers, and maintenance staff. Where dieticians or nurses were hired from outside, they were paid very nominal salaries, if at all.

George's views have mellowed with the year:, "I had a delayed response to the patient and thoughtful and courageous support of the American Friends Service Committee. I was a difficult dissident during the experience."

Many people commented about the high calibre of local managers. While James' reaction was not typical, it was heard frequently: "The people that ran the camp were great. Office people were helpful. Also the government people of the Forest Service that I worked for, and all the rest of the personnel, were wonderful."

The COs generally respected the government and agency people who ran local work programs. These opinions worked both ways. Project foremen, hospital superintendents, almost universally commended the men for the quality of their work (they often said that it was superior to work done by former workers), whether it was in a former CCC camp, a mental hospital, a medical experiment, or a dairy farm. As a result, there were usually cordial relationships at the local level.

Criticism of local directors was either that they gave too much attention to official directives or that they gave too little attention to individuals in isolated locations. In the former case, some assignees thought they were too strict in following rules and regulations. As the years passed, adherence to some directives became more relaxed. Many directors eventually said they would resign if compelled to enforce the more onerous provisions, such as restrictions on weekend leave. One director, for instance, advised his church that he would never sign an AWOL report if this meant the man would be arrested and prosecuted by the FBI.

There were many CPS units, particularly the dairy farm project, where assignees worked alone and were isolated from other COs. Hours were long, and some farm families were quite unfriendly. Restricted wartime travel made it impossible for anyone to see these men very often. David observed: ". . . [there was] too little supervision and support for the individual because of the widespread assignments. As a result, too many young people were lost to the church. . . and, I fear, to the CO position. . . ."

A FELLOWSHIP OF BELIEVERS

CPS was like a gourmet recipe. The individual ingredients could be—and usually were—unpalatable; but when thoroughly mixed and baked, the resulting confection was never forgotten. Following are a few general evaluations as seen fifty years later. Comments on specific aspects of the program are dealt with in later chapters. As you will see, the taste became more pleasant in memory than it was on first bite.

Opinion divides on two issues: first, the <u>system,</u> and second, the <u>people.</u> The system was loathsome; the people great—not always sweet and kind, but challenging and stimulating. Recollections of the people were mostly positive: our fellow assignees, those who supported us with their thoughts and their material contributions, and the administrators who tried to make the best of a bad situation. As Hugh expressed it: "What was significant was not the institution of CPS. It was what individuals managed to do during those years almost in spite of CPS or in addition to CPS."

Ralph's judgement comes about as close as any to summarizing our views: "Positive in that I was both reinforced and educated by some wonderful relationships with some great fellow COs. Negative in the administration of the system; although no fault of the religious sponsors, [there were] . . . stigmas attached which temporarily affected COs."

We hoped our work might have a social or political significance; that it might make it easier for those young men who came after to say "No" when called by their nation to kill. "I no longer feel," Charles said, "that taking the CO position is a politically effective act—though it remains essential as a moral witness."

Affirmation

Opinions ranged from the mild to the eloquent: "indispensable," "the most important decision of my life," "an unmatched human experience," "a profound effect on my life," "extraordinarily stimulating and rewarding," "a key experience," and "a watershed in my life." Many said the experience made them what they were.

Many of us found the roots for our later lives. Our convictions took us to CPS, but from CPS we gained the

vision of a better life for ourselves and our world. For
Nelson the first 6 months were negative, "but the total
experience kept developing into a very positive and significant pilgrimage." Warren probably spoke for many of us, "I
wonder why I griped so much." Earl said, "I rate the penal
aspects and the bitterness of campers . . . as <u>negative</u>, but I
rate the experience of <u>transcending</u> these hardships and
frustrations as <u>positive</u> and the association with like-minded
objectors to war. . . as <u>positive</u>." Rod spoke of "a widening
of horizons, a widening of acquaintances and friendships,
many useful experiences, a lesson in self-discipline, etc."

It was a pervasive influence—affecting the selection of
our spouses, our education, our careers, our volunteer
activities, and our values and moral standards. It affected
not only our individual lives but those of our families and
friends.

For Norman it was "a very important and significant
slice of my life, with memories that will be with me until I
die. I would say it was positive; the experiences were mostly
helpful and useful and DID direct my future path."
For Warren, CPS was "one of the most significant and far-
reaching experiences of my life. It is an experience to which
I return in memory and which gives me guidance and
courage for the way ahead."

"I can't imagine my life without the CPS experience,"
Harold commented, "can't imagine what or who I would be
if I hadn't known some of those people who had a profound
effect on me." Robert agreed: "The kindred souls in CPS—
not the work done—provided a peak episode in my life."
"I was glad I could go," Orie added. "I was hungry for
Christian fellowship. . . . I enjoyed every day of the experience. I felt so sorry for my brother who was 4-F and
couldn't go."

CPS showed us how difficult it is for people to live together, but it also showed us that it is possible to get along. Indeed, the confining group life made us realize the absolute necessity of harmony.

Canby saw people work through tremendous differences. He felt "a disillusionment with how incredibly different people can be in their beliefs and behavior patterns and yet . . . [he was able] to accept them all in all that incredible variation." For Royce it was "a period of learning to live and work with many men of varying backgrounds and experiences; learning to cooperate with supervisors who did not share the CO belief; learning to adjust to situations over which I had no control."

It was not easy to absorb all those new ideas. Taber learned "meeting people . . . from different backgrounds, but similar beliefs, showed me how . . . regard for others' beliefs take time to develop." Vernon commented on how we had all come from different areas with different backgrounds and yet were " determined to live out the peaceful nonviolent life in the middle of a world gone mad with hate and war. We were encouraged by each other's faith and actions as we served side by side among government men and local community."

We also learned how to get along without money. Material things became a great deal less important. It blunted our ambition for physical comforts and gave us a healthy disrespect for materialism. "The greatest distortion CPS had on my life," Kent said, "was to minimize my concern for money; I got so used to having very little and nevertheless content . . . that I forget that I need money . . . I am proud of it. The Pentagon got very little of my money."

Living the simple life gave real meaning to the old adage, "the best things in life are free". Reed "was strongly influenced by the ideas of the simple life. . . . I did not want to become a monk, but a simpler life, closer to God, one might hope, and to nature, had a strong appeal for me."

PUBLIC POLICY

The debate over CPS goes on. It was apparent from the beginning that church objectives and public policy were at cross purposes. It was soon evident that the government wanted to keep COs as isolated as possible; the public had to be insulated from any criticism of the war. With increasing numbers of families suffering the loss of husbands, brothers, sons, and cousins, it was imperative that objectors be put out of the way. As Lester saw it, CPS was a "strategically brilliant maneuver by a militarized democratic government to isolate but not make martyrs of dissidents during a 'popular' war. . . ."

In the minds of many men, the purpose of the program was primarily punitive. Any constructive work was achieved in spite of the government.

CPS was a story of contradiction and contention. The government served its purpose by keeping us out of the way. It was, nonetheless, a short-sighted policy. The country could have benefitted so much more from this group of dedicated, hardworking, and well-trained people. It was an unconscionable waste.

CONCLUSION

Most of the people who speak in this book believed that CPS was the correct course for them. The churches were respected for underwriting the program even while they were criticized for getting into it in the first place. They respected their fellow COs, warts and all. There were many critics in the one thousand respondents; but again, I caution the reader to remember that the thoughts of the other eleven thousand are unknown, except as they can be inferred from what these men said.

Most said they would accept alternative service if placed in the same situation again, provided it was completely separated from the military. A substantial number of others, however, said they would either refuse to register or refuse any draft order if called up. For these people, once was one too many. Spencer explained, "In retrospect, I conclude that I should have taken the non-registrant position, since I now realize that conscription is the enemy."

The experience gave Donald, "strong doubts about the compromise of cooperation with conscription. . . . [I] refused to register for the 1948 draft and became imprisoned. I served eight months of an eighteen months sentence. . . . "

It is doubtful that CPS ever would—or should—be repeated. National service programs with young people giving a year or two of their lives for community service have been proposed in the U.S. Congress from time to time. The pros and cons deserve serious debate, for there is merit to the idea that citizens have an opportunity to contribute to their communities. If funds were available to the many volunteer service missions already in place, the positive aspects of CPS could serve as a guide.

1.   Stephen M. Kohn, *Jailed For Peace*. New York: Praeger Publishers, 1987. p. 10.
2.   NSBRO, *Congress Looks at the Conscientious Objector*. Washington: NSBRO, 1943. page 11.
3.   Ibid., p. 12.
4.   Ibid, p. 56.
5.   Ibid, p. 61.
6.   NSBRO, *Tolerance*. Washington: NSBRO, 1943. p. 2.

7.   Robert E. S. Thompson, "Onward, Christian Soldiers!", in
        Saturday Evening Post, August 16, 1941. p. 27.
8.   Frank Olmstead, *Conscience Compels Them*. New York: Fellowship
        of Reconciliation and Others, 1942. p. 7.
9.   Selective Service System, Camp Operations Division. Mimeo-
        graphed government document. p. 6   From CPS 21 camp
        files.

3
Work of National Importance

A s Chapter one ended we had just arrived at Civilian Public Service Camp No. 21 in Cascade Locks, Oregon. The day was December 5, 1941. We were greeted by the Camp director and his staff, given a brief tour of the facility, and assigned to our bunks in the barracks that would be our home for the next many months. (Our living quarters would be called dormitories—"barrack" was from another world.)

We arose the next day, Saturday, December 6, 1941, to a cold and blustery day that we came to learn was typical of winter in the Columbia River Gorge. But the mile-wide river with the rock and shale slopes of Wind Mountain beyond welcomed us to one of the Northwest's natural wonders. After some brief wanderings to explore this jewel of nature, the Forest Service superintendent described the various forest projects we would be performing and explained that work would be divided among crews headed by Forest Service foremen. We had interviews with the Camp Director and

Forest Service foremen to determine our work assignments.

The director's wife, a warm and kindly woman, would be the camp dietitian. As the months passed, she also became an informal counselor and "house mother". Having the director's family with four small children on the premises was a marvelous tonic for a group of young men separated from their families in the isolation of a forestry camp.

On Sunday, December 7, 1941, most of the camp attended chapel in a recently converted storage building. Little did we know that forces being unleashed that very hour across the Pacific Ocean would drastically change our lives. Following the service, we gathered in the dormitories for more get-acquainted conversation. As we sat on our bunks enjoying lively speculations about our new life, a man from the next dorm rushed in, calling out that the radio reported a Japanese military attack. Japanese bomber planes had just struck Pearl Harbor, Hawaii, on that day which "will live in infamy". Realizing that the United States would now be at war, we talked about the uncertainties that lay ahead. A grim apprehension spread across the land that dreadful day as the country lurched itself into war, and that foreboding surrounded our lives, too. Our pacifist faith would be challenged on every side.

In the weeks and months to come we would search our souls for grim truth of our belief. Could we still refuse to fight after "our country was attacked"? We would wrestle with the question and turn it over in our minds as families and friends would urge us to join the fight. But ultimately we renewed our resolve and settled down for the work ahead, anxious to demonstrate our faith in nonviolence. The war would be prosecuted in other places, but we hoped to demonstrate in our small way that man has a higher destiny.

BOON OR BOONDOGGLE

In the early days there was great hope and much idealism about the work we would be doing. This March, 1943, article in *Fellowship* magazine captures that spirit:

They [the Peace Churches] believe that the spirit of Christianity . . . requires that they . . . do constructive work; they believe that work undertaken in that spirit is redemptive in its effect upon society. Far from feeling complete freedom from the rest of the country's war guilt, they realize that they, because of their weakness and imperfection, share responsibility for war and for conscription. They know that the problems concerning the war are not something belonging exclusively to the state but are 'their babies', too. [1]

Much was said about the salutary benefits of physical work.

As they worked out the plans, it was agreed that a program of manual labor would be the order of things no matter who conducted the camp—Church or State—the planners of CPS were convinced that the real builders of a peaceful society will need to know as much about using their hands as their hearts and heads.[2]

This talk sounded a little hollow coming from people outside the program, but it was said with great sincerity. And there was a firm determination to prove to the world that we meant business. Stories of unusual deeds challenged us all. Rudy's tree planting prowess in a Michigan forestry camp, for example, became a legend. He broke all records for the number of trees planted in one day, and each day he was determined to plant more than the day before. Rudy explained:

> This area had been plagued with erosion, and foresters figured out that trees were the only hope of saving the land. I was born and raised in Michigan, and I wanted to see what we could do to improve the state's economy. My family had a tough time during the Great Depression of the 1930's; and if our work would help prevent future generations from going through what we did, I was all for it. My imagination was sparked when they told us how many trees a person could be expected to plant in a day. I decided right then that I would double that number, and I usually did—a few times even tripling it.

CPSers wanted their work to amount to something. David's comments are typical, "I felt that when a democracy decided to go to war and an individual felt he/she could not conscientiously work in that war effort, it was good for the society and for the individual conscientious objector to perform some work of social benefit instead—and at some cost to himself."

It was not easy to overlook the trivial nature of many projects, but we were determined to put in a good day's work. Canby spoke for many, "I was confirmed in my determination to do a good job on project . . . even if Selective Service was boss and I got no pay." Bernard echoed the same sentiment, "I am glad I was able to contribute to my government and country in a constructive way."

Martin agreed: "I wanted to obey and do my share of the work as I was told, hard work or not, and do an honest job without complaining. I always counted it a privilege to serve my country through the CPS way. In this way I was willing to do the work that they asked me to do."

We measured the quality of a project by how well it contributed to the well-being of people. Each person, of course, had his own idea as to what that meant. What was worthwhile for one might be meaningless for another. Everyone "marched to his own drummer", and growing seedlings could be a joy to one and an agony to another.

In Frank's opinion, "It did create a challenge to make of that experience a positive one . . . one that contributed service to society. . . . [It was] very valuable . . . in subordinating one's own ends for a period in service to mankind."

Someone else said, "What I did for the government agency, I did because I was required to do it. Whatever I did after that freed me."

To rail against the system, LeRoy thought, was not worth the stress: "COs could well feel they got off to a bad start and be bitter for many years, feeling they lost all that time, money, etc. Or they could determine to work . . . for the good of mankind."

The most aggravating aspects of the work came when governmental agencies filled in time with make-work projects. In the total balance of things, this probably happened no more than it would in any other place of employment. But when projects were marginal even at best, meaningless fill-in time was an insult. It is true, also, that the CPS men were probably overly sensitive to such things.

Young men everywhere were being drafted for tasks they did not choose. Military draftees spent a great deal of their time in menial chores, too. That did not stop us, however, from asking why a country would waste its human resources in such a reckless way, whether they were soldiers or COs.

As the war continued, the pressure mounted for more meaningful work. In the base camps much work was reminiscent of WPA leaf raking in the 1930's. Some government project managers seemed to say, "let's see how long they can stand this". When assignments were described as "important to the country" by project superintendents who knew they were simply filling time, the transparent deception was very demoralizing.

The situation became intolerable for one camp director who was being pressured by a project superintendent to expel an assignee for his criticism of a work project. The assignee, the superintendent charged, was agitating against him. The camp director had some pointed comments:

We operate under a system of conscription for war, which is basically obnoxious to most of our men. It becomes only partially satisfactory when they are permitted to engage in satisfying work under conditions geared to use their abilities and offering opportunities for growth and satisfactory relationships.

The Forest Service has had first claim on the time and attention of the men here and were given opportunity to win their interest and loyalty, so that other work opportunities would have remained less attractive. If it has not succeeded in holding the men by inspiring them with a sense of importance of the work here, it is obvious it can do nothing but estrange the men further.

Why cannot the Forest Service make use of the peculiar resources which are inherent in the kind of men who have for the most part made up our camp and particularly that class of men who have furnished leadership in the past? Some of these men have been accustomed to sharing in the management of the stores, schools, farms, and other enterprises of which they have

been a part. They have a unique desire to make their
work socially significant to the maximum. They have
been impelled to seek efficient means of operating.
Here they have not been impressed that the work is as
beneficial to the race as forestry can be made. They
have evidence that the work is not even efficiently
planned, and rightly or wrongly, they have the hunch
that if some of their number were invited to share in
the overall planning and particularly in the use and
disposition of men, it would be possible to achieve
more of the goals of the Forest Service and more of the
concerns of the men.

Why should the Forest Service, which has been
ready to adjust to various types of equipment, weather
conditions, terrain, and vegetation find it difficult to
recognize variations in groups of men and adjust its
methods to fit? I venture to predict that the understanding use of the men will be fully as rewarding as
the same attitude is when applied to other elements.

The action of the Forest Service in attempting to
force [the assignee's] removal very largely succeeded in
alienating the men of our camp who are convinced that
the Forest Service was operating with the spirit of
vindictive retaliation.

It is my resolute intention to correct, as far as
possible, my past blunders; and I invite the Forest
Service to share in this venture in redeeming the
situation which is at present neither the most pleasant
nor most conducive to a good work record.[3]

Early in the war, the church agencies were assured
that COs would be assigned to relief and rehabilitation
service in areas devastated by the war. When the program
was finally established, a group of eager men gathered for

training in overseas relief. A small contingent was placed aboard a steamer and was in Africa on its way to China when word came that Congress had passed a resolution prohibiting the expenditure of public funds for the program. The cost of operating the relief unit was to be borne by the Church agencies, but public monies would be expended for governmental oversight. The total program was canceled before it could get started, and the churches were even compelled to pay the cost of returning the men from Africa.

The collapse of the such hoped-for relief program shattered the hopes of men throughout the camps. To rub salt in the wounds, Walter told about this public meeting with then-Senator Harry Truman: "On the occasion of Senator Truman's appearance at Iowa State, one CO asked if COs would have opportunity to serve in . . . [foreign reconstruction after the war]. The Senator had a quick, flat 'NO'. Why? 'Because they're unfit for it'."

As frustration piled on frustration, CPS became unbearable for some men. "After two years at three different camps," Arthur declared, "I decided that CPS was controlled by Selective Service, was really a form of forced labor, and was largely irrelevant to peacemaking. Therefore, I walked out . . . ."

Walt made the same decision: "During a year in CPS I came to the conclusion that my position should oppose military conscription as well as military service. I informed the hospital administrator . . . and wrote the Attorney General that I would do 'work of national importance'. . . but not under conscription. . . . I received a two-year sentence to Lewisburg Penitentiary. . . ."

Edward carried his resistance a step further, "If I had a son, I would try to dissuade him from jail or camp and would encourage him to flee the country [rather than register for the draft]. . . ."

In the summer of 1942, a group of CPSers addressed the problem in, *Toward Greater Opportunity in CPS*:

We consider conscription to be a process of involuntary servitude, which denies the freedom of occupational choice basic to democracy; but we have acquiesced to service under the Civilian Public Service program in the hope of having an opportunity to make a positive contribution toward solving the major problems of our society. Instead of being employed on projects affording this opportunity, however, we have been almost completely shunted aside, where we remain in safety and impotence, with very little use made of our abilities.[4]

Men building a stock pond for the Soil Conservation Service described their project:

With shovels and wheelbarrows, six to a dozen men work steadily . . . for three days and still may not complete the scalping. One of these men was formerly a university instructor in physics, another a graduate student in political science, another was formerly a machine operator on a large Kansas farm. And so on. Each man knows that the work could have been finished by two men and a tractor in half a day. . . . The job is big enough for steam shovels and caterpillar tractors, and the Government admits that it owns many idle machines, easily available. . . . Almost to a man, conscientious objectors protest easy artificial work, demanding instead, power and equipment to staunch the rapid ebb of America's basic vitality—her soil.[5]

Selective Service maintained a strong fire fighting capability by keeping men in camps run by the Soil Conservation Service, the National Park Service, and the Forest Service. There had been widespread fear that the Japanese would plant incendiary bombs in the country's forests, particularly on the West Coast. Such a threat never did materialize, but there were two or three reports of such hostile action. In any event, in order to maintain a strong fire fighting force, the work force was concentrated in the base camps.

Discontent and restlessness continued to grow; and in April, 1943, a group of CPS men called a Conference on Social Action in Chicago to formulate demands for better work projects. This action so distressed General Hershey that he froze all furloughs, hoping to scuttle the conference. Hershey's action intensified interest in the conference that ultimately drew people from all over the country. The conference was delayed by a week, finally being held on April 19-25, 1943. The published Proceedings of the conference, while giving a tolerant nod to CPS—"It is undeniable that those in CPS are making a witness against war by their presence in the camps"—emphasized the long term evils of conscription and the shortcomings of alternative service for COs. The churches and NSBRO came in for their share of criticism for cooperating with Selective Service.[6]

The Chicago meeting had hoped to create a protest movement within CPS. Most of the CPS participants returned to their units, vowing to work for expanded project opportunities. With a public hostile to complaining COs, not everyone agreed on the value of protests. There can be little doubt, however, that protests did have an impact. The government did not want the public reminded of any war resistance.

Many public agencies, faced with acute labor shortages, pleaded with Selective Service for help from conscientious objectors. They received requests from mental hospitals, homes for mentally deficient children, children's centers, homes for the deaf, work camps, social settlements, educational institutions, housing agencies, Red Cross, youth centers, YMCA's, and a myriad of other such enterprises. At the height of war in 1943, General Hershey said he was unable to meet the labor needs of so many worthy organizations, "I haven't anywhere near enough conscientious objectors to meet the demands for use in places which really need them." [7] Selective Service responded to some of these requests, and a number of worthwhile projects were established. (A list of these projects will be found in Appendix B.)

All this did not lessen the frustrations of work in the base camps, and sentiment about the work program became more bitter.

At one of the government camps this past winter the men inaugurated the custom of singing Negro spirituals, substituting, however, words appropriate to their own status. These melancholy tunes, sung in unison at meals or in the trucks going to work were a forcible reminder of the parallels between civilian public service and Negro slavery in the United States before the Civil War. . . . no matter how veiled, there is still no essential difference between conscript labor and slavery. . . . The old slave codes, which regulated the Negroes' conduct, have their replica in the detailed Selective Service regulations.[8]

Late in the war, when the government took over some of the base camps, discontent grew into demonstrations and slowdowns. The protests against insignificant work intensified.

Later, when assignee demobilization lagged behind that of soldiers after the war, assignees changed their focus from the shortcomings of CPS to the evils of conscription. Protests now concentrated on the harm of conscription in peacetime.

An assignee from the Lapine, Oregon, camp described the purpose of their protest:

> The Lapine episode was a demonstration, not a slow-down or a strike. . . . We . . . substantiated our thesis that conscription itself, unalloyed and unvarnished, is completely destructive and adds nothing to human welfare.

> Never once was there any disobedience, but the foremen were pressed for every decision, and they soon saw that the situation was utterly hopeless. Without our help—voluntary help—they were powerless to make us produce. . . .

> Conscription adds nothing . . . it merely imprisons the laborer and steals the product of his labor.

> Yes, conscription works. It is a powerful force and one that cannot be brushed aside. But it is not [a] constructive force . . . . It is all negative. It breeds obedience and stagnation, not intelligence and growth. . . . We know that it can kill just as surely as a rifle bullet—but more deadly than that is the danger that in accepting it as necessary we stamp man a 'commodity' and kill the mind.[9]

Nonviolent resistance in the government-operated Minersville, California, camp in 1946 received considerable media attention. In May, 1946, Jack Foise, staff writer for the San Francisco Chronicle, wrote a three-part story on the episode.

In commenting on a similar slow-down in Glendora, California, the American Civil Liberties Union said:

The fundamental grievance of discrimination arouses the sympathy of all lovers of fair play. This but adds to the discrimination of the Selective Service Act and its administration in which no provision was made for the care of dependents, and men have been compelled to work on projects of far less than national importance without compensation.[10]

In summary, most COs would say that the work was not the most significant aspect of the CPS program. More important was their testimony against war by their refusal of military service. If they could do something worthwhile in their alternative service, so much the better; but the primary purpose was to send an unequivocal message to the governments of the world that citizens cannot be coerced into killing their brothers. CPS was our way of sending that message.

THE RESULTS

Early in the war Colonel Kosch, Selective Service Director of Camp Operations, said that COs did two to two-and-a-half times as much work as CCC men did. The agencies sponsoring the special detached service projects were universally satisfied that COs had performed their work in an honest and thorough manner. In chronicling CPS achievements, the Selective Service System emphasized the quantities of work performed. The church organizations, while acknowledging the physical results, saw the results differently.

The government recorded: miles of trails maintained, number of fires fought, number of trees planted, and the like. Selective Service tabulated a total of 8,237,866 man days of labor in the six years from May 15, 1941 to March 31, 1947.

Here are some typical projects: 100,266 man days in forest fire fighting for the U.S. Forest Service; 1,070,170 trees planted for the Soil Conservation Service; 156,173 square yards of bank sloping for the National Park Service; 25,232 man days in fire suppression for the National Park Service; 18,440 man days to land surveys for the General Land Office; 1,347,363 man days in mental hospitals; 150,713 man days in scientific research such as the "guinea pig" projects; 54,193 man days on public health projects in Mississippi and Florida and 51,280 in Puerto Rico. No dollar value was placed on all this work, nor was any mention made that this labor cost the government not one red cent.[11]

The assignees and the church organizations who paid the bills saw the accomplishments quite differently. They were much more interested in how the projects contributed to the quality of life. Tree planting in the rains of Michigan or Oregon would not have been a city-dweller's choice. However, one of those tree planters who visited the scene many years later was able to say, "When we were planting thousands of little trees on that burned-off mountain, I never thought it would look like this; it is just simply beautiful." Others had similar reactions to their work in soil conservation, park preservation, and agricultural development. The projects with more direct human service such as mental hospitals, homes for the handicapped, public health, and scientific experiments offered more immediate satisfaction.

One observer-participant (a Quaker lady who was dietitian in several CPS camps) remarked:

> The camp life offers them not so much the opportunity of doing anything important; but does offer them the opportunity to become citizens of incalculable importance to the community. It all depends on what

they make of <u>themselves</u>—and even picking up litter can be used as an opportunity for growth if they shift their minds from the litter to themselves.[12]

The Director of the agricultural experiment station at Ames, Iowa, wrote to Colonel Kosch: "This group of men have probably made, through their work during the past year, as great a contribution as any equal number of men in the State of Iowa."[13]

The Chief Forester for the state of Oregon reported on the work done at the Elkton camp in 1944. "Their fine attitude has always been most commendable, and we believe has been of great importance in achieving the good results that have been attained."[14]

The director of the Commission on Acute Respiratory Diseases in the Surgeon General's office wrote to each man who participated in the Atypical Pneumonia Experiment: "I should like to express appreciation for the contribution you made in the course of the recent experiment conducted by CPS Camp No. 108 in Gatlinburg. Your willingness to serve as a volunteer in the attempt to transmit atypical pneumonia in human beings was a courageous act of the very highest order."[15]

The mental hospital work was especially notable, not only within CPS but throughout the mental health profession. (See Chapter 10 for a discussion of men who devoted their careers to the mental health profession, much of it as a result of their wartime experiences.) The men were often commended not only for their accomplishments but for their gentle and compassionate manner. One visitor to a CPS mental hospital unit observed,

> One thing I wanted to find out was whether a conscientious objector, through his methods of nonviolent good will, has something to contribute to the

mental hospital. . . . [Before the COs arrived] there were attendants who used violence. A number were heartless and brutal. As a matter of record, no patient was ever injured in a hospital except by 'accident' or as 'the result of a fall'. When the COs were introduced into one of the hospitals the number of 'accidents' decreased forty percent in three months' time!

One objector assigned to the violent ward refused to take the broomstick offered by the Charge. When he entered the ward the patients crowded round asking, "where is your broomstick?" He said he thought he would not need it. "But suppose some of us gang up on you?" The CO guessed they wouldn't do that and started talking about other things. Within two or three days the patients were seen gathered around the unarmed attendant, telling him their troubles. He felt much safer than the Charge who had only his broomstick for company.[16]

The final Selective Service report on CPS contained a number of comments from mental hospital superintendents. This one is typical:

I can speak most favorably as to the value of the work performed. With practically no exception the men have been diligent, compatible, conscientious, and well-behaved. . . . After the first few months of the unit's assignment to the hospital there was very little opposition expressed and no overt antagonism displayed.[17]

. . . Looking Back

Malcolm described the shock of his first day on a CPS work project, "My first work day . . . hoeing a garden at

Powellsville, Maryland . . . when the world was on fire made
me disillusioned indeed."

"I am not starry-eyed about the tremendous amount
of good that was accomplished," Peter said. "Except for
special projects such as mental hospital service, most CPS
work was work of national 'impotence'."

John explained the evolution of his thought: "A period
of intense frustration, anguish, anger, and impotence. . . .
Much of the work was merely a part of a boondoggle and
effort by the government to keep conscientious objectors out
of sight and out of mind. Fire suppression duties . . .
provided some opportunity for plainly worthwhile service
and work. . . . Massive tree-planting efforts also were seen as
an effective contribution. . . . Only in later years did I come
to a realization of my good fortune at being in a safe and
productive environment during the horrible violence and
destruction of World War II."

"The two camp experiences," Carl said, "weren't
worth much. However, the three years I spent in Presbyterian Hospital in New York proved to be very valuable in my
pastoral calling. . . ."

Paul thought we could have made more of our
opportunities, "In a camp in Virginia . . . much time was
spent in a constructive rather than destructive manner, but I
believe we failed to minister to mankind in an effective way.
My . . . work in a mental hospital . . . contributed much in a
positive way to the welfare of humanity."

For Lloyd the base camp years were worthless, "I felt
that most of my CPS experience was a waste of time (i.e., I
did nothing significant to help my country and my fellow
man); although my time at NSBRO did seem more significant."

Jack found one redeeming feature to base camp. "I entered camp with great expectation of doing 'work of national importance'. That feeling soon dissipated with 'made' work projects. Fighting forest fires was always uplifting. . . ."

In spite of it all, many were able to say, as Gregg did. "I think that . . . with all its limitations . . . I did do work of national importance."

With the world gripped in a devastating war, everyone was supposed to be doing noble and heroic things; so to be put "out of the way" was frustrating and aggravating. Looking back fifty years later, it does not seem nearly as useless as it did at the time. Many emphasized the <u>constructive</u> nature of the work in contrast to the destruction of war. We were at least building rather than destroying.

For Donald "The projects we worked on were for the well-being of people rather than the sadness and destruction caused by warfare."

Paul concurred: "The emphasis of CPS was on 'building up', doing good or helping rather than tearing down. . . . I wanted to be in a unit that made a contribution of some kind rather than simply passing time."

Eugene found purpose in what he did: "Of immediate significance was the work in soil conservation by taking corrective measures to prevent erosion of land. Directly related was the work in tree nurseries, growing seedlings for mass and isolated plantings. . . . teaching and caring for the mentally ill has brought about profound changes in the approaches for the treatment and care of those requiring psychiatric attention. . . . The relief training unit made deep and lasting impacts immediately following the war and for many years thereafter."

Experimental projects for the Surgeon General's Office, Public Health Service, and Office of Scientific Research and Development resulted in a considerable body of scientific knowledge. This knowledge is still making contributions to the health of people all around the world.

Berle recalls his participation in one of these projects, "The last six months at Rochester were the most significant to me. It is becoming more significant. . . . We have had the rewarding experience of being informed of the significance of this basic research in the medical profession. Thousands upon thousands of lives have been saved by the cardio research work done. . . . One of University of Rochester's physiologists [who had served in the Navy during World War II] discovered the research and suggested the Peace Center idea [as a tribute to the men of peace who served there]." The Peace Center was ultimately established at the University of Rochester and named for Peter Watson, one of the participants. (See Chapter 10.)

Work in a mental hospital was, for Walter, "the opportunity to try to bring help to a group of people we found to be much worse off than we were: people locked up in state institutions."

LeRoy's work in a mental hospital unit was rewarded by a number of letters from the families of his former patients. He shared one of those letters with us:

Mother wanted me to write to you and let you know that my father, Dave, passed away March 12, 1947. You were so very kind to him when you were at the hospital, and we have felt that we could never thank you enough for all you did for him. He often talked about you and missed you after you had gone,

as no one took care of him as you did. . . . /s/ Mary
McFadden and Family

What did the public know about the work of CPS, and
when did it know it? We often wondered if anyone cared.
We now know that it did matter and that the results are still
evident.

Norman reported visiting the site of his project many
years later, "Last week I travelled through the Merom,
Indiana, area and saw some large pine trees I helped plant
instead of killing people in the war."

We did think that not many people even cared, but
John reports this episode in an unexpected place:

"At the conclusion of my services on the Malaria Unit
at Massachusetts General . . . an Army officer presented each
of us with a fancily embossed certificate signed by the
Secretary of War and heads of the Army, Navy, and Air
Force citing us for 'valiant service to the war effort'. Here I
had spent four years trying to witness against exactly that,
and here was my reward! I wanted to tear it up. . . . Some
others . . . were delighted to have it as they faced more
hostile reception in their home communities."

Personal Rewards

Whatever the quality of the work, there were other
satisfactions.

"I am an outdoor person," Joel said, "so assignment to
CCC camps [was] a delightful experience for me . . . to be
parked in the midst of the White Mountains cutting firewood
was basically a delight."

Worden was rewarded by "new experiences: fighting
forest fires . . . developing confidence and enjoyment in
forests and other outdoors activities."

Howard, tongue in cheek, observed, "I . . . can thank CPS for obliging me to do physical labor in the wild out-of-doors. . . [which] provided me with so much exercise that I have never needed any in later life."

Many of our projects gave us a view of the human condition that we had never seen and probably never would have seen. The vast majority of us—still in our twenties or younger—knew little of environmental problems or the poverty in which so many people live.

"The hookworm project", Harold said, "was a big eye-opener for me. It was there that I first learned how the blacks and poor whites were treated. Without this much experience, I doubt that I would have ever really known or understood the problem."

Reed relished the physical work—and a great deal more. "I learned things from the work projects, despite our gripes about them. I learned how to handle an axe fairly well, how to cut down trees, how to use a scythe, how to do some carpentry. . . . how to cook, how to keep coal fires. . . I learned about cows and pigs and chickens, and milking, and laundry work, and teaching and supervision, and institutional social work, and mental deficiency. . . I learned about state institutions and their problems and abuses."

Many men had their first brush with manual labor and learned what to expect from it—after blisters and sun burn.

"It was my first contact with hard physical work," Bill said, "and I learned to like it."

"I learned basic carpentry and building skills," Canby said, "which have saved me thousands in the years since."

Channing's CPS work prepared him for his career. "It propelled me into UNRRA, UNRWA, Africa, etc."

"My CO assignment did get me into hospital laboratory work," Norman said, "and eventually I became a biochemist with my own private clinical lab. So my career was really the result of my CO assignment."

"My project work as a ground water geologist," said Robert, "began my professional career."

As a CPS administrator, Bob "received a lot of help on human relations skills and affirmation of my organizational gifts."

Reinhardt told how his work in soil conservation influenced his farming: "The Soil Conservation Service . . . experience made me realize that we need to be stewards of the privilege we have in farming the unstable land we were living on, and I almost immediately put that concept into practice as I began farming after my return from CPS . . . . I experienced ridicule. . .[from] neighbors and passers-by . . . when they saw my terraces around rather than up and down the hills. . . . After about eight years of this practice, [people] could tell that I could raise good crops on the hillsides. . . . After that I had dozens of converts who began to do the same thing."

Bob had grown to love the mountains in his youth, but CPS broadened his knowledge of the natural world, "It added to my love for the mountains and forests . . . [and gave me] an appreciation of the prairie."

THE FINAL BALANCE

In spite of our objections to the way CPS work projects were handled, we knew that the fate of 12,000 conscientious objectors was not high on the national priorities. There is no doubt, too, that CPS was at times an annoyance to Selective Service and the governmental agencies running the projects.

And most of the time Selective Service and the project agencies were an annoyance to the Church organizations.

Both sides had good reasons to make the best of the situation—the government, to keep COs out of the public eye, and the churches and individual COs, to salvage some of their hopes. The conflicts and misunderstandings usually resulted from differences in perception rather than from deliberate obstruction. Selective Service, for its part, saw CPS facilities as miniature military reservations and COs as peculiar (or malicious) ingrates, people who were willing to let others "do their fighting for them". Most of us in CPS probably never fully comprehended the animosity toward us. We saw ample evidence of it, but we did not know how deep it was. We did, however, learn what minorities face in times of stress.

In the heart of every CO is the conviction that we must make a position and and hold to it. In a pragmatic world where decisions are expected to be "realistic", standing on principle is at least "quaint"; some would have much stronger terms. The crises and conflicts in the CPS work projects nearly always arose out of different ways of looking at fundamental issues. The camp director's letter to Forest Service officials above is a classic example.

The term, "work of national importance" was a favorite topic of discussion and the butt of a good many jokes, some leaning on the term "impotence". Whatever the writers of the original draft law had in mind, the reality was a mockery of those words. After the Church founders had committed themselves and the work program was actually begun, they learned that Selective Service had no inclination to help the Church sponsors realize their goals.

Indeed, church administrators on more than one occasion found Selective Service annoyed by the continual talk about "socially significant" projects.

The COs themselves were eager for what they thought would be an opportunity to perform some meaningful work to help alleviate some of the world's miseries. The skills and capabilities of the CPS work force was high, with above average education level, prewar work experience, and motivation. In a world at war, they were looking for something worthwhile to do. It was a foolish waste of talent, as the prejudices of government bureaucrats compromised their ability to make optimum use of the skills they had available to them. This is the real tragedy of the CPS work program.

1. Dick Brown, Chuck Ludwig, and Dave Salstrom, "In Defense of CPS", in *Fellowship.* March, 1943. p. 56.
2. Richard C. Mills "Civilian Public Service, An Experiment in Personal Discipline", April 6, 1943. From CPS Camp 21 files.
3. Mark Y. Schrock, *Memorandum to James C. Iler, Supervisor, Mt. Hood National Forest from Mark Y. Schrock, Director, CPS Camp No. 21, July 16, 1943.* From CPS Camp 21 files.
4. William Henderson et al. *Toward Greater Opportunity in C.P.S.*, August 5, 1942. From CPS Camp 21 files.
5. Lester Mattison, "Inside Looking In!" in *Fellowship*, November, 1942, p. 190.
6. *Proceedings -- Chicago Conference on Social Action.* The Chicago Conference on Social Action, Chicago, 1943. p. 10. From CPS Camp 21 files.
7. "Lack of 'Conchies' Worries Hershey," in *Portland Oregonian*, October 3, 1943. From CPS Camp 21 files.
8. Arthur A. Ekirch, Jr., "CPS and Slavery," in *Pacifica Views*. Glendora, California, August 25, 1944. pp. 1 & 4. From CPS Camp 21 Camp files.

9.   George Baird, "Experiment in Conscription"", in *Fellowship*, March, 1945, pp. 41-43.

10.   Glendora Strikers' Defense Committee, *Five Years* . . . . , Los Angeles, 1946. From CPS Camp 21 files.

11.   Selective Service System, *Conscientious Objection, Special Monograph No. 11, Vol. II*, Washington: U.S. Government Printing Office, 1950. pp 180-199.

12.   Nancy Neumann, letter written during World War II. From CPS Camp 21 files.

13.   American Friends Service Committee, *The Experience of the American Friends Service Committee in Civilian Public Service*. Philadelphia, 1945. pp. 26.

14.   Ibid., p. 27.

15.   Ibid., p. 27-28.

16.   Frank Olmstead, "They Asked for a Hard Job," in *Fellowship*, November, 1943, pp. 192-193.

17.   Selective Service System, *Conscientious Objection, Special Monograph No. ll, Volume I*, Washington: U. S. Government Printing Office, 1950. pp. 175.

4
The Hope
and
the Reality

Who do you think you are? Don't you know I'm in charge of these camps under Selective Service?" Colonel Kosch was getting things straightened out for Thomas Jones, director of Friends Civilian Public Service camps. Jones had been talking about the "creative pioneering" that COs were anticipating. "My dear man," Kosch continued, "the draft is under the United States government operation. Conscientious objectors are draftees just as soldiers are. Their activities are responsible to the government. The Peace Churches are only camp managers. Do you understand that?"[1] (Some months later, as we saw above, Col. McLean gave us his version of that script.)

That was a cruel blow to the man who only a short time before had written so passionately about the great adventure for COs who

As 'Creative Pioneers' joyously accept the opportunity to demonstrate a spirit of love in wartime through constructive service to humanity. . . .

The present opportunity for alternative service in Civilian Public Service camps is not an imposition but a privilege accorded by the government to persons who seek to defend individual sovereignty, the right of conscience and freedom of religion. It is a manifestation of state cooperation in the preservation of democracy and the restoration of international good-will through physical and spiritual sharing in the responsibilities of a new age. Motivated by an inner compulsion, these 'Creative Pioneers', gladly pay the cost of an opportunity to discover themselves in 'Living Fellowships'—where work and service are rendered without reservation and earthly gain.[2]

So began the rocky relationship between the churches and the U.S. government. In effect, the colonel was telling the churches that the game score was already known—or perhaps that the game had been called because of rain. The illusion of civilian direction was revealed once and for all—just as the first inning began. The church members who scrimped and saved to pay for this adventure never fully understood this ominous beginning. It did not take the assignees long to figure it out.

The churches were compelled to approach Selective Service with hat in hand for approval of projects they thought were part of the original agreement. Selective Service was holding all the cards, and they had no patience with "whining" complaints from COs. Indeed, they knew that a wartime Congress saw things quite differently from the Congress that approved the CO Section 5(g) in the Selective Training and Service Act. During the war some Congressmen urged the abolition of Section 5(g), and only when the military complained that they did not want these people was Congress persuaded to leave things alone.

Many of us learned for the first time what it meant to be a minority. We learned that constitutional provisions for equal rights will not protect a minority from a vengeful majority. The Blacks had known this for generations, and Japanese Americans were soon to learn it. "Civilian direction" meant nothing to a governmental bureaucracy determined to keep dissidents "in the closet".

Early in the war Col. Kosch visited CPS facilities from time to time. On one visit he proclaimed, "We must respect the army because they protect and preserve this program. [This was not much comfort for men who saw few redeeming qualities in the program anyway.] We must keep out of the limelight to prevent the public from becoming antagonistic."[3] Selective Service was reflecting the sentiments of the American Legion and similar groups. However, a major public opinion survey conducted during the war found that the general public—especially soldiers who had actually been at a warfront—had few negative opinions about COs.[4]   (See Chapter 5 below.)

The churches' visions were described in a pamphlet by the Church of the Brethren:

A large number of religious objectors, whose conscience makes military service impossible for them, are entering Civilian Public Service camps to train in the arts of peace and brotherliness. The soldier beats plowshares into swords and goes forth to kill and destroy. The conscientious objector beats swords into plowshares—into hoes, picks, shovels—and goes forth to preserve the soil, protect the forests, rebuild shattered homes, preserve health, and defend foundations upon which democracy rests.[5]

Harold Row, director of the Brethren CPS program was full of hope. "This is the first time in our church's history (indeed of world history) that we have been allowed to give a *positive* testimony of our peace doctrines in time of war. . . to demonstrate that Brethren who refuse to kill, love their country deeply, and are willing to sacrifice for its good."[6]

Paul Comly French expressed the Friends' view: "I think most of the people who participated in the decision to accept the responsibility felt that it would give them an opportunity to prepare men for the tasks that would come with the ending of the war and the reconstruction period that would face us at home and abroad."[7]

Henry Fast, an early Mennonite participant, believed that the young men assigned to CPS would, "learn how to help people . . . repair their minds and feelings and to work together to lift the level of their living for... the good and happiness of everyone."

For the founders of the program, CPS was: " . . . an opportunity for the members of the three peace churches to express their national loyalty without the necessity of killing in battle or of going to jail for their beliefs. . . . Men of good will . . . fashioned from their dreams a concept of Civilian Public Service which would be a laboratory where men could learn to live together harmoniously and constructively even in the midst of a great war."[8]

In the heat of the war, many citizens hated to see able-bodied young men working in the woods while others were risking their lives in battle. Many of us wondered about that, too. We had hoped for much more significant work. For families who suffered the pain of killed brothers, sisters, husbands, and wives, tolerance of the CO wore thin. However, returning soldiers who had seen war at first hand were much more understanding. Having experienced the horrors of war, they were open to the idea that refusal to take part in war may be a way of bringing the madness to an end.

Those of us who came from families with brothers and sisters in the military knew the anguish of having a CO in the family. A man who volunteered for the CPS smoke jumper unit said that his family was "disgraced" by his CO stand, and by participating in a dangerous endeavor he hoped to atone for refusing military service. Many of the men who volunteered for the "guinea pig" projects were showing their willingness to put their lives on the line for a positive good.

Wilbur had felt a "sting of safety" in being shunted off to the wilderness,

The way of nonviolence was an appropriate response to war [for me]. I had a brother who served in the Air Force and was exposed to life threatening situations. I lived and served in a very secure environment. I thought it somewhat unfair that my position did not require that I make a similar sacrifice. . . . I would have been willing to experience such a condition.

WHOSE PROGRAM WAS IT?

As Selective Service tightened its control over CPS operations, people who saw the positive side of CPS in 1941 became more critical. Early supporters began to question the wisdom of Church participation. Frank Olmstead, who had earlier expressed such high expectations, began to see ominous consequences:

We come to an appraisal of the arrangement which the Church leaders made with the government in establishing CPS. Some men feel keenly that the government is violating a most vital principle when they compel men under the Selective Service law to work under a Church board. They see this as linking church and state. Many of them know their history and realize what the union of church and state has done to religion in Europe. They are perturbed about the already apparent influence of the present set-up upon religion in the camps. Others feel most keenly the fact that the church imposes upon the COs a far more rigorous standard than was demanded by Congress. The church leaders raised the bars to compel every CO to work for nothing and to support himself or be supported through private gifts.[9]

One of the strongest indictments came from Evan Thomas of the Fellowship of Reconciliation in October, 1944:

The time has come, I think, when some of us must openly renounce the leadership of the Historic Peace Churches and make a public issue of the failure of the Service Committees to achieve the kind of challenge that some of us have in mind. . . . After years of waiting it is now my considered judgment that pacifists must break away from the leadership of the Historic Peace Churches, if they are to be most effective.

I am aware of the emphasis of religious pacifists on love, but it is indeed disconcerting when love turns to the paths of expediency and is more anxious to understand and excuse the devious methods of practical politics than of conscientious objectors who are prepared to risk their all in opposing war. . . .

It is common knowledge among men in CPS camps that one of the favorite arguments used by NSBRO representatives in defense of their policies is, "if we don't do it this way, you will get something worse." That, of course, is the outstanding argument of the supporters of war and is based on pure expediency. . .

Through its financial obligations in directing and supporting camps for COs granted alternative service under conscription, the NSBRO has created a vested interest in conscription.[10]

This language seems intemperate in the light of what we later learned about NSBRO's efforts to expand the project work. It was, however, a sentiment widely held at the height of the war.

These condemnations must have seemed like double jeopardy to the church administrators who faced a terrible inequity in dealing with the quagmire of the Washington bureaucracy. For example, the church agencies were required to post bonds for government property occasionally loaned to them (old army blankets, for instance). Thousands of people were working without pay, yet the government posted no bond for their protection. In short, the government wanted guarantees for the protection of its <u>property</u>; but it was unwilling to guarantee protection of the <u>people.</u>

Always short of money, camp directors were cautioned in their requests for governmental property. Here are the guidelines for the 1943 Budget Planning document:

> The National Service Board has posted a bond of $500,000 with the government to assure that they will pay reimbursement to the U.S. Treasury for each item of government property that is lost or destroyed WITHOUT ADEQUATE EXPLANATION BEING MADE.

> [To make matters worse, Selective Service decided whether an explanation was adequate, further underscoring the degree to which the church organizations were beholden to Selective Service:]

> In case of losses FOR WHICH EXPLANATION CAN BE GIVEN, the NSBRO is freed of responsibility upon specific authorization from Selective Service. (Adequate explanation means that explanation must be made immediately after loss or damage.)[11]

WORTHY OF THEIR HIRE

The lack of compensation was never far from our minds. For some, it was a vital issue and for others relatively unimportant. Whether the lack of money created a hardship or whether it did not, it was seen as a symbol of discrimination. For some people—particularly those with dependents—the absence of income was a calamity; for others it was merely an inconvenience. But to everyone involuntary servitude was an outrage.

In Congressional hearings on the draft law in 1940, the lawmakers assumed COs would be compensated for their "work of national importance" in the same manner as soldiers. By 1941 the political climate in Washington was changing rapidly, and the President is reputed to have said that he would not ask Congress for appropriations to pay COs. Those who had nursed the CO provision through Congress feared that hostile forces could destroy everything if they made an issue of it.

As late as 1942 Congress declared its intention to support the CPS program. Public Law 630 of June 27, 1942, stated:

Such amounts as may be necessary shall be available for the planning, directing, and operations of a program of work of national importance under civilian direction . . . [for] individuals found to be conscientiously opposed to participation in work of the land or naval forces . . . including also the pay and allowances of such individuals at rates not in excess of those paid to persons inducted into the Army under the Selective Service System, and such privileges as are accorded such inductees. . . .[12]

In light of this specific declaration by Congress, it is now clear that the military officers of Selective Service were determined to see that COs were not compensated.

In a Congressional hearing on February 17, 1943, General Hershey explained his view of compensation for COs:

I had a request from the governor of one state for over 5,000 men for a hospital for the insane.

I could use—how many—50,000, if we had them.

[Senator Wallgren: Do you feel that they should be paid?]

Definitely not. It would destroy the best public relations. The thing we have to consider is they have not received any pay so far, and I think I would be supported by 60 to 70 percent of these people, who consider that is one of the contributions they are making to show that they are really conscientious objectors and conscientiously believe what they came to believe, and I know some that will not accept, under any circumstances, government money.

On the same day General Hershey saw another dimension to the issue of pay for COs:

I do not believe that the government as an employer can escape its responsibility to an employee. I think, after the war is over—before it is over—we have got to face the problem of, if they are injured, that they have some claim as an employee.

[Senator O'Mahoney: . . . since the Congress, by a law which was properly approved, granted exemption . . . [and] authorized their employment in a civilian capacity—this Congress should not punish them by denying them the benefits that come from the compensation law?]

"That is right."[13]

These apparent inconsistencies in the director's position are further compounded by the recommendations in the final Selective Service report on CPS in 1950. In this report Selective Service said that men should not be expected to work without pay in any future alternative service program.

In a separate hearing, Congressman Kilday questioned Colonels Keesling and Kosch:

Mr. Kilday: They are not paid, are they, Colonel?

Col. Keesling: No sir, Mr. Kilday: they are not paid anything; nor do they get family allowances. . . .

Mr. Kilday: They get food and clothing. Who pays for that?

Col. Keesling: In the camps, the fee is taken care of by the Church groups. . . .

Mr. Kilday: Of course they get no family allowances?

Col. Kosch: No, Sir, there is no pay or allowances.

Mr. Kilday: Now on this question of having refused to fight; of course all of these men have been processed by their own Selective Service Boards, and have been held to be conscientious objectors?

Col. Kosch: Yes, Sir.

Mr. Kilday: In other words, they were prevented from participating in the Armed Services because of their own conscientious objections?

Col. Kosch: They are serving their country under the provisions of the Selective Service law.

Mr. Kilday: It is not a case of a man who refuses to fight. It is a group of people, recognized by law as being exempt from the necessity of participating in combat, but who were required to participate in essential civilian service, is that right?

Col. Kosch: That is right.

Mr. Kilday: Primarily at the expense of their own people, their own Church groups?

Col. Kosch: That is right.[14]

On other occasions we were told that COs were not entitled to pay because they were not doing what the government wanted done. Eleanor Roosevelt, who many felt was genuinely sympathetic to COs, in her *My Day* column on June 20, 1944, said that COs should not expect to be compensated because "They are doing what they want to do. . . . That is the price of doing what one believes in."[15] The thrust of her argument seemed to be that since the country wanted its young men to fight and since the CO would not fight, he should not expect to be paid when he was drafted under the same law for non-fighting work. She did not elaborate on how this rationale applied to the other young men who were never drafted and continued working in civilian jobs.

We were told that an injured worker was not entitled to workers compensation because, since he was paid no money, he was not an employee. What was he then? a Serf? a Peasant? a Chattel?

In its May 4, 1945, issue, *Pacifica Views* commented on the work being done in CPS:

These men are neither lazy nor by nature inefficient. It is simply that CPS contains for them no incentive or obligation. They work under compulsion, as conscripts. For them, CPS is not a channel for service, but a form of legalized submission to slavery imposed by the State, over which the glamour of "service" has cast a specious disguise.

Service rendered without thought of compensation is probably a natural expression of the ideas of most COs. But such service can have no rigid definition, nor can it be extracted mechanically as a legal requirement . . . . Neither compelled nor servile submission to injustice is identical with the spirit of service, and no amount of pious platitudes can make it so.

Pay of $50 a month for COs would no more solve all the problems of CPS men than it has removed the frustrations and maladjustments of men in the armed forces. But pay for COs would remove the taint of undemocratic discrimination, the slur of imposed penury, and much of the deliberate punishment of conscience in the United States. In refusing these men pay, the Government has hit below the belt, has degraded the American tradition of fair treatment of unpopular minorities.[16]

There were many men who would not have wanted to receive any money from the government. However, the work-without-pay policy established two very dangerous precedents: first, a conscripted laborer is not worth his hire; second, and even more ominous, minorities—simply by being law-abiding minorities—can, when a majority so decides, be pressed into service and compelled to work without pay.

The manager of the Germfask, Michigan, government camp had a few words of his own to say about the no-pay policy:

Paul G. Voelker, manager of the Germfask camp, resigned his position on March 17. In his letter of resignation, he said: "This action is taken only after thoroughly familiarizing myself with the situation. I have found the Selective Service treatment of men in CPS camp to be the re-establishment of slavery in our nation and the punishment of men whose conscience does not permit their participation in war. As a liberty-loving American citizen and ex-serviceman, I cannot take part in the administering of a system of unpaid, forced labor.

Mr. Voelker resigned only two weeks after accepting the position.[17]

Farmers, faced with severe labor shortages during the war, petitioned Selective Service for help. Up to that time, all CPS projects were within governmental agencies. This presented Selective Service with a potentially explosive issue: could labor from CPS be provided without charge to privately operated businesses? Probably not. But if farmers paid for the labor, what would be done with the money? The CPS men could not receive pay because they were already "employed" by the government. To "release" men for work on the farms, NSBRO and Selective Service entered into a contract that required farmers to pay the going wage rate. All wages would be placed in a special trust fund in the U.S. Treasury and held until after the war. At that time, the monies would be turned over to the church organizations for relief and rehabilitation.

"Release" did not mean that men were discharged from CPS. Most of the work was done near existing CPS units. Men were transported to the fields in the same way they were taken to government projects, returning to their camps at the end of the day. The men were satisfied with this arrangement because of the government's commitment to place the funds in a committed account, and for several years monies paid for the labor of CPS men went into the Federal treasury.

Church administrators were led to believe that these monies would be identified as a relief trust fund for release to the religious organizations after the war. When the religious agencies sought to obtain the frozen funds after the war, they were told by the United States Comptroller that specific Congressional action would be required before he could disburse the funds. The monies had never been deposited into a special fund but instead had gone into the U.S. Treasury General Fund.

Several attempts have been made to "unfreeze" these funds for humanitarian purposes (at one time it was proposed to give the money to the United Nations Children's Relief Fund), but all such efforts have failed. A number of sympathetic Congressmen have introduced legislation to release the funds, but nothing has ever come of it. So far as can be determined, the money has been lost forever in the complex budgetary and appropriation processes of the U.S. Congress. The commitment made to the COs has been long forgotten.

So much for the vagaries of bureaucracy and the breach of faith with this little band of dissenters. While the issue of compensation aroused considerable emotion during the war, fifty years later it was rarely mentioned. When it did come up, there was still a variety of opinion.

One respondent had a change of heart, and many other men shared that view, "[During CPS I thought] it was all right not to get the pay and benefits of anyone who was drafted into the military," Wilbur said. "I now think that was most unjust." On the other hand, Joel found, "receiving no pay had no meaning." Many others felt that the lack of pay was not worth getting excited about.

The issue did not go unnoticed in the halls of Congress. Senator Mon C. Wallgren of Washington chided General Hershey when he was told that COs received no compensation. "You are treating these fellows worse than the Japs."[18]

Congressman John M. Coffee (Washington) addressed the issue from the floor of Congress on February 9, 1944:

> Congress made definite provisions in the Selective Service Act for sincere, religious conscientious objectors by setting up for them work of national

importance under civilian direction. In doing this it was guided by the American heritage of protecting the freedom of belief and worship even of those unpopular minorities whose ideas seem to most people to run directly counter to the safety and best interests of the Nation. . . .

Since the Selective Service Act was made law, however, Congress has not followed up its original intent to grant freedom of conscience to those religiously opposed to war. It has failed to provide for the basic needs of men in civilian public service despite the fact that this was established as a legal and recognized alternative to military service. . . .

Men in civilian public service have at no time been paid for their work. . . .

The Government does not provide maintenance, beyond loaning the men vacant C.C.C. camps and setting up their work programs which are rigidly enforced. Food, clothing, and incidentals are supplied in the main by three historic peace churches: Mennonites, Brethren, and Friends(Quakers). . . .

CPS men do not receive accident compensation.

Neither are CPS men included in any of the dependency legislation for servicemen, despite the fact that the draft of fathers affects both groups equally and their rates of dependency are about the same. . . .

As the matter now stands, a conscientious objector is granted legal standing by the Selective Service Act, but at the same time is fined, in effect, for his views.[19]

To make matters worse, Selective Service saw the CO's economic hardship as a device for forcing men into the military. Sibley and Jacobs in their landmark book, *Conscription of Conscience: The American State and the Conscientious*

Objector, 1940-1947, dealt with this issue. General Hershey, in testimony before Congress, said that the uncompensated labor policy was a way of "reclaiming" CPS men for the army.[20] At another time Hershey described how his administration had "salvaged" COs for the military.[21]

Illegitimus Non Carborundum

Many men came to believe that compensation was not the fundamental issue. Conscription was.

While soldiers were compensated, the pay was meager; and even the dependency benefits, health care, insurance, and post-war benefits hardly matched what civilians had earned during the war. Both soldiers and COs were subject to involuntary servitude. This was the pervasive evil. The U.S. Supreme Court rationalizes conscription as necessary for the general welfare. The Constitution, in this line of reasoning, allows the subordination of individual rights in time of "national emergency". Conscription, the Court says, follows from the duty of citizenship; so it is not involuntary servitude. The notion of civic duty is deeply rooted in the history of constitutional law, with ample precedent to support the Supreme Court's opinions. Impressment for military service, however, violates the intentions of the nation's founders who fled from enforced military service in the old world.

There is little doubt that the Supreme Court reflects popular sentiment; and until conscription itself is seen as a threat to freedom, it will remain a tool of government. Just as universal conscription is seen as a legitimate institution of society, so at one time was slavery and the slave trade, and so still is capital punishment. At another time, in another era, a new interpretation of individual liberty will fulfill the dream of freedom envisioned by those who founded the nation and who thought they had enshrined that freedom in the U.S. Constitution. In time, men of conscience will redeem their claim to freedom just as did their black slave brethren.

1.   Mitchell Lee Robinson, *Civilian Public Service During World War II: The Dilemmas of Conscience and Conscription in a Free Society.* Ann Arbor, MI., University Microfilms International, 1990. p. 354.
2.   Thomas E. Jones, Creative Pioneering., Philadelphia: American Friends Service Committee, 1941. pp. 1, 4.
3.   R.C.A. *Camp Notes,* April 24, 1942
4.   Leo P. Crespi, "Public Opinion Toward Conscientious Objectors," in *The Journal of Psychology,* 19, 1945, pp 209-310.
5.   Brethren Service Committee, *Civilian Public Service.* Elgin, IL., Brethren Service Committee, 1942.
6.   W. Harold Row, *Fulfilling Our Heritage.* Elgin, IL, Brethren Service Committee, 1942.
7.   Paul Comly French, *Civilian Public Service.* Washington, NSBRO, 1943.
8.   Richard C. Mills, From CPS Camp 21 files. July, 1942, and April, 1943.
9.   Frank Olmstead, *C.P.S. After Eighteen Months.* New York, War Resisters League, 1942. p.6.
10.   Evan W. Thomas, "The Assumptions of Reformers," in *Pacifica Views,* October 20, 1944. po. 1, 4. From CPS Camp 21 files.
11.   *Budget Planning,* 11/20/43 Accounts 11, 12, & 16. From CPS Camp 21 Files.
12.   U. S. Public Law 630, June 27, 1942. 54 Stat. 885.
13.   NSBRO, *Congress Looks at the Conscientious Objector.* Washington: 1943. pp 56, 59.
14.   NSBRO, *General Letter No. 124,* July 13, 1945. Hearings on H.R. 3597, House Committee on Military Affairs, Room 1310, House Office Building, July 8, 1945.
15.   Eleanor Roosevelt, *My Day.* Hyde Park, New York, June 20, 1944.

16. "The Service Philosophy"'" in *Pacifica Views,* May 4, 1945. pp. 1, 4.

17. "Germfask COs Say *Time* Missed Real Story," in *Fellowship*, April, 1945.

18. NSBRO, *Congress Looks at the Conscientious Objector.* Washington, D.C., 1943. Congressional hearing, February 17, 1943. p. 57.

19. John M. Coffee, Congressman from the state of Washington, "Conscientious Objectors," in *Congressional Record.* February 9, 1944.

20. Mulford Q. Sibley and Phillip E. Jacobs, *Conscription of Conscience: The American State and the Conscientious Objector, 1940-1947.* Ithaca, N.Y.: Cornell University Press, 1952. pp. 89-90.

21. NSBRO, *Congress Looks at the Conscientious Objector.* Washington, 1943. p. 56.

5

In the Backwaters

We lost out on the "main event". For the rest of our lives many of us would see ourselves on the outside looking in; we would never again be a full member of the community. Oh, we had our compatriots and would continue to share that companionship, but we would forever be "different". Indeed, being in an "out" group may explain why CPS reunions have had such wide appeal. There have been scores of reunions since World War II, at least one group meeting for over 40 years. Even after long absences, "it was like I saw them yesterday."

While we knew our cause was unpopular, we were often bewildered by the intensity of some reactions. Our religious education had taught us that war was a violation of human decency and an offense to God. It seemed incredible that those who had taught us to hate war would urge us to reject those lessons. We did not understand how others could enthusiastically join in killing people they had never seen. We understood how Henry David Thoreau must have felt when asked if he had made peace with God, "Well, I have had no quarrel with Him."

We were told that pacifism is irrational because force and violence are facts of life. Tyrants understand only force, and force must be met with stronger force. On the other hand, it was said that pacifism is rational, but the world is irrational. In other words, since the world is irrational, rational behavior is irrational. These two lines of reasoning apparently seem plausible to apologists for war, but they do stretch the bounds of common sense. In the first instance, people close their eyes to the conditions that create tyrants; then they ignore the fact that wars plant seeds for other wars. In the second instance, nations perpetuate war in the same way that drug addicts perpetuate their habit; namely by "doing drugs".

Both of us—warrior and pacifist—face the dilemma in Joe's story (Joe did his CO time in prison): A group of prison inmates were complaining about the injustice of their sentences. One man had shot his wife when he found her in bed with his best friend (it was not clear whether he shot the friend, too). Another killed a drug dealer who had "hooked" his young brother on heroin. A third prisoner spoke up, "Well, if you think your cases are crazy, look at Joe here; he's in prison because he <u>refused</u> to kill anybody."

We have seen how General Hershey wanted to keep COs out of sight. He explains:

> I have opposed publicizing that sort of thing [CO "guinea pig" projects] because the conscientious objector, by my theory, is best handled if no one hears of him.[1]

It also helps if COs are seen to be a little strange. General Hershey told about a CO who had been incorrectly inducted into the army:

> We had a peculiar case of one man who had got inducted. . . . He spent several weeks at Fort Sill. He will not receive any money. He will not wear a uniform . . . , and he is in the peculiar position of both

refusing to accept money and of refusing to wear a uniform, but yet he is nonbelligerent. That is, he went to any place that they wanted him to go, but he is simply unwilling to bear arms, that is all. He has worked free, and will not accept money because he thinks it would compromise his position. . . . he got inducted before he made his appeal, and it shows what some of them will do. They are a most peculiar kind of people. [2]

A peculiar people indeed: holding to their beliefs against pressure from military commanders; pressure from fellow draftees who do not want to appear sympathetic; and pressure from home because of "what our friends will think."

Pressure also came from Congress. At the height of the war in 1943 Senator Elmer Thomas of Oklahoma introduced legislation to eliminate the conscientious objection provision Section 5(g) from the Selective Service Act.

Senator Thomas read a petition sent him by the Oklahoma American Legion:

We petition. . . the Congress of the United States of America for a change in the Selective Service Act, so as to eliminate the classification of "conscientious objectors", and amend the law so as to provide that all men subject to the draft shall do service in the armed forces of the United States.

In the hearings on the Thomas amendment, General Hershey stated, as he had on other occasions, that keeping COs out of the military was a wise policy. He also said that the New Jersey American Legion supported a CPS unit for a veterans' hospital in that state. The Thomas amendment was never enacted.

When the military began demobilizing the armed forces in May, 1945, Selective Service planned to release COs under the same formula used for military releases; that is, when 10% of the military were released, 10% of the COs would be released.   Congressman Winstead proposed legislation to restrict the release of COs.   Hearings on the Winstead bill in July, 1945, revealed some flashpoints of animosity.

Congressman Durham asked Colonel Keesling, *"How do you arrive at the conclusion as to why any of them should be released, Colonel? They all refused to fight."*   After a discussion of the civilian work done by COs without pay, this exchange took place between Congressman Durham and Colonel Kosch:

Mr. Durham: If 75% of the people felt that way, you would not be able to get much of an army, would you?

Col. Kosch: *If 75% of the people felt that way, we probably would not have had the law in the first place.*

Later in the same hearing, Colonel Keesling explained that some men had been discharged for reasons of disability, dependency, occupation, etc.   In answer to a question from Congressman Durham, the Colonel said, "If you look at the . . . men that have been discharged, the tests for discharge were comparable, or even stiffer, than those used for discharging men from the armed forces for comparable reasons."[3]

OUT OF SIGHT . . . NOT OUT OF MIND

While it was not front page news, there were occasional newspaper stories about CPS.   The public learned:

The early Quakers in England did not believe that it was enough simply to refuse to fight.   They believed that through good works they could convince their fellow men that peace and brotherly love could accomplish more than could be attained through war.

A committee of Quakers, Mennonites, and Brethren called on him [Clarence Dykstra, director of Selective Service] and said, "We do not think the Government should pay the support of conscientious objectors. We will raise five hundred thousand dollars to establish work camps throughout the nation for them.[4]

As was seen in the previous chapter, Selective Service policy was to keep COs as far from public view as possible, with General Hershey declaring that the less they are seen the better. Hershey's freezing of furloughs in April, 1943, to stall the Chicago protest meeting was an example of Selective Service anxiety. The year before, the inflammatory "Yamada Incident" aroused a firestorm when assignees protested the evacuation of a Japanese CO from the Cascade Locks, Oregon, camp. Colonel Kosch was reported to have alerted the Portland, Oregon, sheriff's office to ready the county jail for protesting COs. The affair was compounded by the Camp Director's refusal to sign the transfer papers, and this created a mini-firestorm in the Church bureaucracy, too. The matter was ultimately resolved by transferring Yamada to a Colorado CPS facility instead of a Japanese Relocation Center, but Selective Service was forever after alert to the slightest possibility of publicity over the antics of COs.

Most media coverage was strictly reportorial, with little editorializing. Conscientious objectors were not "hot copy", but there were occasional curious reporters who wanted to know about these people. The treatment of one CO was so flagrant, however, that the editor of the *Washington Post* condemned the government's action.

In 1941 Don Charles DeVault, who held a PhD in chemistry, was conducting penicillin research at Stanford University. He had registered as a conscientious objector and had been deferred twice because of the critical nature of his work. His deferment was later revoked, and his CO classification was denied. When ordered to report to the Army, he refused induction and was sentenced to prison. He was ultimately paroled to a CPS camp where he resumed his penicillin research in his spare time. After a few weeks he asked for detached service to concentrate on the penicillin studies. The request was denied, and he was transferred to a government camp for "trouble makers". He continued his research at the new camp and eventually devoted full time to the research, declining to work on forestry projects. That led to his arrest and a second incarceration, this time a three-and-one-half year term in a Federal penitentiary.

Washington Post editorials on November 22, 1944, "Pangs of Conscience", and January 2, 1945, "What Price Conscience?" (©The Washington Post) brought national attention to the case:

[DeVault explained his position]: As I work with a shovel or lean on it or drive a truck during the 51 hours per week, I am prevented from being useful in any way comparable to what I can do. . . . It is not that we object to making sacrifices, because we do not. It is the uselessness of the particular sacrifices that the authorities designate for us.

When the Army finds a man physically unfit for military service, it sends him back to civilian life with the hope that his abilities will make a contribution to the war effort. When it finds a man psychologically unfit for military service, it does the same thing. But when it finds a man conscientiously unfit—that is, unable to render military service because of conscientious scruples—it treats him in quite different fashion. It packs him off to something called a Civilian Public Service Camp and assigns him to something called 'work of national importance' without taking any account whatever of his ability to render more useful service in some other sphere. . . .

If there is any sense in this wasting of a man's skill [in the case of Dr. DeVault], we cannot see it. If there is any justice in this punishment of a man because of his conscience, it is beyond our discernment. We say that this is stupid and ugly—and unbecoming to a great free people engaged in a war for the freedom of the human conscience. [November 22, 1944]

Dr. DeVault's conscience is no doubt a peculiarly intractable and nonconformist one. Yet it is hard for us to understand how the war effort will be advanced by punishing him for his singular scruples or by denying him an opportunity to contribute his talents to the general welfare. . . .

3-1/2 years in jail seems a somewhat drastic penalty for an action which did no injury to his fellow-men and which was taken at the dictate of his conscience and of common sense. We recount the story of Don Charles DeVault because it illustrates, we think, the absurdity of a system which wastes the skills of men because it deals with conscience as though it were a crime. . . . Their potentialities are wastefully ignored when they are put to work at unskilled manual jobs. And they are assigned to such jobs, it seems clear, because Selective Service wants to punish them. [January 2, 1945][5]

Much press coverage was like this *Boston Herald* story in 1942:

Only criticism I ever heard around here was when I went to Ashburnham the other day. . . .

A little boy looked up at me in a store, when I charged something and exclaimed, "Oh, You're one of them sissies at the camp."

The COs often hitchhike back to camp from their frequent visits to Boston and New York. Usually they feel obliged to tell motorists who offer them rides that they are conscientious objectors. Invariably, it is said, the motorist takes them in and plies them with questions about their stand.[6] (Reprinted by permission of the *Boston Herald*.)

We were perhaps overly sensitive in our contacts with the public, but we had numerous rebuffs that made us cautious: Ministers requesting that we not attend services; restaurant owners demanding that we leave; school officials asking that we not attend public functions; merchants refusing to sell us products; and the like. Prices would sometimes double when store proprietors learned we were from a "Conchie" camp. Housing for our wives was difficult, and a number of women lost their jobs when employers learned that their husbands were COs. There were no "lynching" parties; but the local toughs near one forestry camp, liquored up on Saturday nights, would invade the dorms and threaten to "tear the place up".

One CO newspaper reporter was told that a paper would need to be "discreet" about publishing his story:

Inasmuch as we heard your name mentioned over the radio in a rather delicate situation, we think it best to use another name. We feel that we must do this in order not to incur any unfavorable comment from our readers.[7]

In recalling those years, Roy said, "What bothered me especially was running into the bigotry in the towns near camp."

Overt hostility was difficult enough, but even more unnerving were the subtle, unspoken resentments. Wallace Hamilton in his pamphlet, *Clash By Night,* explained the price of rejection:

Thus the CO finds himself apart from his work community, his home community, and the experience of his generation. That constant, omnipresent social pressure is enhanced by the running guerilla warfare which he carries on with practically everything contemporary which he reads, sees at the movies, listens to on the radio, sees on the bill boards. Given time, of course, he acquires a certain immunity and does not feel obligated to carry on a debate with every political orator or recruiting poster. . . .

The CO inside or outside of camp, inside or outside of jail, is a segregated being. He is segregated not merely by physical isolation, but by the fact that he is a CO in wartime. And as a segregated being, the CO reacts.

Through incidents and public pressure, the CO begins to think that there is some sort of invisible picket fence that separates him from the rest of the citizenry. When he sees that his natural actions are sometimes misinterpreted and twisted by people on the other side of the fence, he begins to watch his step and substitute for his natural actions a what-is-expected-of-him set of artificial reactions. He guards himself against any twistable flippancy, even though that flippancy may be the better part of his sense of humor. He guards himself against getting into arguments about the war where he might get mad and lose his head. He guards himself against too close association with people because the closer the association, the bigger the possible rift. For such a rift the whole group might pay. He guards himself behind the picket fence.

Hence the CO, always conscious of his relationship with other people not merely as an individual but as a CO, finds it difficult to be really mentally at ease with other people, even people he has known before he was a CO.[8]

Morris had felt the sting of rejection that many of us experienced:

The impact of living in camp with a group of COs in a hostile community over a period of time *created a real erosion of my self-hood.* In this camp it was commonplace to have rowdy, half-inebriated young men bust into the dorm at night and give every appearance of threatening our well-being. I never suffered actual physical harm, but it was psychological and took many months to get it out of my system. In the daylight hours when going from this same camp into the little town, even on an official task like to get the mail, one needed to watch and walk carefully.

But it was not all negative. Senator Robert A. Taft believed that freedom of conscience was a bedrock issue in American democracy:

The religious convictions of several denominations, such as the Quakers, Mennonites, and Brethren forbid them to take part in military service. While I do not agree with a theory of complete pacifism, I think that all should recognize the sincerity of these groups. Tolerance is an essential part of American democracy. Congress has recognized that it requires the recognition of religious views. The decision of Congress should be wholeheartedly supported by all Americans.[9]

In February, 1945, a minister reported to his congregation on the work of CPS:

> In some of the mental hospital units the paid help will not speak to the COs. Even after weeks and months of working together and eating in the same room, no word is passed. By a curiosity it has been discovered that one of the best ways to break the ice in that frigid situation comes when some soldier friend comes to visit his CPS buddy and they fraternize as brothers. That ought to be a cue for those of us on the home front who are wondering how CPS men will be received when they come home.
>
> No aspect of the home front problem is so revealing of prejudices as this. Frankly, the problem does not seem to exist in the military. If you think that the man in uniform will belittle the man who did not wear the uniform, you do not understand the mettle of either of them. So often the expression of this concern is but the voicing of a fear that they will get along well. We on the home front ought to be careful that we are not less understanding in this than those on the war front.[10]

The public was curious—and perhaps skeptical—about our sincerity. Were COs simply looking for a soft berth? On the other side of that query was another question: could a man "con" others—or more to the point, himself—for three or four years while working at sometimes boring and repetitive tasks without any pay? The universal opinion among governmental and public officials was that, while they disagreed with the stand, COs were not "conning" anyone.

Colonel Keesling (Selective Service) went out of his way in one congressional hearing to comment on this. After describing the overseas relief work which COs had hoped to perform, he observed:

> It is not what we consider would be a very soft job. . . . These people, if they are sincere, are actually not afraid of danger. It is merely that they do not want to kill anybody.[11]

Rabbi Abraham Cronback told about COs in Great Britain during World War II:

> It has been reported that, owing to the tremendous peril connected with mine sweeping in the waters adjacent to Great Britain, such work is never assigned on command but is performed by men who specifically volunteer for the task. Conspicuous among such volunteers have been the British conscientious objectors—adverse to destroying life, yet risking their lives to save life—true heroes and patriots. Similarly, those whom our nation has, out of regard for religious scruples, exempted from military service may yet come to rank among our bravest and most loyal citizens.[12]

Bishop Lawrence of the Protestant Episcopal Diocese of Western Massachusetts, observed:

> It takes courage to live according to one's conscience. It takes nerve to stand for an unpopular cause. Such courage and nerve is the very fiber and fabric of democracy, and must be cultivated, not condemned. In our anxiety to crush out intolerance and totalitarianism abroad, let us not fall victim to practicing these things at home. The right of individual conscience has been recognized in the Selective Service Act. As citizens, we can do no less than accord the same recognition and respect to all those with whose convictions we may fundamentally disagree, but who

have as much right to hold their convictions as we have ours. Tolerance is bred in mutual respect.[13]

U.S. Supreme Court Justice Frank Murphy spoke about the importance of individual conscience in a democratic society:

It is not the man who follows the dictates of his conscience who is a menace to the Republic; it is the man who doesn't.[14]

Many government officials in Washington appear to have believed that the public was hostile toward COs. In the perspective of fifty years, public acrimony was much less intense than had been supposed. In Stuart's opinion, "We were paranoid in thinking that we were powerless in our situation."

In March of 1944 the Office of Public Opinion Research conducted a national survey of the American people on various issues relating to conscientious objection. In 1945 the results were reported by Leo P. Crespi in *The Journal of Psychology*. Respondents were asked a series of questions.

1. In general, do you approve or disapprove of conscientious objectors? . . . . [p. 212]

Seventy-four percent of the subjects interviewed expressed disapproval of COs; 18.1 per cent expressed approval; and 7.8 per cent had no opinion on the issue. . . .This average attitude of the public the writer has interpreted as substantial disapproval, but definitely short of the "crushing disapproval" and "popular contempt and hostility" which seems to be the prevailing stereotype of public feeling about COs. [p. 248]

2. [The author separates approval/disapproval from rejection and finds that, while there is a large proportion of disapproval, there is a lesser proportion of outright rejection.] The largest proportion of the public evinces. . . *no rejection whatsoever.* . . . A majority

of the public will accept COs during this war as friends or closer—in most cases with no reservations; i.e., as close relatives by marriage. [p. 258]

The prevailing conception about public attitude toward COs is social ostracism—the public wants "nothing to do with COs." This stereotype contrasts sharply with the actual fact that the largest proportion of the public expresses no rejection of COs whatsoever, and more than a majority would accept them during this war as closely as friends, or closer. [p. 260]

3. To the question as to whether or not COs assigned to camps should receive wages and money for their families from the government, over three-fourths of the general public answered in the affirmative. . . This support should be, the majority feels, the same as that received by a private in the Army. [p. 290-291]

4. Policies of treatment for COs have been formulated on the basis of the stereotype—social ostracism—rather than on the basis of the public attitude toward COs. Justice would seem to demand a reconsideration of policies based upon such a mistaken assumption. [p. 275][15]

There were occasional sympathetic accounts from the "outside".

Let the CO see himself as we see him, and he may feel differently about his witness [the writer is responding to CO complaints about the insignificance of CPS work assignments].

We feel he is our representative. He stands for all of us who feel the way of war is not the right way. He refuses to take part in the war system, and his presence in a CPS camp makes him an active force in the struggle for the freedom of men. In his refusal to be part of the war machine, he protests the use of conscripts for war in all countries. When enough men refuse to be used as tools of death, there can be no more wars. It is because of this that governments fear and persecute the CO.

He may feel thwarted in CPS camp, as he cannot but be conscious of the great need for his services in other fields. Yet to some of us he seems to be making a contribution to humanity simply by being steadfast in his allegiance to spiritual forces, to the right means to the right end.

To some of us also it seems that the CO represents the spirit of the Church. Although there is reason to be happy over the thousands of ministers who registered their faith as pacifists, the Church has not taken as brave a part as she might in standing by her own. We wonder at churches, paying honor to the men who were forced into military service and not honoring the men who remained loyal to the teachings they had received from the Church in their youth.[16]

The mother of one CO told about meeting his former teacher: "My first grade teacher, a Quaker lady, met my mother one day during the war and asked, 'What is Arthur doing now?' 'He is a conscientious objector and is in a camp for COs.' 'Thank God! Thank God!' responded the teacher, 'I have prayed for this.'"

Minorities make majorities uncomfortable because they are constantly poking at cherished ideas; so the majority likes to remind minorities that they are outside the warmth and glow of acceptance. If a minority can be made to believe that it is outnumbered, it may keep its ideas to itself. This was the lot of the CO in World War II, for the government—and indeed most of the community—did not want any discord. Even when the public later learned some of the unholy aspects about that war, World War II was still the great crusade.

We did learn, though, that minorities have some satisfactions. Majorities enjoy the comfort of numbers. But so long as there is disagreement, the majority has a faint doubt: are we overlooking something? Even for the majority, it is comforting to have some extra ideas around just as it is nice to have a spare tire in the car trunk or rusty bolts in an old tin can. Advertising is based on the premise that people need products they do not yet know about; so consumers are conditioned to look for a better mousetrap. But there is a limit to toleration. When someone is digging a trench to divert a coming flood, he does not want anyone telling him he is putting the dirt on the wrong side of the hole.

In the post-war world, minority complaints were not so muffled; and when American foreign policy supported oppressive regimes, the people began to see how such policies lead to military conflicts. People are learning that prudent action can avert war just as intrusive actions can cause it.

THE CONSEQUENCES

Someone once said that CPS was a combination of prison, school, and monastery. Joe found it "boring;" to Jim it was "traumatic;" Bill was taken almost to the "breaking point;" the confining life completely demoralized Ed; the granite canyon walls surrounding his camp "imprisoned" John; the lack of privacy was misery for Philip; and the uncertainty of the end was deadly to Bill. Jim's sense of humor enabled him to find the experience "hilarious."

"Some people looked down on me." "I was scorned." "I have been chastened." "No one wanted to hear what we had to say." "Some experiences generated intense enmity." "I paid a high price for my religious beliefs." "Makes one wary." "I am still being censured."

The separation from family and community were uncomfortable, but they were no more so for us than for the millions of other draftees. We were much more concerned about the quality of the time we invested in those years. For one it was a "blank four years," and for many it had little constructive value. Gilbert found, "The whole experience kind of rolled off of me."

The war had put our lives on hold just as it had for others. Many draftees—military and CO—felt they had a legitimate grievance against a system that enabled some people to profit from the wartime boom. But that was largely forgotten in the new post-war world. The COs' complaint was not so much in the delay of our careers, but rather in the inequities that followed. We were specifically excluded from governmental support programs in spite of the fact we had worked for up to four and a half years on public projects without compensation.

When we returned to civilian life, our "past" followed us as we searched for employment, for housing, and for continuing education. "The CPS man," commented Dulan, "was willing to take rebuff, and he usually got it, too." While we bore no physical scars from our wartime service, many felt as Norm did, "Having been a 'conchie' has marked me as surely as the Jews were tattooed. . . "

For years it was difficult for many of us to return to our home communities. Wesley observed, "I have felt the sting of public opinion. For nonconformity the world whips you." Someone painted a yellow stripe around one CO's house.

Ironically, it was often an ex-soldier who gave us the warmest welcome. Most COs found that the average soldier—particularly the one who had been in combat—was friendly. Some soldiers who had gone through front-line combat said they would never do it again.

Ex-GIs were often curious about CPS. Some encounters generated more heat than light. For the most part, however, they were quite congenial. It was evident that many soldiers had been attracted to the idea themselves. "I felt no unpopularity," William said. "[I] continued to be close friends with my friends who went into the armed forces. In travelling . . . [I] found businessmen and those in the armed forces interested in my position and was asked frequently how one gets into this kind of service."

One man told about meeting an old schoolmate immediately after the war (in those days, the first question asked was, "Where were you in the war?"), and when he said he had been a CO, the acquaintance said, "Well, Bob, you always were a little different." No rancor, but a bit of discord.

Richard had just returned home and was walking on a downtown street when he heard a familiar voice from the past, "Hi, Dick, are you living here now?" It was Margaret, a girl he had known since childhood. It was a joy to get a cheerful greeting. "It's so good to see you, Dick. You'll just have to come by the house this afternoon. Bill would love to see you." Margaret and Bill, an exceptional athlete with charisma in his every pore, were married the summer they graduated from college. He joined the Air Force early in the war, and advanced rapidly to the rank of colonel. "When I entered their apartment that afternoon, all the memories of the college football hero returned in that handsome square-jawed face. Well, when he saw me, the temperature dropped to 10 below zero. After some sharp glances and a stiff hand-shake, Bill told Margaret they were late for an appointment across town. We said very few more words to each other, and I left. That was the last time I ever saw either one of them."

When Andrew attended college after the war, a number of men told him that they had intended to ask for a CO classification when first registered for the draft, but they were persuaded by their families to drop the idea. Jim had actually registered as a CO; but, at the insistence of his father when the war finally came, he went into the army. His father "just knew that his legal practice would be destroyed if he had a son in a CO camp."

"I'm still careful," Bill offered, "about revealing my wartime experience when it will take a lot of explaining." "Only now [after fifty years]," Dale added, "do I freely express being a CO, and most people regard it as being eccentric." Well, it could be a lot worse than "eccentric".

Probably the most painful consequence was the reaction of our own families. Many men, of course, came from homes where being a CO was expected. For others, it required that we defy family custom. One man was shunned by his sister all his life , and others were grudgingly accepted only because they were considered "a little odd".

Clashes of opinion within families occur on many issues, but the images of courage and bravery conjured up by war are especially emotional. Charles commented on the split with his family, "CPS was the vehicle by which I broke with my family, my church. . . ." In Howard's case there was a happy ending, "At first my father thought I was yellow; but when I explained it to him, he loved me and admired me—and that was all I needed (my mother, too)."

"I longed for peace," Robert said, "and thought everyone else did, too, and anything I did toward achieving it would be commended/lauded. . . . I felt the following experiences nagging and incredible: Our family doctor refused to examine us for alternative service because of our CO stand. . . . Our watch repair man and [his] son read of our answering to 'another drummer' in the local paper and said, 'You fellows just want some cheap publicity; don't bring any more work to us.'. . . My college president notified me to come to his office and said, 'Robert, I read your letter to The Star on a better way than war to solve international problems. I don't agree with your point of view.' The Dean, Miss T, called me to her office and asked me to cease and desist from writing 'your kind of articles' in the college paper. 'How did you come by your ideas?'. . . Both of these meetings . . . stunned me; I thought these persons would be—in their leadership capacities—on my side. I tried to explain things. Oh, how naive was I."

We often withdrew and restricted our associations. Whitfield said what many of us felt, "I am perhaps less sanguine and less 'aggressive' in my views after being made to feel alienated during W. W II." After the CPS experience, Worden developed a pattern of "maintaining a low profile—being inconspicuous."

We also experienced that ultimate indignity; namely, indifference. If people would simply scream at us, we would at least know they heard. "Associates and friends," George offered, "don't give a [hoot about my convictions]. . . . In the event of another conflagration their attitudes could change toward me. I am tolerated."

Reinhardt's experience is familiar: "I did severely curtail my exposure to the public because of their attitude to[ward] a CO. I did avoid confrontation wherever possible . . . . [A father of a friend] let me know that I will always be labeled and will be ridiculed for the rest of my life, which I admit bothered me at first; but it did not happen."

Robert, the son of a famous missionary family, changed his approach, "During the 1950's, 60's, and 70's I avoided mentioning the [CPS] experience. Now (perhaps because of the long perspective) I put it in my biographical notes. . . ."

We lost a great deal of our "herd" instinct. We discovered that "it is a big step to get out of step," but we spurned popular perceptions when it was necessary to do so. Robert said, "Having taken a strong stand in World War II, I found myself a little drained in taking activist stands in the years following." "I often found myself rationalizing that I had done my bit on one big issue," Dan said, "and it was now someone else's turn to take on other issues." Michael declared, "After four years, including two in a state hospital, I'd had enough self-sacrifice for quite awhile."

Those "years of retirement" did not last long, and the energetic pursuits of former CPSers is a story in itself. These experiences will be told in Chapter 10, *The Impossible Ideal.*

As the years passed, we found more sympathetic listeners. When the full impact of World War II penetrated peoples' consciousness and particularly as the public came to appreciate the awesome possibilities of atomic war, more people were willing to listen to another viewpoint. During the Vietnam War, conscientious objection was dramatized as young men "refused to go", burned draft cards on court house steps, and emigrated to Canada. Much of that protest was aimed at Vietnam, not at all wars. But the idea that individual citizens could have an impact on governmental war policies began to sink in.

We learned to balance candor with prudence. We discovered that there was a time to speak and a time to wait—never giving in or giving up, but waiting for the appropriate time and place. Harold explained, "[As a minister] in the United Methodist Church, my convictions, being non-belligerent, were initially either questioned or rejected by parishes, but ultimately accepted." And Gabriel was able to say, "People accepted me for it much better than I had anticipated."

CPS had made some of us too compliant. Someone else took care of such tasks as shopping, cooking, laundry, and the like. This softened our sense of personal responsibility. Art noticed, "For the first year or so after I got out, I had to get used to being responsible for my own decisions again." This loss of independence, of course, afflicted returning soldiers, too.

"My behavior," Ralph said, "was conditioned to be less aggressive in personal life which I now consider to have been a negative development. (Too much consideration for the viewpoints of others)."

Occupational Opportunities

Many men returned to family farms and businesses after the war, but most of us became job-seekers. The special privileges and governmental benefits given to returning "GIs" were not extended to us. We had been out of the job market for several years; so we faced many of the same problems that returning servicemen had to deal with. Fifty years later those hardships had been largely forgotten.

We avoided certain types of jobs—particularly in governmental agencies—because veteran applicants had priority. "My life-long struggle," Wilbur said, "to make a living for myself was affected negatively—many, many, many times." Others observed that their careers were slowed down, their choices narrowed, or their occupations changed. Harold changed his career: "It was ultimately the spineless upper echelons which caused me to leave the parish ministry for teaching—a change advised by a parishioner." Aretas "was turned down for medical school. . . . My interviewer was an ex-Navy man who had less than no use for COs."

Interviews terminated when our wartime service was reported; pressure from veterans groups intimidated some employers; former employers refused to take us back; and other less qualified applicants were given preference. Eugene learned to play down the CO connection: "Difficult to find a teaching position 'til advised not to offer freely my past CO position."

Russell's determination paid off: "Getting a job in public education was a study in persistence since I listed in my resume four and one half years in CPS. . . . It took nineteen interviews before I uncovered an administrator who said he would take a chance on me!"

Even after we finally landed a job, we were not always welcome. "In my work and elsewhere I was treated with disrespect," Charles said. "Many opportunities for advancement came, but I was denied them. When they found out I was a CO, I was branded." Edward discovered that he had worked for many years at less salary than others were paid for the same job, "I was 'punished' with regard to the pay I received for about seven years after returning to my employment (so I was told). . . . I attribute this to my rejection of war."

Some were fired from jobs when it was learned they had been COs; others lost clients and patients; and people told an electrical contractor that a CO could not work for them. Allen and Lewis believed they lost teaching jobs because they had been COs. Eldo's employer made conditions very unpleasant—including four transfers—until he finally quit.

Some of us abandoned our original careers. John took up "a private handicraft and eventually became a small capitalist in order to survive." Samuel "turned down a chance to enter medical school in 1942, because I would have had to be in the military. [But I completed medical school after the war, and] I have had a very good career and have no regrets about having gone to CPS."

Although a few were elected to political office, many others gave up political ambitions. Michael abandoned any political aspirations, "[I] never thought I could be a political leader . . . as I might otherwise have been."

Einar dropped his interest in public service for a slightly different reason: "I deliberately turned away [from political office] after assessing . . . that a background of conscientious objection to war would be an ongoing campaign obstacle. . . when confronted with the demands for compromising and deal-making endemic in the political arena."

It worked both ways for Elmo: "There is no doubt that it opened some doors to me that would otherwise have remained closed; nor can it be denied that it closed some doors that I would have liked to enter." It meant very little to John, "Probably lost a few job offers and the like—but that has not made much difference."

Loren's electrical contracting business prospered, "I have not lost any business that I know of because of my stand. I've worked for many veterans and parents of lost soldiers and never a comeback of any kind." A man in the plumbing business had a similar observation, "If people have a stopped up water line, they don't care who fixes it."

Some of us followed professions that were in high demand by the military; but as Herb found, it was possible to pursue those careers without contributing to the military,

"Following of a career in space sciences necessitated working for 'defense contractors' . . . without working on any of our country's weapon systems."

The academic world was quite open. "I was actually hired out of the CO camps," Francis explained. "The Department head who hired me [as a college professor] respected my religious convictions and my legal exercise of the CO stand. He considered me professionally well trained and highly motivated."

Charles was well accepted. "When I was asked by my school board what my status was in the war, I responded with full truth. I never had any difficulty with adverse criticism." Geographic locality and, to a lesser extent, the type of occupation had some affect. An Amish farmer would be a pillar in his home community, whereas a northern professional attempting to practice in the rural South might get a pretty cold treatment.

Some men felt they carried "marks" that kept them from the better jobs. We were conditioned to think we were not wanted in "good" society and that we should be content with second rate jobs. It took us many years to shake these images. Eventually, of course, the wartime experience became irrelevant.

The no-pay situation did have one oblique benefit. Henry explained, "When . . . I've given speeches concerning some of the times we spent in camp as COs, . . . seldom do we get into a heated discussion when [it is] . . . explained that our 'work of national importance' was free of pay and tribute. . . . "

CPS. . .SOME MINUSES

As one listens to the wide range of comments which follow, one might ask, are these people talking about the same places and the same people? In one respect they are, but in another they are not. As any family member knows, each person in the family has "different" parents, brothers, sisters, uncles, aunts, grandparents. It all depends on one's place in the family, one's age, one's sex, one's individual temperaments and interests, and the family's economic or social situation.

So it was with CPS. We came into CPS at different times and places—some of us before the war started, others in the middle, and still others near the end—and we were assigned to different types of projects operated by different government agencies and administered by different religious groups. We might have been assigned to a Mennonite camp on the midwest prairies, a Brethren camp in the forests of California, or a Friends hospital unit in an Eastern city. A midwestern farmer going to a Friends camp in New England would find an environment quite different from any he had known before, as would a Princeton graduate assigned to a Mennonite camp in Virginia.

For many men the great diversity of people was an exciting aspect of CPS, but the differences could be startling. Earl left a new bride behind. But, he thought, "I will be among friends that think like I do. That was my first big shock. I had nothing in common with about 90% of them."

George was surprised: "The biggest letdown of my life. I had expected that a group dedicated to nonviolence would be the closest thing to heaven on earth . . . . I realized I was just a dreamer."

Wilmer had some lofty notions, "We were too idealistic at the outset. . . . I shared a fantasy [that] CPS could have an important influence on the shortening of the war and possibly even develop some kind of leadership that could change the world situation."

One thing we did learn: one need not be a saint to be a conscientious objector. As Corny observed: "The experience shattered my naivete about the motives and dedication of my fellow inmates (and myself). I found out we are all humans, not angels." We were among seekers, and there were plenty of rough diamonds.

There was more than a little pessimism. Jay explains: "My inclination to skepticism and negative outlook were both strongly reinforced in camp. These inclinations had unfortunate repercussions throughout my life . . . ."

"I had great anticipations for the CPS experience," Jack said, "but being young was readily rendered disappointed and resentful." For William, "Close camp life is no help to me. I need space." Roger also spoke about the confinement, ". . . the experience of group life left me shy of CPS reunions or any other reruns of close community living."

"I was dismayed," Edward said, "that I found many of my fellow CPSers neither as serious nor as dedicated as I was. I felt little in common with many of them. I recall being shocked when a young Quaker . . . told me . . . that he wasn't sure he'd be there if he had not been a Quaker."

"I had to go through an appeal and other hurdles to get my classification." Everett said, "and felt some gratitude for finally getting to go to CPS rather than to jail; . . . [others] tended to take their status for granted. . . . Many had received their classifications rather automatically without being forced to think through their beliefs and had gone into CPS for the same reason that most . . . , I think, went into the armed services—not from personal conviction, but because it was expected of them."

Ted "was disappointed because what [he] found was a disparate group of men with different backgrounds, beliefs strange and unformed . . . . It was sort of like a group of orthodox Talmudic scholars outshouting each other in their attempts to get at the truth."

"Not all ideological pacifists," Paul observed, "had pacifist or even kindly natures. Some were less likeable . . . than some GIs I knew. . . . Some guys seemed to love mankind much more than they loved their fellow campers. . . . Strictly religious pacifists . . . had the most nearly Christian spirit."

"I was appalled," Bill said, " by the way many so-called liberals treated the so-called conservatives, such as the fundamentalists. I often found the 'liberal' so locked in his beliefs that he could not accept the values and faith a 'conservative fundamentalist' lived by, while many 'conservatives' could accept the 'liberals'."

. . . SOME PLUSES

It was a great consolation to be with other men who shared our perceptions, our convictions, and our commitments. In looking back on those years, Herb was able to say, "[It was] undoubtedly the most positive, valuable, and intellectually challenging experience in my life to that time. It was the last time in my life that I knew with certainty the correctness and value of what I was doing."

Several men said that while the consequences were negative for them personally, it was an important testimony. Anyone who confronts a problem will at some time be forced to take an unpopular stand—whether at a school board meeting, a political campaign, a county farm bureau, a church board of elders, a company workers meeting, or a minority rights picket line. "Hanging in" against the war made it easier to hold firm on other causes. Opposing the established order is not a pleasant thing to do; but there are times when it is necessary to sign a recall petition on a corrupt official, refuse to sign a discriminatory covenant in housing, or protest environmental contamination.

CPS gave Donald "strong doubts about the compromise of cooperation with conscription. . . . [I] refused to register for the 1948 draft and became imprisoned. I served eight months of an eighteen months sentence. . . . "

All in all, we took the bad with the good. Standing against the tide of opinion taught us a good deal about ourselves. In spite of the shortcomings all around, the experience strengthened our faith. We learned our weaknesses and our strengths. But we also found that even with all those shortcomings, amicable human relationships are possible because survival—physical and psychological—depends on it.

In Chapter two, pages 37 to 40, COs talked about the meaning of the CPS years in their later lives. The impression of this writer is that, at least in the perspective of fifty years, that time had a far-reaching impact. The years immediately after the war, for most exCPSers, were filled with pain, disappointment, and distress. But as the emotion of the war faded and as individual careers matured, the unpleasantries disappeared. As we emerged from the shadow of rejection, we were able to savor the successes of our individual careers. We came to be evaluated by how we lived our lives and what we did with our talents, and our wartime resistance was seen in a broader perspective by ourselves and by others. This is not to say that all of us lived a life of misery in those interim years.. Some of us never did experience resentment, most of us shook it off, but others never did recover from it.

CONCLUSION

While CPS separated us from the mainstream of society, being a CO was a matter of conviction and loyalty to our consciences. We were compelled to stand by those obligations and to take the slings and arrows that came with it. Nevertheless, in the climate of wartime, many felt they had to demonstrate their courage in some tangible form. Many men welcomed the opportunity to do just that by volunteering for hazardous health experiments and other physically challenging activities such as smoke jumping into forest fires.

We saw courage in standing by our convictions and refusing compromise with principle. We reject, for example, the type of behavior displayed by members of the U.S. Congress who in the 1950s allowed Senator Joseph McCarthy to ride rough shod over innocent people in his reckless charges of Communism. It took Joseph Welch, a citizen lawyer from Boston and Edward R. Murrow, a television commentator to challenge the Senator and unmask him for the demagogue that he was.

While we learned to live in the backwaters during the war and afterwards, we always felt that there was in the wider community a bedrock belief in the same principles in which we believed. We knew that our particular way of living out our faith placed us at odds with most of our fellow citizens, but we also knew that we were drawing our beliefs from a common reservoir of principle. We believe that most people most of the time accept the concept that all humanity is one. We learned that, in our own lives, our behavior is not always consistent with what we believe; so we know that if the broader community does not always abide by its approved covenants, it does not mean that those covenants have failed. Indeed, it is the function of a minority to hold and preserve values that the frenzy of immediate events often put aside.

All this is not to minimize the discomfort and loneliness of being out of the mainstream. But living according to one's perception of things is really not so unusual. It is what most people do to some degree or another. Indeed, for all of us, our thoughts are within; and many of our occupations are performed in isolation. Even those jobs done in company with others depend upon our individual perceptions and motivations. Whether a person does a good job or a fair job is determined not by what others have prescribed but by what each person decides.

Most people, and this certainly applies to COs, do not like to reject the consensus of their communities; for in the end, harmony and unity determine a society's strength. But when a family, a community, or a nation adopts standards or practices that destroy that group's fundamental values, individual members will resist. The practice of slavery in the United States was condoned for over two hundred years, even by that most hallowed of institutions, the U.S. Supreme Court. People knew in their hearts what a heinous institution slavery was, but it was practiced even by those who professed loyalty to the cherished principles of human freedom. The abolitionists made absolute pests of themselves reminding their fellow citizens that this practice must be abolished! They met opposition on every score: social, political, and economic (why, the country's total economic structure depended on the labor of slaves).

COs saw their refusal to kill as the the same type of ultimate loyalty to a broader human family. But, further, they saw that war undermines a country's heritage, sows the seeds for other wars, and saps a nation's moral fiber. The American society, over one hundred years after its abolition, still suffered from the impact of that diabolical practice. War is no different.

As these men neared the end of their lives, the sense of isolation and rejection faded for most of them. They believed they had shown by their lives what it meant to stand for principle, and they were content with their accomplishments.

1. NSBRO, *Congress Looks at the Conscientious Objector*, Washington, 1943. p. 61.
2. Ibid, p. 35. Congressional testimony of General Lewis B. Hershey. December 11, 1941.
3. Ibid. pp 53-62.
4. Robert E.S. Thompson, "Onward Christian Soldiers,", in *Saturday Evening Post*, August 16, 1941. pp. 27, 53.
5. *The Washington Post*. Washington, D. C., November 22, 1944 and January 2, 1945.
6. *Boston Herald*, Sunday, August 16, 1942, p. 1.
7. Curtis Zahn, "A Pacifist Publicist Takes Stock", in *Pacifica Views*, June 29, 1945. pp. 1, 4.
8. Wallace Hamilton, *Clash By Night*, Lebanon, Pennsylvania. Pendle Hill Pamphlet No. 23, 1945. pp. 22, 29.
9. Robert A. Taft, United States Senator, Ohio, in *Tolerance*. Washington, D.C., NSBRO, n/d. p. 3.
10. Harry K. Zeller, Jr., *Lamps That Never Go Out*, Elgin, Illinois. Highland Avenue Church of the Brethren, February 15, 1945. p. 5.

11.   NSBRO, *Congress Looks at the Conscientious Objector*, Washington, 1943.   Testimony before the Senate Committee on Appropriations, June 24, 1943. p. 69, 70.

12.   Rabbi Abraham Cronback, The Hebrew Union College, Cincinnati, Ohio, in *Tolerance*. NSBRO, Washington, D.C., nd, p. 6.

13.   W. Appleton Lawrence, Bishop, Protestant Episcopal Diocese of Western Massachusetts, Springfield, Mass., in *Tolerance*. NSBRO. Washington, D.C., p. 7.

14.   Ibid, p. 4.

15.   Leo P. Crespi, "Public Opinion Toward Conscientious Objectors", in *The Journal of Psychology*, 1945, 19, pp. 209-310. Reprinted by permission of the Helen Dwight Reid Educational Foundation. Published by Heldref Publications, 1319 18th St. NW. Washington, D.C. 20036-1802. Copyright, 1945.

16.   Eloise Hollett Davison, "Credit to COs", in *Fellowship*, July, 1945.

6
The Honing
of
Beliefs

By the time he arrived in CPS, a CO had been through the rigors of self examination, the challenge of a draft board, and the anxieties of friends and family. But not many of us had known the range of people we encountered in CPS. The varieties of personalities, diversity of backgrounds, and profusion of philosophies, ideas, and beliefs was astounding. It was as if someone had collected people from every culture, every race, every religion, and every occupation; from the highly educated, self educated, and barely educated; from the physically strong to the frail; from the artistic and the literary; from the skilled craftsman, the business entrepreneur, the farmer, and the professional; and from the sincere and straightforward to the designing and shrewd.

We found ourselves in a richly diverse flock, and each unit was small enough—never more than about 250 men—for each of us to know at least a little bit about everybody. Men drafted into the military also found themselves in a great melting pot. Indeed, World War II was a tremendous eye-opener for an entire generation of youth all around the world.

"I entered CPS," Richard said, "as a very naive young man who expected to find all COs to be like-minded individuals who, given the opportunity of national and world leadership, could soon have all nations living in peace and harmony. It didn't take long in CPS to learn of the many divergent opinions held by pacifists, political objectors, JWs [Jehovah's Witnesses], and others who constituted the CO community."

We met men whose education had ended at the eighth grade and others who had doctorate degrees from some of the world's most prestigious universities. We rubbed elbows with farmers, carpenters, ministers, doctors, business men, lawyers, salesmen, teachers, and every occupation in between. There were followers of Father Divine, devout scholars of Christian faiths, devotees of obscure religious orders, disbelievers and nonbelievers, skeptics, and iconoclasts.

Lloyd Frankenberg in a 1947 article in *Harpers Magazine* summarized the complex environment:

Just about every denomination was represented. These included several Fundamentalist sects: First Century Gospel, Christadelphian, Seventh Day Adventist. One man belonged to a single-church sect called "The Church of the Four-Leafed Clover", which preached the gospel of optimism. Appropriately he was a Fuller Brush salesman. Another sect believed that a religion should have no name. Consequently its members were officially listed as having no religion.[1]

A complete list of the denominations represented is in Appendix A.

THE ORIGINS OF FAITH

How one <u>feels</u> and <u>thinks</u> about the affairs of life come from the "codes" of a person's beliefs. While many people can accommodate warfare within their codes, the conscientious objector cannot. The CO is exceptionally fastidious about the demands of conscience, but no more so than other people on issues vital to them. COs become nonconformists not simply because they follow the dictates of conscience but because their particular "code" demands a form of behavior not shared by many of their fellow citizens.

Does the conscientious objector see a different world? Does he see the same world through foggy glasses—or through sharpened lenses? While the CO's solutions may be different, the yearning for a world of peace, freedom, and social justice is universal. The CO simply believes that society has been going about it in the wrong way. We are told about "good" wars; then we see the virus of war spreading and becoming ever more terrifying. Tyranny is purged in one place only to be implanted in more deadly form someplace else.

In this chapter we will listen in on a four year debate as COs honed their beliefs on fundamental issues of peace and freedom. The dialogue was long and spirited as we sought to form our "impossible dream".

Religious Belief

As pointed out above, the basis for a conscientious objector classification in the 1940 draft law was "religious training and belief". While Selective Service attempted to guide local draft boards in interpreting the word "religious", it was a constant source of difficulty. Most people on the draft boards had their own definitions, and they preferred their ideas to the directives from Washington. If a draft board was not very sympathetic to conscientious objection in the first place, religion was given a very narrow definition—belief in a God, church membership (and even specific denominations), or a particular family background. In other cases, when members of certain religious colonies—such as Amish in Pennsylvania or Ohio—were being drafted, it was understood that conscientious objection was a tradition for these "unique" people. CO classifications in these cases were relatively routine.

When draft boards refused CO classifications and COs appealed to the courts, the courts usually interpreted Congressional intent liberally and applied a broad definition in approving CO classifications. Long after the war, the U.S. Supreme Court established its own relatively liberal definition. (U.S. v. Seeger, 380 US 163, March 18, 1965, and Welsh v. U.S., 398 US 333, June 15, 1976.)

For many, conscientious objection was based on the word of God. Their belief was a matter of personal salvation. Percy expressed it most succinctly, "God said it; I believe it; and that settles it." It was a lifetime commitment, and there were no compromises.

Christian pacifists were bewildered when nearly all churches supported the war. While we were criticized for taking the Christian teaching "too literally", we learned with some dismay—and some comfort—that some men in the military services shared our concern about the Church's compromise with war. Many of us had personal experiences with friends—and strangers—who quietly supported us for holding to our religious faith.

People citing Biblical support for war usually cite the Old Testament dogma such as an "eye for an eye and a tooth for a tooth." Our understanding of the New Testament, however, is that Jesus taught us to "turn the other cheek" and to forgive "seventy times seven."

Harry K. Zeller from the Highland Avenue Church of the Brethren in Elgin, Illinois, told of meeting a group of military officers during the war:

> The train was sold out the night I went east. I got on without reservation and took a seat in the club car. I prepared to "sit the night up" in company with the army colonel, the navy lieutenant, and the ordnance inspector who shared the booth-like corner in which we were crowded. We talked about the war and more . . . the last one and the next one. After some hours I told the men that I was a minister. The colonel let out a roar, "Well, boys, let's give him the works. We will tell you what kind of church the boys want after the war is over." Then with blistering irony he began to satirize the way ministers had invoked God into the war. In Germany they say—he said—"God is on our side." Here we say the same. "You ministers do not understand much, do you? You cry wolf when you think you need to," he said. By this time a crowd had gathered around our corner. In high glee he rode on castigating the ministry for its evils in the matter. I was smiling—for he was going right down my alley, and he didn't know it. So I let him have it full force. "Now you are talking my stuff. I am not only a minister, I am a pacifist minister. I am occupying this precious travel space to visit in the camps with the men who are conscientious objectors to war." There was a solemnizing moment of quiet before he said, "That's the only message the church has in such an hour as this."[2]

Traditionally, members of "historic peace churches"—the Brethren, the Friends (Quakers), and the Mennonites—were "birthright" pacifists, opposed to violence in any form. It was their religious heritage, and their heroes came from their church history.

"Being from the Church of the Brethren background," Paul said, "my attitudes on war and peace were already well established."

"My CO stand," Spencer said, "was the result of childhood conditioning in a Quaker household. This conditioning has contributed to my generally nonconformist attitude."

Speaking from the humility of his Mennonite roots, Ora expressed faith in what, "My Anabaptist fathers taught and lived. [We have] . . . pride in ourselves in that we were allowed this heritage of a gift from our Lord and not pride in ourselves."

While not all members of even these churches followed their church's teaching, the course was clear for those who did. Stephen's path was well trod by those who went before: "As a Quaker, I . . . inherited my CO status. I did not have to do the extensive search for the rationale that made me a CO as others without this background did." "The CO position," Robert said, "was simply one rather dramatic outcome of my Christian persuasion and commitment."

For the Christian, Jesus' Sermon on the Mount was a creed for life. The way of Christ was the way of love and peace, not hatred and war. CPS was a way of fulfilling this belief.

The greatest number of COs in CPS were members of churches and considered themselves religious objectors. There were some, however, who professed no religion at all. A few of these enjoyed the shock of announcing that they had "moved beyond" religion. They relished their status as camp iconoclasts and enjoyed the consternation created by their dissent. One of these rebels told me that a dormitory mate, in the mate's nightly prayers, included his name, asking for God's forgiveness. This intrusion into his rebellion annoyed him at first; but the neighbor's gentle manner won him over, and they eventually became friends. (The one for whom the prayers were rendered never confessed to joining in the prayers—and it is unlikely that he ever did.)

While most religious COs were Christians, pacifism has its roots in most religions and philosophies. As Ed said, "Becoming a CO is a very logical extension of being a Christian. . . . That belief has broadened so that now I see myself not so much as a Christian, but as part of a universal spirit."

Many men had social, political, and economic objections to war that overrode or replaced religious beliefs. In their minds these were sufficient justifications for refusing war. They were not, however, recognized by draft boards; so it was necessary to couch claims in religious terms. It did not take much imagination to broaden the meaning of "religious", since draft boards knew the military did not want to bother with these people anyway.

Values and Ideals

"I was a birthright CO," Eliot said, "since both parents were ministers and both were ardent pacifists. . . . A commitment to the struggle for social justice was practically a condition for membership in my family."

Whatever the basis for our conscientious objection, we saw that war breeds social, political, and economic disorder. It not only results from the breakdown of social order; it is also the cause of those breakdowns.

Conscientious objection, then, is not an isolated act. It is a way of challenging the dislocations of social order. It is a commitment to action, a covenant with an ideal. "I do not regard being a CO as being virtuous," John said, "except as it is but a small part of a whole inventory of concerns and involvements."

Richard's convictions grew out of his family's life: "We were a large family that had a terrific struggle during the great depression of the 1930's. We had to learn to live by faith and trust God. My values, positions, disposition and some character traits were forged by these hardships. . . . I had to fight to get my CO position recognized. I plainly told them [the draft board] I would go to prison—go to jail—rather than go to the army. When they saw I meant it, they granted my CO status."

Many of us had been inspired by the dedicated lives of other pacifists. Gandhi's name was often mentioned, as was Albert Schweitzer's. Historical figures included Thoreau, William Lloyd Garrison, and the founders of the historic pacifist denominations, George Fox (Friends), Menno Simons (Mennonites), and Alexander Mack (Church of the Brethren). There were great pacifist leaders in most Christian denominations, some well-known such as Harry Emerson Fosdick and John Haynes Holmes and others less well-known but equally committed.

COs are as persistent as they are independent. "I have been from the start an independent person," Bryn said, "so I have no trouble taking a stand no matter how unusual."

THE FOUR YEAR DEBATE

The diversity of people offered us a rich menu of ideas, beliefs, disbeliefs, objections, contentions, and counter-contentions. There was never an idea without its challengers; no beliefs were left undisputed; and we were expected to defend every pronouncement with line, verse, and chapter of authority. Some of us relished the dialogue; others were dismayed and intimidated by it—at first; and still others withdrew to watch the fireworks, occasionally attempting to referee or arbitrate. But would-be conciliators could not stand aloof; they would either join the fray or be ignored. Our discussions and our camp meetings lasted until everyone was out of breath, causing some to declare that CPS had met their lifetime quotas for meetings and debate. A wit observed, "We split wood all day and hairs all night." He would not find much disagreement—but of course he would be required to define "wood" and "hair".

We were visited continually by members from church organizations, religious societies, peace organizations, civil liberties groups, public welfare agencies, and the like. These people brought us a wide range of ideas, philosophies, and opinions; and they kept us abreast of affairs in the world outside. We were eager for any fresh ideas, and we were delighted to see new faces. People from educational and religious organizations brought us what often amounted to short courses on all manner of topics. Politicians, governmental officials, and journalists who shared our convictions urged us not to give up on the political process or to reject what came to be called The Establishment. People from all social, political, and economic persuasions brought their causes, looking for converts in a receptive audience. Some people simply wanted us to know that we were not forgotten. Others lived among us for short periods, offering classes in history, economics, psychology, cooperatives, and the like. In one camp we were visited by a roving woman preacher traveling with her young son. She entertained us with her sweet, gentle songs, accompanied by her charismatic little boy.

A number of special schools were established in various camps where assignees studied one topic for several weeks. We had concentrated courses on Cooperatives, Pacifist Living, and Fine Arts conducted during evenings and weekends.

Selective Service military officers called to reacquaint us with their rules and regulations. Even these meetings were well attended—cordially, but not with much agreement. The officers were not looking for agreement; but their perspective on things was always a source of amazement (and on occasion, amusement) to us. They took themselves and their positions so seriously! We attempted to understand the military mind but probably without much success. We also realized that it was difficult for them to comprehend ours.

Our seeking opened our minds to a new world of thought. Many of us had not heard about social, economic, or political objectors before entering CPS. "It widened my perspective," John said, "to include 'political (non-religious) objectors' who I did not realize existed. It also exposed me to a wide scope of religions with peace and reconciliation doctrines." We were "unified by dynamic dissension."

We learned that there were many paths to the same end. We took comfort in knowing that people from all walks of life and all ranges of belief can reach the same conclusion. "I gained a greater tolerance," Dan said, "for the variety of ways one can arrive at the CO position and difficulties of holding to that position—especially for those without a birthright within one of the 'historic peace churches'."

Curtis came to CPS with strict interpretations of Christian duty, "I went from a somewhat literal, Biblical basis for my beliefs about war to a more comprehensive attitude toward violence and the connection of violence to racism, sexism, poverty, and other oppressions."

"It changed my attitude of religious belief," Jonas said. "[I discovered] that other denominations that differed from our Old Order Amish denomination hold the same cherished hope of Eternal Life through Jesus Christ as we do, though we differ in our mode of dress, etc."

There was a generous tolerance of dissenters, for in the wider world we were all dissenters. Carroll remarked, "Although I am a Church person, I feel a kinship and respect for others whose CO position is not, at least openly, based on religion,. Some 'non-religious' objectors work harder than we 'religious' objectors."

CPS was a time to re-examine values, to rid ourselves of prejudices, and to think through what we wanted to do with our lives. "Living and working with men of a number of different religions and lifestyle persuasions," Dan observed, "caused me to think through many of the biases and traditions I had grown up with."

"When I entered CPS," Leonard said, "I had been a farmer and had not had the opportunity to attend college; so my faith in the way of love had not been tested by differing interpretations. I knew that I could not kill other humans and participate in any kind of warfare. During CPS I had the opportunity to test my beliefs through intense conversations with persons of many different persuasions. As a result, my convictions became deeper and broader, helping me to relate to many other areas of life."

We were anxious to test our views on nonbelievers, too. Hitchhiking, the only transportation available to us in those fuel short years, gave us that chance because we were usually asked why a healthy young man was not in uniform. The discreet rider would stall the conversation until he reached town, anticipating that an irate driver would put him out of the car—which did happen. The less timid person jumped at the chance to try out some new wrinkle in his argument.

One of our more ingenious brothers told about one of his rides, "The first question out of the box was, 'Why aren't you in uniform?'. 'Well,' I said, 'I'm from that "Conchie" camp up the road.' 'Oh, you work there. What kind of people are those guys?' 'Well, yes, I work there; but I'm a CO myself.' I could see fire in his eyes, and I knew I had to talk fast or be stranded on the highway. 'I can see,' I said, 'that you are an open minded person; so if you want me to, I'll try to explain why I am a CO.' That seemed to defuse the situation, and he said he would like to hear what I had to say. 'Well', I said, 'I'll tell you; but only if you agree to give me twenty uninterrupted minutes.' (I knew by that time we would be in town where I wanted to go.) 'O.K., go ahead.'

"I started by explaining to him that I had made it a policy never to kill anybody that I wasn't going to eat. While he shuddered a little at that, I could see that my flip remark amused him. So I told my story. I explained that I took education seriously and believed that war was brought on by greed and that wars only cause more wars. He tried to interrupt me a couple of times, but I reminded him of his promise and continued my story. I covered all the reasons I could think of but left out some of the more abstract ideas. By the time I got through, we were in town; so I didn't care if he let me out. But, to my surprise he said, 'I can see that you are sincere; and while I can't see things the way you do, I respect your right to have your own views.' With that, he drove me to where I wanted to go, shook my hand, and let me out."

As challenging as it was to joust with nonbelievers, it was even more rewarding to talk with fellow believers because someone was always ready to take the opposite side of an argument. No claim went uncontested. We had to answer the tough questions and explain our refusal to fight.

We also learned to listen and to see as many viewpoints as possible. The one-on-one and two-by-four discussions clarified and broadened our outlook. The older men had more seasoned explanations, and the younger men showed more fervor and excitement. "The beliefs I had as an eighteen year old," Harold said, "were not very grounded. Associating with fine Christians at Terry, Montana, taught me a lot both in Christian faith and ideals and in trying to live out a positive peace witness."

Some of our work assignments affirmed our convictions. Ray described his work in a mental hospital: " I found confirmation arising from the daily routines, especially in our relationships with mental patients and our demonstration of the superior methods of treatment based on respect and Christian commitment."

Opposition to war meant more than refusing to kill. It led us to seek better ways of dealing with people in our day-to-day lives, conducting business affairs, participating in community activities—churches, schools, public services, charities, peace organizations, and the like. We searched ways of living that would make violence impossible "Meeting 'non-religious' objectors caused me," Robert said, "to realize that I was a pacifist, not just a CO."

We enlarged our view of the world. Lee explained the change in his outlook: "I was not a confirmed pacifist when was drafted. I took the Mosaic commandment seriously. To me it meant 'thou shall not kill,' period. All I was sure of at the point of induction was, I should not go to the army. Early on in camp, the philosophy of nonviolence took hold."

When we entered CPS, we may have been COs by impulse, by heredity, or by emulation; but we ultimately became COs in our own right. "I was a Church CO when I entered," Wesley said. "In three years I became a CO by conviction."

We became less naive, but our idealism was strengthened. We became more realistic, more practical, and more firm. We had hardened our beliefs, and we had emerged with a clearer vision. We were enriched in the knowledge that societies which can overcome cannibalism, feudalism, slavery, and tyranny can certainly overcome warfare.

Our eyes and our minds were opened to broader possibilities. Paul changed, "from Baptist to Quaker; from tentative CO to pacifist; from conservative per family to liberal per new experience; from patriotic to world loyalties; from college graduate specialization to new concern for ecology and the mentally ill; from callow to concerned."

The CPS years lifted us from the humdrum of normal life and gave us a new vision for our lives. For Morris, it was "an antidote to becoming too heavily focused on just my profession." "The intense, confined living experience," Steve said, "provided a huge opportunity to learn about and experience a range of societal conditions. The CPS experience—with all its trials and tribulations—provided an environment whose cultural richness has never been matched, before or since."

CPS was a generous mind stretcher for Spencer: "The camp did introduce me to a wider range of COs than I had known, and helped me overcome some of the class snobbishness and self-righteousness I brought with me." Harold . . . became more accepting of various lifestyles, less prudish. . ."

We learned to understand the plight of the permanent minorities—those whose race, color, or religions fixes them forever in their disadvantaged position. When the war was over, our differences passed unnoticed. Other minorities who carry their permanent "markers" are not so fortunate.

We became, as Canby expressed it, "emotionally very intolerant of rednecks, KKK,. . . and any other aristocentric group out to exploit, murder, or do violence to others for their own aggrandizement."

The positive impact on our personal lives was expressed in many ways: "greatest experience in my life," "most significant event," "maybe the best thing that ever happened to me," "best years of my life," "meaningful and memorable," and "highest light of my life—next to my marriage." It was "unique," "unforgettable," "indispensable," One person confessed to being "still elated" over the experience.

Bill explained how it was for the world to "find him out," "Suddenly I was brought into the real world. Having taken an unpopular position, being challenged at home by a family of conventional persuasions, and discovering (or being told, in any case) that I was not welcome in such places as the American Legion Hall . . . I was now required to function in the real world."

"I entered CPS as a simple farm boy with only an eighth grade education," Virgil said. "I left with 18 hours of college credit and skills such as typing, cooking, fighting forest fires, outdoor living skills. I went to CPS socially handicapped, timid, and fearful. I had never dated. I left CPS with a fiancee whom I later married. . . ."

For many, CPS was their "college education." "It was more significant than my college," "it was higher than graduate school," "it was my college," "it was six years of college in two years," and "I would not trade it for four years of college."

"CPS is more my alma mater than my college," said Neil, "the turning point in my life." Gordon said it was his "best education, including four years at college . . . and a PhD." Mervin explained, *"I got my degree in college but my education in CPS."*

For Wilbur, "CPS was a great University By Example. I have never found a better one or one that was more interesting." "Had it not been for CPS," Eugene said, "I most likely would not have gone on to college. . . . "

It was a time of new beginnings: a "watershed," a "pivotal time," a "turning point," a "springboard," a "point of departure," and a "kickoff to everything that followed." It was a "life transforming" time that "turned our lives around."

We learned how to cut ourselves loose from social pressures. "I was made aware I had to stand for something," Francis said, "or I'd fall for anything that came along. . . Have a purpose and dare to make it known!"

Mark explained: "It was the first thing I did out of deep conviction. That opened the door to later position-taking and action,"

Being a CO gave Jarrott: "1) an understanding of being in a minority and unpopular class; 2) an appreciation of the plight of poor blacks in Arkansas; 3) an empathy with the impoverished when out of money; 4) an education in mental illness at a state hospital; 5) firsthand observation of the effects of starvation."

Arthur had a highly unusual CPS assignment with the National Park Service in Hawaii, and this led to a long career in forestry management and erosion control. After the war he worked as a Forestry and Erosion Control advisor in Korea, Watershed Management advisor in Jamaica, and Soil Conservation Specialist and Forestry Officer in watershed management in Australia. Immediately after the war he went to China as an agricultural specialist with the Brethren Service Committee and with UNRRA. His concern for human life, he says, extends to the life of the planet.

Andrew summarized it for us: "One's Faith journey is an endless search for truth. As the search goes on, attitudes and beliefs are enriched—and changed."

Finally, we have a soldier's perspective, told by a visitor to his friend in a CPS camp: "You know, when you are part of the military, you are continually indoctrinated to the ways of the military. You are told first that the enemy out there is something less than human and that he is determined to kill you. Then you are taught how to kill-kill-kill in order to save your life and those of your buddies. Finally you are educated—propagandized—to think and react like every other soldier. You are all to look alike, dress alike, think alike, and act alike. You are told that the camaraderie of soldiering is the highest and noblest duty to which a man can be called. Before you know it, you are just like every other guy in the outfit, ready to go anyplace and to do anything that you are ordered to do. It was a real breath of fresh air to be here and see that you guys can question anything you hear and can give your own opinions about things whenever you want to. You don't have to swallow anything until it makes sense to you. There is no way that a military organization could operate on that basis because if you were able to question an order in a certain suicide mission, the whole military system would collapse."

TO STAY OR TO WALK

Most of the comments in this book come from men who stayed in CPS, but there were some who found CPS unbearable. A few of those went into the military and others "walked out", usually ending up in jail.

Considerable heat can still be generated on the pros and cons of CPS. In August, 1990, a Celebration of Conscience was held at Bryn Mawr College to commemorate the 50th anniversary of conscientious objection under the 1940 Selective Service law. A number of people who had refused to cooperate with the draft law during the war were bitter about wartime conscription and about those who had sponsored CPS and about those who participated in it. Did those who chose CPS betray pacifism by accepting that alternative? It was evident that 50 years had not reduced the emotion about those years. The men who stayed in CPS were satisfied that they had done the right thing, and those who left were sure that CPS was a "cop out".

Those Who Stayed

In the modern world of powerful nation-states all citizens accommodate themselves to the power of the State in one manner or another. There is no doubt that COs in CPS *compromised* with the conscription system, just as did everyone else who accepted the draft. At what point does one draw the line of compromise? Some COs drew that line within the military by accepting non-combatant service; some accepted the muddy waters of CPS; others accepted the right of the government to prosecute them for failing to live up to their draft classifications; some refused to register for the draft but accepted the government's right to prosecute; and still others refused to accept any government jurisdiction and either went underground or emigrated to other countries. So we were not totally without choices. Those choices, however, were severely narrowed by the society's commitment to war.

Whether we accepted CPS or some other course, the issues were the same: First, what is best for my integrity and for the preservation and well-being of my own person.

Second, where should I spend my energies, recognizing that I probably will not be doing what I want to do in any case.

For those who stayed, CPS met the two conditions better than other alternatives.

In 1944 Carl Soule assembled statements from CPS men describing their reasons for entering and staying in CPS.

It is dangerous both for the individual's psychic welfare and for social organization generally for him to extend his conscientious objection to the CPS program, withdrawing from the fellowship of the already small minority. . . . A mature CPS citizen might say, "I believe that CPS is insufficiently under civilian direction and the work is not always of much importance, but in order to exemplify to a disunited world unity in spite of earnest difference of opinion, I shall remain in CPS. . . ." This argument concerning unity does not deal directly with the charge that conscription as embodied in CPS is wrong, but it points out the danger of making conscience such a fine and tender point that one becomes overly critical and socially negative.

CPS represents a proper recognition by the state of the supremacy of conscience and a proper recognition by the church that the state rightfully has some control over the lives of its citizens. Niemoller's position may well be ours: a combination of warm appreciation and bold criticism of government. . . .

Most of us expect to live out our lives in an unjust social order in a wicked world. . . . We must protest and endure at the same time. It is in the working of this dual process that the religious man saves both himself and the situation. I may not be a literal subscriber to the doctrine of original sin, but I support the effectiveness of the curse which followed it. Man must work, and sometimes at unpleasant tasks or deteriorate. We have a very long way to go; we should take the historical view. . . .

In spite of its inconveniences CPS is a potent force. . ."[3]

For Levi, CPS "contributed to my Christian life and experience. I praise God for the privilege of serving in this capacity and have no regrets."

No one had any illusions about this flawed system, but our reaction to it was more important than the system itself. To maintain their own integrity and to remove the sting of compulsion, some people went "the second mile" and worked in excess of what was expected. What they were directed to do, they could not control; but what they did on their own, they did control. Willard explained, "I was willing to make it as positive as possible."

Those Who Left
A number of people changed their minds about CPS. Some abandoned their conscientious objection and joined the military. Others "walked out" because they had compromised their consciences by complying with conscription in the first place or by accepting the flawed CPS alternative.

For the Military
COs in World War I were assigned to noncombatant duties in the army. It became a nuisance for the army to sort out the noncombat men, and COs were harassed for insisting on noncombat jobs. Early in World War II, noncombatant COs (l-A-Os) were in much the same position. When Lew Ayres, the actor who gained fame in the motion picture, *All Quiet on the Western Front*, registered as a CO, he requested service in the military medical corps. The military would not guarantee him that assignment; so he went to CPS. The government, embarrassed by the publicity Ayres received,

changed its policy on non-combatant assignments and agreed to place him in the medical corps. Thereafter, any 1-A-O draftee requesting it was assigned to the medical corps.

Robert explained his change of heart about CPS during the summer of 1944:

We must beware that in living the somewhat sheltered lives we do in CPS we do not lose sight of our oneness with the present national and world situation, and also our responsibilities in helping to solve it, and so live mentally that we run away from ourselves and the real issues of life. . . .

What we need is some clear thinking and unselfish courageous action. What we need is vision and the WILL to DO, in the spirit of love, tolerance, and service. It is only upon the foundation of Right Thought and Right Action that the temple of Universal Brotherhood will be raised. . . .

In the light of true Justice we cannot accept the privileges of physical life and the opportunities of living in this country without recognizing and fulfilling corresponding responsibilities and obligations in some definite form, or through some definite channel.
Personally, I have changed my views as regards the rightness of, or the good that can be done by serving in the medical or other non-combatant units in the Armed Forces.[4]

Writing to friends after his decision to abandon CPS, Don explained:

My change of heart was really a loss of faith . . . if I ever had the faith. I think anyone who takes any other view of Christianity and war is coming danger-ously close to warping Christianity to fit his desires and in the process weakening whatever power Jesus' life exerts in the sphere where it seems to apply. I can no longer be at peace within myself and continue to accept exemption. But in spite of that, neither do I think I can be entirely at peace within myself in the armed services. I'm entering the Army with almost a sense of shame— not because I've changed my mind but because shame seems to me the only spirit with which anyone can approach a terrible conflict which he himself has had more than a little responsibility in causing. I can't feel, as some men do, that I am helping fight a just and righteous war; I can't feel that there could be any glory in my victory over someone very little more responsible for the conflict than I; I can't be convinced that I should have pride in a uniform and weapons that would never have been conceived had you and I and those like us lived a truly Christian life in the prewar world; I can go into the war believing only that Jesus plods on toward peace and justice on a road other than ours, far more difficult, far less easily discerned—a figure sadly and indescribably alone. We, having lost that road, found it too difficult, abandoned it as impractical, or not bothered to search for it at all, took the broad, obvious highway of violence and destruction which may never lead to the goal we seek.[5]

Some who joined the military lost all interest in pacifism. Others came back to it in later life.

Hamilton abandoned CPS for the military but never lost faith in the wisdom of nonviolence. "As news of the holocaust was confirmed," he said, "I volunteered for the infantry and landed on 'the Bulge'. [I still have a] . . . . distaste of violence in the workplace and on T.V. . . . [I] participate in such religious groups as Quakers, American Friends Service Committee, Mennonite Central Committee, various Brethren, along with Amnesty International, etc."

Everett explained, "I left . . . for the Army only because, (1) I felt obligated to go as far with the government as conscience would permit, and Medical [Corps] was now guaranteed to 1-A-O's; (2) I wanted the postwar educational benefits; and (3) I felt out of the mainstream of life. I turned down . . .the Army Specialist Training Program . . . it might compromise my CO status."

Herbert left CPS for the Army "because I became increasingly convinced that I would not refrain from violence in case of personal attack. . . . My CPS experience confirmed my feeling that war would never settle anything satisfactorily, and it changed my beliefs by showing me that pacifism for me was a political force and not necessarily only a personal one.

". . . People have simply got to learn that they cannot expect to get desirable and long-term beneficial results by using force in response to social and political problems, and COs start with that point of view."

For Louis, "going into CPS was more of a social service feeling than pacifist. Since I left for the army in summer, 1942, my commitment to pacifism apparently wasn't that deep. . . . I am proud that I was the only officer who refused to carry a weapon. . . . [Before the war] I had been working for the American Friends Service Committee since college graduation. . . . If my life ever had meaning, it was during those years with the Service Committee. . . . I still think life is precious."

Through his Army service, George retained his ideals: "I left CPS and joined the U.S. Army without the slightest bit of enthusiasm. . . . I knew I was morally opposed to war, but I wasn't able to convince myself that my pacifist beliefs were strong enough to sustain me through the period of the war. . . . I felt increased pressure to be and do like other people. . . . The ideals, however, remain with me, and I regret my inability to stick out CPS. . . ."

Robert had spent three months in CPS in 1941, but was released for being overage. After Pearl Harbor he was again drafted, this time into the Army. "Refusal to participate takes more fortitude than I have. I still admire those with strong CO feelings, and I send a little money each year to NISBCO and CCCO."

For Prison
The people who "walked out" became AWOLs (Absent Without Leave) and knew they would be arrested for violating the Selective Service law. Indeed, they were scrupulously straightforward about it, informing the government where they would be and what they would be doing after they left.

In his 1942 statement Philip described the evolution of his thinking:

Always I have considered conscription to be a process of involuntary servitude, contrary to the freedom of choice basic to democracy. The compromise in accepting assignment to CPS was made because I wanted to work constructively rather than spend my time in protest. I saw the possibility of a regimentory regime extending far into the future—so that instead of jail, I sought thru CPS to find a way to work within the framework of conscription. But it has become apparent to me that a peaceful and cooperative society cannot be built if the conscription process becomes all-pervasive. . . . The strongest action against conscription is non-compliance. In addition, when we refuse to comply with conscription, we also strike at war—since conscription is an integral part of war activity.[6]

Seven men who jointly walked out explained their reasons:

CONSCRIPTION, TOTALITARIANISM, AND WAR . . . are complementary evils. They are based on violence: outright physical slaughter, the curbing of the mind, and the crushing of the spirit. Conscription as an integral and necessary part of this picture is based on the claim that the individual and social institutions do not themselves know best how they can contribute to society, but that they must follow the dictates of the state.

CPS . . . is an integral part of the conscription system, and we believe that in it pacifists are accepting, cooperating, and giving tacit and moral approval to, rather than nonviolently opposing, the trend toward totalitarianism.

After a period of intensive discussion and careful thought, we have decided that in honesty we must dissociate ourselves from the CPS program.[7]

John explained that his decision to leave CPS had grown "out of three years of special concern. . . . It seems clear to me that CPS does not begin to allow most COs the freedom to apply the positive aspects of Pacifism. . . . I hope to fulfill my social responsibility by making the strongest possible protest against conscription. . . . I do this with the faith that this behavior more strongly proves my sincerity and brings to society's attention the error it makes in conscription. . . . I feel compelled to actively protest conscription because of the part it plays in placing military activities at the pinnacle of importance over all other aspects of our entire culture. . . . A further quarrel with the principle of conscription is that forced labor under any circumstances does more harm than good."[8]

Assuming that prison would be the consequence, most walk-outs resigned themselves to prison life and adjusted to its regimen, just as did those who remained in CPS. But to others, noncooperation with the prison system became the next form of resistance. They rejected prison authority and spoke out against the evils of the system. The Absolutist, a journal identifying itself as the OFFICIAL ORGAN OF THE ABSOLUTIST WAR OBJECTORS ASSOCIATION, publicized the plight of CO prison inmates. In the June 19, 1945, issue, John Hampton, an inmate at McNeil Federal Penitentiary, told of his resistance:

I have tried to avoid punishment or physical injury to myself wherever possible, but I cannot spare myself in my fight for the truth that God is the sole lord of conscience, and an individual or group who seeks to usurp God's authority is a liar, a thief, and a hypocrite. I am encouraged in my fight by the knowledge that this is a basic and integral part of our American democracy, and the First Amendment to our Constitution sought to guarantee to every man the right to worship God and order his life according to the dictates of his conscience.

As a Christian I cannot cooperate with Selective Service's prison program of punishment, "correction", "rehabilitation", or of using me for the purpose of building war morale or of deterrence to the conscientious objectors.

I will not accept my criminal status.

I will not subject myself to prison rules or regulations.

I will not submit to the authority of prison guards or officials.

I have never stood in the way of any conscientious soldier or war worker in the following of his conscientious convictions. I give every man the right to his opinions—and I expect the right to mine; and when any individual or group attempts to cram their opinions down my throat, I do not intend to let threats, intimidation, or punishment deter me from obeying God.[9]

As a pacifist Christian minister, Jim Bristol refused a ministerial deferment and ignored the Selective Service law. He had this to say about COs who served in CPS:

The acceptable objector stance was to perform alternative service under the law. Although . . . those of us who rejected conscription altogether *did* receive support, most of the pacifist community treated us "absolutists" like second-class citizens. I think that often we [absolutists] were an embarrassment to our fellow pacifists, and frequently they were hurt by our rejection of the law, with its hard-won and rejoiced-over provisions for COs.[10]

Bristol spoke with such fervor, it is painful to disagree; but no such sentiments were expressed by the thousand CPSers quoted in this book. Nor do I have any memory that this was the attitude of CPS men during the war. In my experience and the experience of my associates, there was never anything but the utmost respect for these men. Indeed, as noted above, several people came around to the absolutist position themselves in later years.

RENUNCIATION OF CO BELIEFS

There were seven among the thousand respondents in the CPS Survey who renounced their conscientious objection. Victor's comments were the strongest of the seven: "The folly of the whole idea. Exchanging a Commission in the

Quartermaster Corps for tree planting in Northern Michigan appears to illustrate an extreme lack of perspective. . . . The biggest mistake of my life. A decidedly negative impact on professional, personal & family existence."

Many of the seven said that their change of mind came after learning about the Nazi extermination camps. They did not think the pacifist had a credible response to such conditions. Others said that while they were no longer pacifists, they still believed in the credibility of nonviolence and in the wisdom of such apostles as Martin Luther King, Jr. One man said he admired the "principled men" who took the CO position and respected the integrity and sincerity of pacifist believers even though he abandoned pacifism himself.

Six of the respondents were among those mentioned above who left CPS for the military. Five of these said that despite changing their minds about conscientious objection, CPS had been a positive experience. They continued their interest in the peace movement after the war and participated in various peace activities. One of these said, "Refusal to participate takes more fortitude than I have." Another said he still felt very good about having been a CO, "It was the one time in my life when I stood up for my convictions." A third man, in expressing his continued interest in pacifist ideas, said he hoped ex-CPSers would maintain contact with him, "if you don't mind communicating with an ex-mule officer."

1.   Lloyd Frankenberg, "Conscience Free"'", in *Harpers Magazine.* November, 1947. p. 471.
2.   Harry K. Zeller, *Lamps That Never Go Out.* Elgin, Illinois, February 15, 1945.
3.   Carl Soule, *Reasons for Entering and Staying in C.P.S.*, 1944. From CPS Camp 21 files.
4.   Robert Stewart, Letter written from CPS Camp 76, Arcadia, California. August 5, 1944. From CPS Camp 21 files.

5.   Ted Kandle, letter to Nancy [Foster/Neumann], Camp Antelope, Coleville, California, August 29, 1942. From CPS Camp 21 files.

6.   Philip Isely, *To Make A Positive Affirmation*. February 1942. From CPS Camp 21 files.

7.   Jim Bristah, et. al., *WE SEVEN ARE WALKING OUT OF CPS*......... June 7, 1943. From CPS Camp 21 files.

8.   John Magee, *ANOTHER JULY "WALKOUT"*. July 17, 1944. From CPS Camp 21 files.

9.   John Hampton, *The Absolutist*. Vol III, No. 6, June 16, 1945, pp. 2 - 3. From CPS Camp 21 files.

10.   Jim Bristol, "Conscription, Conscience, and Resistance", in *Friends Journal*, January, 1992, p. 21.

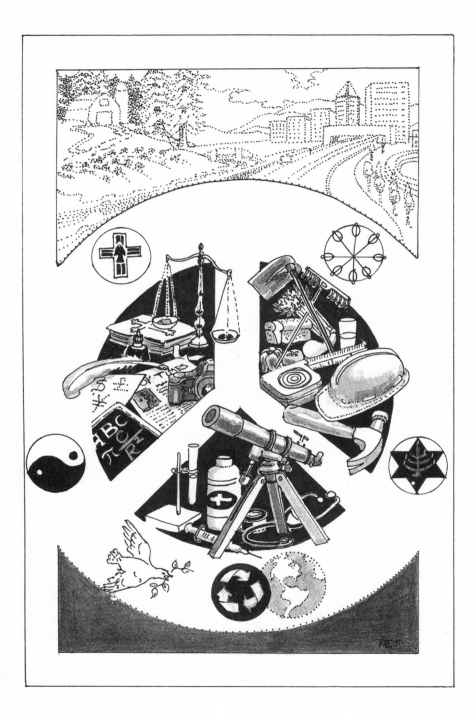

7
An
Undaunted
Minority

There always have been people willing to pay the price for rejecting society's customs. When COs refused to participate in what their world saw as a just war, we knew we were in the company of many like-minded people who had gone before. Our ancestors had paved our way when they fled the military tyrannies of Europe and established the freedom of conscience in the new world. They also brought with them a conviction in the power of democracy and its new ways of thinking. This, in turn, rested on a belief in the fundamental dignity of each person. These notions were later codified in the Constitution, the statutes, and the common law in the New World. So in the twentieth century the freedom of conscience was protected from a community that did not welcome deviant ideas. But we offered more than a different idea. We condemned one of mankind's most popular institutions.

Our minority status did not end with World War II because we continued to speak out against wars whenever the occasion required it. Although the Vietnam war came to be seen as a mistake, in its early years it was a great crusade against the Communist "threat". Philip was fired from his church pastorship when he opposed that war. Leonard lost his minister's position for a similar indiscretion: "speaking out and standing firmly on principle.."

THE SOCIAL CONSEQUENCES

Did "bucking the tide" against a "just" war have any lasting impact on a world obsessed with war? As inheritors of the pacifist tradition, we have been waiting a long time for the answer to that question.

Pacifists insist on looking at human conflict in fundamentally different ways. The CO, John explains, ". . . sets up a different center of values, a competing set of claims, a differing and arguable set of conclusions." This approach may rock the boat or slow down the engine, but it is not intended to capsize the vessel. The purpose is to bring about a change of course.

The CO, by objecting to what we see as the illusion in war, arouses intense resistance. "Any Christian stance in the name of Christ," Lee felt, "creates stresses and strains because we are dealing with two kingdoms—Kingdom of God and Kingdom of Evil."

As Edward expressed it, "We are an irritating minority and may create both fear and anger in people who see their way of life, power, privilege challenged." In short, the CO is a pain to the established order.

If a minority's message is false, it will disappear. When it perseveres, however, it will be heard. The CO raises fundamental questions that people would rather not deal with. The aim, William explains, is to call, "attention to a fact that has always bothered thinking people; namely, what is in the make-up of man that makes him want to destroy himself and his fellow beings."

The CO is a purveyor of tensions; and the hope is that people will <u>think</u> about what they are doing. "The CO approach and techniques," Joe said, " . . . are part of the stress and strain as they focus on the need for changes. Change, even toward the 'good', is stressful; and in-as-much as we push for change, we are part of the reality of modern life. Our hope is that appropriate changes in the long run result in a less stressful society."

The Promise of Change
The wars that followed World War II—at one time there were as many as thirty wars around the world—increased the skepticism about military adventures. The marvel of communications brought the horrors of war into people's homes all over the world, and there was a widening revulsion against the madness of it all. The reality of war was sinking into the public consciousness, leading John to observe, "I do not feel as alone today as I did in 1945."

The failure of military solutions has opened people's minds. "I was the first objector in my county," Paul re-marked. "People didn't have too much time for me. The attitude of the people has made a complete turnaround toward me." Other World War II COs commented on how earlier resentments have softened; and while people may still not agree, COs have increasingly been able to say,"I have been respected."

Waldo took the long view, "If it doesn't happen today, there is tomorrow. Let's give it time." The atomic bomb created a great many nuclear pacifists; and if the movement against nuclear war does not merely eliminate those weapons to make the world safe for conventional weapons, the world may have taken a giant step toward preserving civilization.

The power of nonviolence has caught the imagination of many people as a result of nonviolent struggles by Mohandas Gandhi in India, Martin Luther King, Jr. in the United States, underground resistance movements in Europe during World War II, and social movements in Korea, the Philippines, Latin America, China, South Africa, and Russia.

People increasingly proclaim their support for the nonviolent solutions, and many are beginning to believe what they say. At the same time, there is a growing belief that modern military institutions are obsolete. Sandy summarized the issue: "The 'silent majority' really doesn't care for war and prefers to see conflicts resolved peacefully. When someone is willing to stand up and present reasoned views on the matter, it cannot help but have a positive effect."

The supreme irony is that nonviolence is even today the most widely used strategy for solving all manner of conflicts throughout society. "The cultivated ability," George points out, "to say NO on the basis of principle and compassion is applicable to many social situations, and society urgently needs it." Nonviolence is discussed again in Chapter 11.

The message of human brotherhood, Royce says "offers an alternative to the stresses and strains of competitive, selfish living by encouraging appreciation and respect for every person, by offering to mediate in strife situations, by refusing to show anger or to retaliate, by taking a stand against injustice, by affirming persons who make the right choices."

8

A Covenant
of
Solidarity

No one who went through the CPS years would characterize them as a love feast, nor was it a gathering of angels. But for Alex, "being with a group of individuals, all striking sparks off one another, was thrilling."

We had two things in common: first, our belief that there is only one human family; and second, our abhorrence of violence. These convictions bound us together during the war and cemented relationships in the years which followed. The strength of these connections is quite remarkable when one considers the differences in religion, family background, education, social perceptions, and economic condition, to say nothing of the differences in personality.

How the bond among such a disparate group of individualistic people could survive—and grow—is one of the most fascinating aspects of the story. We had come by these ideas on our own, and we did not easily retreat. We were always willing to let others know where we stood, and it took very little to start us off. Robert was pleased to get acquainted with other points of view, but he was also "amazed at how zealous many of the fundamentalists were."

The quiet ones could fool you. If you thought they lacked conviction, you soon found that no one was swayed by frivolous argument. A quiet demeanor did not mean a lukewarm conviction. Joel described one of the more quiet men: "His answers were hesitant, but he exuded an aura of commitment that surpassed his verbal abilities."

We found thoughtful, intelligent, serious, and committed men who knew why they were there and what they expected to do with their lives. "For the first time," Robert said, "I met people willing to go to jail for . . . beliefs. That impressed me."

Howard saw in his fellow COs, a "dedication to human welfare, with absolute disregard of racial and national distinctions . . . integrity, devotion, open-ended search for peace on every level of human life . . . good-humored, an often ironic capacity to 'hang in' for the sake of the cause."

Yet for all this, we were about as average a cross-section of people as you would find anywhere. We were as self-centered, as cantankerous, as ill-tempered, and as difficult to get along with as any other slice of society. We were also friendly, affable, and cooperative when conditions called for that. In short, we were not much different from any other group of restless young men. Indeed, as John expressed it, we were glad to find that we had not left the real world, "I expected fellow CPSers would probably be several cuts above me spiritually and was relieved to find they weren't."

We were not totally immune to the violence of our society, but we had made a conscious decision to reject violence in every aspect of our lives. While we were not above occasional flares of temper and anger over the daily irritations of life, serious altercations were rarely heard of. (It was reported that deprivations in the starvation experiment led to some friction toward the end of the program.)

We met people from groups we had never known before. Congregationalists learned about Mennonites; fundamentalist Baptists rubbed elbows with Quakers; and Catholics encountered Unitarians. James "discovered non-academic groups respond to everything more personally, requiring [us to be more sensitive] . . . to how things are said."

THE COMMUNITY

"I had something wonderful and beautiful that I wouldn't have except for the experience of CPS," said Vic. "It was warm and close and sharing." "When the world was going one way," Alvin commented, "it was a relief and a wonderful bond and kinship to live, work, and relate as a close and compatible group."

We formed many special friendships, friendships that were "a critical influence in my life," that were "hard to equal," that were "closer than any others," that were "tremendous." For Vincent CPS "created a host of friends and places of interest which, without CPS, I wouldn''t have had."

"They are the only people," Elmo said, " with whom I can be completely open and uninhibited." You felt "at home." It was a common story among CPSers that we could leave our few personal possessions—money, watches, rings, and the like—in open sight at our individual bunks and know they would remain where we left them.

Kinship

Leroy spoke of the family tie, "They are my brothers, because of being together and sharing our beliefs, convictions, and ideas and encouraging each other." Robert was emphatic, "If you didn't share a feeling of close kinship with other CO's, you would be a fraud."

For Mark, "There is a feeling of solidarity because: (1) we all chose that path, no matter what the reason; (2) it was unpopular; (3) generally we managed to get along reasonably well; (4) a large number of assignees were basically worth knowing."

"The camaraderie of the CPS experience," Bob said, "provided a community of friends and co-workers that has lasted my entire life. Having been through that experience was the cement that held us together."

In a world consumed with war, we were a literal non-entity, a mere grain of sand on the plain of life. Our brotherhood was our shield against the winds of war. We learned to cast our lot with other minorities and to champion the cause of "the least of these". Howard explained, "The solidarity of my fellow pacifists made it easier for me to align myself with a number of unpopular causes."

"Coming in, as I did," said Van Cleve, "from a totally non-pacifist family and tradition, I felt quite alone . . . . Thus, it was a great joy and relief . . .to find myself daily working and living with others who shared the same convictions . . ." At last we belonged; we were with kindred souls. The experience renewed our confidence, gave objectivity to our beliefs, and strengthened our convictions.

John explained his life before CPS: "I was a misfit wherever I went; unacceptable to my peers; and I had learned to live with the concept that I could never fit in. CPS changed that for me. I didn't fit in there either, but no one else did—which made it somehow all right." Bill said,

"Being associated with many fine men of similar convictions assured me that I wasn't just 'an odd ball'."

Diversity

Malcolm explained his surprise—and delight: "Rubbing shoulders with Appalachians, Hoosiers, Rednecks, et. al. was revealing, but it was contact with Boston Brahmins, Main Line Philadelphians, and Southern aristocrats which introduced me to the world of art, music, libraries, museums, etc., thereby enriching my life and giving me an appreciation for something besides hard work."

"I was raised a pacifist," said Dan, "and living in the traditional Mennonite community, it was easy to be one. But in camp we met [people] from many cultures and ethnic backgrounds. Some were not pacifists for religious or Biblical reasons, but just because it was human. There were many differences. But we were able to live in harmony and peace with one another."

Virgil was pleased to find "compatriots who, while sharing similar beliefs, were also different—both on the basis for the belief and the depth of the conviction. That was stimulating and prompted further study and reading."

"[From] the endless hours of listening to/participating in discussions of all kinds," Harry said, "we eventually became accepting of or even appreciative of the uniqueness of each one and of the contributions each could make to building community."

"We educated each other," Robert said, "by sharing our knowledge and experiences informally as well as sometimes in scheduled study . . . in music, drama. . . concerts . . . play or poetry readings. I would not likely have developed an appreciation for such things on my own."

A Generous Esteem

The at-ease comradeship left us with fond memories of the people we knew. It was an environment of stimulation and learning. Dull it was not. Richard spoke for many of us, "I am honored and grateful to be a part of that noble group. . . ." John found, "an amazing set of individualistic, brilliant, eccentric men." For Lee, "CPS men were quality people. I don't remember a mean one. I encountered a number of stimulating individuals."

Here are some of the other things these men said about each other: "many great people," "people of honorable convictions," "a great range of men," "so many wonderful fellows." "people I could trust," "so many dedicated people," "an unusual group", "a rich variety of folks", "superb people," and "a camp full of characters."

Comparing his CPS days with his later life, John recalls, "The sweetest of all memories and experiences are some of the relationships we enjoyed with CPS men. . . . The long philosophical, theological, and political discussions with men of high learning and purpose in life provided us with deep inspiration. Our assignment brought us in touch with cultural practices, strong convictions, and brilliant minds. "

Harlan: "[I] met many of the finest people I know in camp." "CPS men," Howard learned, "were people I could trust without any long period of getting acquainted." And Canby "admired the basic honesty of all the men. . . ." "Living with like-minded men," John said, "sharing their ups and downs, seeing the same liabilities, were all important. Also, many of them were really good guys. . . . I felt almost ennobled by their committed work that I shared."

9
For a Lifetime

C onscientious objection was only one part of our lives, but
it taught us the value of firm convictions. Frequently
heard remarks were: "I learned to be steadfast." "Neither
my beliefs nor my convictions have ever wavered."

Standing against war matured us and strengthened
our convictions. Sheldon explained, "Before I was drafted I
was a very bashful and shy person. . . . When I stood up
before the judge and told him I would not serve in the
military and he could send me to prison or a CPS camp, I
lost my shyness. . . ."

We welcomed the chance to do something constructive. "I feel somewhat proud," John said, "that I didn't help
mess things up." "I was able to live with myself more
easily," Bill agreed, "having taken a stand that set me against
the slaughter of people in war."

"The person who resists war on Christian principles,"
Leroy said, "has the feeling of peace and satisfaction of
having a conscience that is free of guilt and compromise.
This knowledge outweighs the stress." "It is a measure of
satisfaction," Carlton added, "to have demonstrated my

desire for peace. . . . My conscience has given me more peace in later life. . . ."

Our determination to "stick it out" added a dimension of adventure. "It does reduce the boredom of going along with the stream flow . . . [it] adds a dynamic to life. It has a purpose that demands a response."

Nourishing that "still small voice" earned us a degree of serenity. We faced the risk, paid the price, and reaped the reward. "Our stubborn insistence on loving each other, regardless of what stupid or wicked things we do, has made for a wonderful and exciting existence."

We were compelled to think about values and priorities. It was a "rite of passage" that enlarged our world. Paul remembers how "it gave new value to my convictions—having to sacrifice money and other conveniences (G.I. benefits) made me look at things more seriously . . . . The experience gave me a new perspective or way of looking at the needs in our world."

"The choice to go the CPS route seems better and better to me," said Arlo. "I am more proud of this decision as the years go by. 'That's one thing', I say to myself, 'that I had the courage to do and am a better person today because of it'."

A RENEWAL OF THE SPIRIT

Many men said that CPS was a turning point in their religious lives and a time of new religious awakening. Sometimes this meant an increased interest in the organized Church; sometimes it did not.

Walter was optimistic: "My faith that God . . . can enable us to live together in love and mutual helpfulness has grown stronger. . . . [God's] will and help are available in . . . many kinds of human social devices."

Rufus emphasized, "My Christian faith became a working basis for making judgments regarding social and political issues." We learned how religious values apply to a broad range of social issues. "The new-found knowledge of the 'peace churches'," Joe said, "broadened my outlook."

CPS was its own seminary, with advocates for every form and shape of religious idea. It was a wondrous religious bazaar, and we saw other churches and denominations in a new light. "I was raised to believe that my church was the only one right," said Sam. "I learned. . . [differently]." "Once a theological conservative," George said, "I later became a liberal and now [am] a hybrid."

Martin explained: "I soon learned what it meant to be a CO. My Christian life changed. I began to learn from other Christians that a Christian life was more than going to church. My love for Jesus Christ grew stronger. . . . As years went by, this same conviction grew stronger; and we are more mature in our Christian life, and we know that God will give us the strength to cope with the strains and stresses in our modern life."

"The mainline protestant churches," Earl said, "and especially the non-liberal fundamental churches are missing the way of life as taught by Jesus by not supporting the CO doctrine." Many of us agreed with Arlo's observation about the Christian Church's drift from its central mission: "Most national leaders seem to believe in the Bible but get no further than the Old Testament. For them, the Sermon on the Mount is not relevant."

When churches abandoned what COs considered a central mission of the Church, many of us drifted away. Norman changed his career as a result of his church's response to conscientious objection. "I had been planning [to enter] the Ministry when I was drafted; and the Lutheran Seminary was afraid to admit a conscientious objector, as it might be perceived as giving sanctuary to a draft dodger. That experience had a negative effect on my attitude toward the Seminary and the Lutheran ministry." (Norman became a biochemist.)

Tom said, "[I] have become more humanitarian and less religious." Religious institutions became less important to Paul; he "challenged the idea that conscience needs the confession of sectarian creeds for validation." George explained, "[I] changed my religious beliefs gradually to skepticism and . . . to agnosticism."

While Lester's is a minority opinion, it came up a number of times: "Though nominally serving significant social needs of [members] . . . religions are essentially corrupt, fraudulent scams, promising things in exchange for faithful tribute that they cannot deliver and for which there is no come back. Their prophets are profitable; their business is to prosper."

A LASTING IMPRINT

Saying what you mean gets to be a habit. "I am a firm believer in saying yes or no," Donald said, "not maybe or straddling the issue." "My Missouri stubbornness came out," Jim said, "when I perceived that other people were trying to control or regulate my thoughts and movements."

CPS had taught Menno that doing what you say was equally important. When in Poland after the war, he saw many relief workers leave before their assignments were completed. "They [the volunteers who left] did not have the stubborn conviction to work . . . in a country completely destroyed." Tenacity "helped me," Clifford said, 'to put my hand to the plow' and stick with a plan of action for my life."

We were in for a lifetime of challenge, and the fellowship of our comrades was never far from our thoughts. Walter acknowledged his debt: "The CO stand required one to say what one thought and to act in conformity with what one said and thought. The CO experience firmed up my formed but largely untested character, and the experience was a great aid in later life."

We learned that people with different views can still be reasonable. Rollin pointed out: ". . . although the actions of others may not be excused, they can be explained. . . . We can seek to find what in our own behavior may be causing others to act and react as they do."

A Way of Life

Many other parts of our lives were affected. "It just became a part of me." "My whole life was different." "It was a lifetime commitment." "My social consciousness was raised."

"Anyone who, at 18 . . . challenged the social necessity and virtue of the war," Tom said, "despite not having belonged to a major support group such as the historic peace churches or the various major antiwar political groups, could not but have such a decision and such an experience affect him forever."

After CPS we found it easier to stake out positions and to speak out on other unpopular issues. As Tony expressed it, "Having crossed a 'big bridge', the little bridges seem easier." George echoed Tony, "I felt freer to take unpopular and even risky stances because of having done it once, faced the consequences, and been able to live with them." Chris found that CO convictions "help provide a measure of all we do in life. We hold that measure up to all we do. . . . "

We learned to "go public" with our views. "Having said 'No!' once", Robert observed, "it is impossible for the establishment to frighten a CO again with ostracism, loss of job, etc." Tom discovered: "It is important that my point of view should be expressed and that I should do it."

Joining the bandwagon had no appeal. "I am skeptical of the . . . 'everybody's doing it' psychology," Wesley said. "I find the lonely road more interesting and challenging." Leonard agreed, "I was able to throw off or refuse to 'go along' with people and activities . . . for personal prestige, recognition, influence, etc." Tom said. "The stresses and strains of modern life are largely trying to keep up with the Joneses. Once you give that up and find your real goal in life, the unpopularity of your thoughts and action causes you little concern." We did not waste a lot of energy meeting others' expectations.

When we rejected convention, we also rejected the materialism that went with it. "I could no longer settle down to a comfortable life of 'making money'," VanCleve said. "I became convinced of the rightness of seeking a simple way of life." Jonas spoke from his Amish heritage: "We gather strength and also peace in living a simple life. . . ."

CPS influenced us to continue an active role in the affairs of our communities, our churches, our schools. "The act of becoming a CO was the dramatic opportunity to express my religious (including my social and philosophical) beliefs," Bill said. "This experience strengthened my view which made it important to put beliefs into action."

We were not intimidated when it was necessary to "fight city hall". "The inner strength that I developed as a CO helped me to cope with ridicule and prejudice," Roy said. "As a Canadian Indian rights activist . . . I never wavered in the face of intimidation by police and others."

While not all COs share the value of such endeavors, many took part in antiwar demonstrations. "[I] was able to hold my ideals despite some nasty situations like peace marches and protesting of nuclear bomb manufacturing, arrests in NYC in Easter Parade, successfully stopping stupid air raid siren drills, peace marching in London and Stockholm."

Francis found himself at odds with his university: "I refused in my University faculty career to be a formal faculty advisor . . . when that would mean being a part of a system that signed up students for ROTC. . . . I objected to signing an oath. . . . After my objection, that routine was dropped . . . I declined to drink alcoholic beverages at social times in the professional setting. . . ."

Leonard was drawn into a controversy when a black family moved into his community. "A 'White Citizens Council' [met] to force them out. . . . I stood up to support them and led other pastors in the community in supporting their living in the community [the family stayed]."

One day Dick received a political campaign contribution card from his employer with the explanation that "everyone" was contributing to the party favored by company's management. It did not happen to be Dick's preferred political party; but even if it had been, he would have objected to being told where to put his political support. When he returned the card without any contribution, he was counseled that his Division would look bad if it did not get a 100% participation. Needless to say, this stiffened Dick's objections, with the consequence that others in the department, encouraged by his resistance, expressed their objections, too. So far as Dick could determine, his action had no detrimental consequences for his position in the company. In later years, of course, such political solicitations were outlawed. At the time it was quite a common practice in American industry.

In his operation of a city sanitary organization, Bill often received requests from politicians for special consideration to favored constituents. "We absolutely refused to do for politicians what we believed to be illegal or unethical."

While he did not elaborate on the particulars—although it would have been quite helpful to many of us—Richard explained: "The convictions that led me to CPS helped me in my marriage relationship."

The Joy and the Pain

We had chosen to stand <u>for</u> something, and that test would last a lifetime. We had rejected conformity, and we would continue to find a wide range of causes to support.

"Conscience," someone said, "can be a great stressor." When we challenge custom, we disturb those who fear change. Herman reminds us, "God did not promise a 'bed of roses' for standing up for what we believe to be right." "There are standards to be maintained", said Kenneth. "Integrity is a constant challenge vis-a-vis family, friends, acquaintances, fellow workers . . . society in general. One is constantly asked to sell oneself."

When asked to explain our "peculiar" ideas, we soon learn that people are rarely looking for new ideas. They usually concentrate on the "unrealistic" nature of ours and the "practical" nature of theirs. At least we are still being asked even though there is not much listening. It helps to remember the entertainer who chastised his colleague for complaining about the crush of autograph seekers, "It's sure a lot better than the alternative."

"People see me as 'different'," Ernest said, "and I feel stress in my relationships. In fact, [being a pacifist] . . . does not in <u>reality</u> cause as much negative reaction toward me as I <u>feel</u> it does. That has been a lifelong struggle for me."

"I am not entirely sure." Walt said, "that the stresses and strains of modern life <u>should</u> be alleviated for privileged people, including most of us, who live beyond the earth's means while hundreds of millions go hungry, homeless, oppressed, even tortured or massacred."

Pacifism reduced the stress in Clyde's life. "It helps develop a less stressful existence because a deep respect for others can promote a deep respect for yourself. Being more 'faith oriented' than 'success oriented' gives a peace of mind that goes beyond the simple acquisition of things."

A WORLD VIEW

We became sensitive to the treatment of other minorities and of women and children; the derelictions of politicians, bureaucrats, and irresponsible industrialists; the environment; and the corrosion of social institutions. "Having been a CO," Roger said, "has undoubtedly influenced, at least subtly, every facet of my life. . . ."

"My views," Homer explained, "are set on eternal values. Society, generally, lives mostly with the present and consequently has a tendency to change its ways and ideas to conform to current standards and modes of life. . . . I find it difficult to accept all the interpretations society comes up with in our day to allow [people] . . . 'to do their thing'."

"Standing apart from the war hysteria," Robert said, "marginalized me and conferred on me the detachment and insight of the marginal man . . . made me a lifelong critic of American society, I trust in a constructive way." "Having been 'marginalized'," Bill said, "I have been less prone to take for granted the 'wisdom' of the majority."

"Having once opposed my government's actions on a fundamental matter as a CO," Ben explained, "probably helps me to see events (and particularly political events) with a less nationalistic slant." Willard concurred, "The CO experience . . . further prepared me for social analysis later in life."

Our social and religious convictions are applied in many aspects of living. "I no longer," said Ted, "see life, society, mankind, the environment, the world, the universe, etc. through the eyes of a single issue mind."

One Human Family

In that rich exchange of CPS dialogue, we learned two valuable lessons: First, people come to different conclusions because they start with different premises. Second, there is a system of *reasoning* even in the most bizarre arguments. So, when trying to understand how others come to their conclusions, we looked for their premises and for the path of their reasoning. That served us in good stead many times in our later years.

When we think of people as "us" and not as "they", the clashing of will can be replaced with the merging of ideas. "We had so many religious beliefs and backgrounds," Elmer said, that it "makes it easier to realize there are other good people out there besides just me and my little gang."

We were sensitive to issues of fairness and equity between individuals, groups, and nations. We are not content to see inequities continue. "I am not accepting or resigned to conditions as they are," Harry reminds us. "My standard of living, my behavior, does affect directly or indirectly the lives of the poor and oppressed. . . . so does everybody else's behavior. We are in the same boat. . . . The violence of economics—of the market place, of banking and finance—may [generate] the most violence of all."

Everybody Belongs

When war conditions compelled us to be a minority, we learned something about the inequities visited upon "different" people. We came to understood that one victim's pain is everyone's pain. We knew what it was like to walk in another's shoes. We chose to be a minority, but most minorities do not have that luxury. They had no choice in their race, color, creed, sex, or condition of birth. We carried no outward marks, and we could keep a low profile because we blended into our communities. But others could not escape from those who hated them for being "different". Ian explained, "I am much more conscious of what it is to be a minority. When they shouted, 'conchie get your gun' or 'CO slacker', I knew I had made the decision willingly while others, called 'nigger', or 'spik', or 'wop' were born that way . . . ."

Whatever our achievements, we were members of a minority on the things that mattered most. "It confirmed in me," Robert commented, "that despite my academic and community acceptance in American society, I am a minority, living on the edges, in the margin, working in the cracks with no expectation of grandeur that I am running the big show. It is the remnant-seed-salt motif. . . . [I am] enjoying it, feeling a sense of worth in being countercultural, committed to 'smaller is beautiful', impacting the larger society in concerns of peace and justice, but abrogating conventional anticipation of success."

"Being part of a disliked and largely rejected minority," Robert said, "fostered a deeper sensitivity to many conditions that I have since seen as a normal condition for many people in our society. It creates a stronger sense of indignation concerning the many injustices that are too frequently taken for granted, or too readily accepted as inevitable." Eugene saw "how little government agencies . . . can or really care to meet the . . . needs of the poor, the homeless, the disfranchised. . . ."

We also discovered that minorities are not totally without influence. The very fact of being a minority engages attention and opens dialogue. Most important of all, the minority rides that most constant of all human phenomena; namely, the inevitability of change. Minorities are society's change agents, ever at the frontier exploring new ways.

Breaking the Barriers

CPS taught us two things about dealing with problems. First, conditions that become problems are usually the *result* of some more fundamental difficulty. Thus, while it is necessary to put out the gas line fire, the most important thing is to find out what caused it. Second, solutions must not only eliminate the present condition, they must attack the root problems. Poverty, for instance, results from a complex of causes, some of which are economic, some psychological, and some so elusive as to be beyond classification. So it is not enough merely to provide shelters for the poor—although in many situations that alone would be a great achievement. Long-term solutions require treatment of the conditions—with the person and with society—that led to the poverty.

For years it was thought that fair educational opportunities required poor children be to be bussed from poor schools in poor neighborhoods to the "rich kids' schools". There were to be two benefits from this: First, children attending integrated schools would know other groups and thus be less likely to grow up with racial prejudice. Second, all children would have equal opportunities for the best education. But why not build and staff high quality schools in all neighborhoods, or why not make it possible for racial minorities to live where the good schools are? Someone also suggested that if bussing were the only option, it would certainly be less complicated to bus the teachers rather than the children.

We refused to believe that the world must stand permanently divided between the "good guys" and the "bad guys". "If one rejects the standard definition of 'enemy'," Louis observed, "one sees almost any social problem, domestic or international, in a far different light."

We retained our idealism but learned to use "way stations" in our quest for the optimum result. While not willing to abandon our goals, we became more willing to accept the possible. "I became much more convinced," said Jacob, "that in most of life's questions the answer must be relative rather than absolute. Life is a compromise, and the question is where and how the compromise shall be made." But if compromise meant loss of principle, we would rather lose than be on the winning side of the wrong cause.

We were in the <u>change</u> business. We were thus involved in the nonviolent movements of the 1960's and 1970's inspired by the work of Martin Luther King, Jr. We saw conciliation and reconciliation as the most effective way of building a lasting consensus, one that would not crumble at the first challenge.

"The knowledge that one <u>could</u> take a strong stand," said David, "even when one knows one isn't likely to convince all the others at once has been a support to me."

We wanted to be counted for our true beliefs. We knew where we stood, and we intended to stay there. There was nothing tentative in our convictions. "My CO experience," Leroy said, "strengthened . . . my Christian convictions . . . to take firm stands on many moral and social issues."

We were not about to lose what we had so resolutely defended during the war years.

We were compelled to find our own solutions. "It sort of forced me," Ray said, "to start coming up with answers. [I had given] . . . too much acceptance to what others told me prior to that."

We also realized the importance of being sure of our ground. "Having to be well informed in order to defend my position as a CO," Robert said, "encouraged me to have a pretty well-informed basis for other stands. . . ."

Many of us had little interest in political and governmental matters before CPS, thinking such things were irrelevant to our lives. While some of us never gained much faith in the instruments of government, others, concerned with the impact of government on people's lives, became more interested in political affairs.

"I am more concerned in what the politicians are doing," Pete said. "I am more concerned in geography, history, and traveling. . . . I don't think I would be if it hadn't been for CPS."

We were exposed to the government's "malarkey" factor, and we learned to recognize propaganda. "Double Speak" did not impress us. Victor summarized what many of us felt about governmental "haze": "Having a conviction about war that goes against the thinking of many people in positions of power or those who follow them, I definitely understand better how public opinion is controlled and for what purpose. It has nothing to do with Christianity." CPS enhanced Sam's "realization that the nation-state is not of primary consideration and that as a Christian pacifist I cannot afford to have my life co-opted by my government."

Our wartime years also kindled some healthy skepticism—and for some, cynicism—about governmental policies and practices. CPS convinced Ottis that the founding fathers had discovered a great truth: "It strengthened my belief in the separation of Church and State, and where to draw the line."

Helmut had some harsh words for the status quo: "I have become increasingly more skeptical about government and bureaucracy. I see them as self-serving power structures, mainly concerned with perpetuating themselves, and services to people . . . [are] a sort of sop to keep the masses content and under control. Enlightened and wholesome social policy is rare." Arthur concurred in Helmut's views, adding, "I consider most institutions (country, company, university, church, etc.) to be basically amoral. They are used by their leaders for personal purposes (cloaked in high phrases), and I am suspicious of them when they take a high moral ground."

Irving was emphatic "The U.S. has used its power to do immeasurable harm around the world. . . . It would have been possible to do a great deal of good in the world, an option which has been greatly undermined by the obsession with military power, erroneously termed 'security'." ". . . My CPS period," Joe said, "contributed to my natural questioning of authority. . . . "

While we have lost faith in conventional structures and systems to prevent war, we have not lost faith in the ability of people to change whatever they decide to change.

10

The Impossible Ideal

This chapter chronicles the travels, the challenges, and the triumphs of CPSers in the years after the war. The breadth and scope of their post-war endeavors is quite remarkable. They found an astounding variety of ways to practice their faith: in their occupations; in their dealings with people on the day-to-day routines of life; and in a broad array of social, political, and economic activities.

We came to CPS in search of peace, and our eyes were opened to the wider opportunities and challenges of our faith. We saw useful work as a social good, but our responsibilities extending beyond the workaday world. The post-war years were full of hurdles and obstacles, but the rewards were enormous.

This story of Uncle Menno illustrates the way these men carried the power of their conviction into every highway and byway of the land. Menno had passed away before the CPS Survey arrived, but a niece saw the questionnaire and sent us this report. He had often talked to her about CPS, she said, and would have wanted to answer our questions.

So, she would tell us why this man had been so important in her life.

"My Uncle Menno," she explained, "never married because he had been called to care for the younger members of his family. He lived in this small town all his life, and everyone knew him as a loving and caring man. In his quiet and compassionate ways, he touched every member of our community at some time or another. After his death I was talking with the editor of the local paper about some matters relating to Menno's estate.

"When we finished, he said to me, 'you know, your uncle was loved by everyone in this county. I have never known anyone like him, and I doubt if I ever will again.' His eyes were wet with emotion, and his voice cracked. He continued, 'Menno always found some way to help other people—with a kind word, a sympathetic deed, or a helping hand to someone in need. He never asked for anything in return, and he would never talk about what he had done for someone else. He will be sorely missed. There will never be another like him.'

"I wanted you to know what my uncle's life meant to all of us here because he was not a famous man; he was not a public figure who people wrote about; and very few people ever knew all the good things he did. He lived quietly and simply, but his life was an inspiration to all who knew him, and he was a model of what a dedicated Christian life can be."

Uncle Menno's life tells us more about the impact of CPS than any statistics could show. From the stories told by and about ex-CPSers it is clear that there were thousands of Uncle Mennos all over this country. Every trade, occupation, and profession is represented in the roster of World War II COs. They carried their ideals to every corner of the land.

OCCUPATIONS

As a result of our wartime experience, many lives were changed as we looked at our future careers in a broader way. We became lifetime activists in the causes of human dignity and peaceful coexistence, both in our jobs and in our community activities. Eugene's experience was not uncommon, "I was fresh off the farm. . . . After CPS I went on to college, seminary, and a doctorate at Boston University."

We were scrupulous to avoid activities or companies with military affiliations. One man gave up flying, one of his great joys, because he could not obtain flight training without participation by the military. Many others refused jobs or assignments connected with the military. In Bill's case, he chose "a worse paid job that seemed more socially useful."

Raymond "turned down a lucrative position as National Coordinator of Disaster Studies when I realized that the studies were actually financed by the Pentagon for the purpose of discovering how best to produce panic in enemy civilian populations."

Bill's career "was in science and engineering. The most fascinating jobs in my area were in aerospace (defense). They paid the best, too. I deliberately went into sanitary chemistry and sanitary engineering. I operated municipal sewage works and collections systems . . . the most fascinating career one could ever have. Totally involved in doing positive things. Making scientific friends all over the world. Working in many places in the world. If I had gone into aerospace, I would have denied my ideals." .

James quit his university teaching job when he failed "to persuade the administration not to install an [ROTC] unit. "

We avoided some professions where public reaction to our having been COs would make our careers impossible. Many men, for instance, avoided politics and elective office; yet others did win election to public office. Eugene thought that "the CO position precluded my entering into local and state politics, as I could not see myself delivering so-called patriotic speeches at Memorial Day parades and appearing at other state rallies of retired armed forces groups. Some years later I feel that I could have worked around this obstacle."

For those who obtained elective office, two conditions made it possible: First, the community contained a relatively significant body of peace sympathizers, people who were not pacifists themselves but who were not bothered by having a pacifist in a public job. Second, the issue of the CO's background never came up in the campaign; or if it did, the individual's standing in the community commanded respect in spite of this "little idiosyncrasy".

Our CPS assignments sometimes influenced our later occupations. For Bill, "The mental hospital experience has been invaluable to my work [as a] country doctor." In his later ministry, Ted said that his CPS experience helped him direct his Church into community service affairs, "I see all this broader understanding growing out of my CO position."

Many found themselves in John C.'s situation. He had "planned to go back after the war [to my former occupation]. I couldn't! CPS opened my eyes to the greater possibilities of life." John R. explained that the CPS years "turned me from a career of earning as much money as possible. I am now . . . teaching Christianity and especially obedience, holiness, and zeal in good works. . . . "

Men changed their occupations from business to medicine; from teaching to the ministry; from entertainment to social work; from teaching to medicine; from physics to social work; from farming to health care; from chemistry to teaching; from teaching to business, and many more. CPS broadened our view of our occupations and encouraged us to "aim for the stars".

"The CO position," Kenneth said, "helped me have the guts to tackle medical school and to want to be a doctor. . ."

"After [my] CO experience," Clyde reported, "I decided to give up my father's very successful bologna business and work with 'people careers'. I have never regretted the decision! I soon discovered, however, that I couldn't get away from bologna by working with people. It's just sliced differently outside the meat shop."

For several years after the war many jobs were hard to come by. "It helped me decide to be a plumber," Chuck said, "and influenced me to locate in a sparsely settled area on a small subsistence farm. . . . When people's toilets are plugged up, they don't much care what your politics are."

Sam found a way to protect himself, "A dissenter should somehow take hold of the economic need for survival [I became a farmer]. You cannot fire a farmer; you can only go broke."

There were occasional stories of COs discriminated against in the work place, but there were also examples of fair play. Alvin stood firmly for his convictions and made them clearly known to a prospective employer: "A committee of officials chose me [over eighteen other applicants, all of whom had war records] . . . to manage the [Pasadena, California] City Pool. . . . When asked what I would do about the black situation, I said I would not take the position unless I could treat all alike. I got the job. Fresh from the CO experience made this an easy decision."

A belief in the ethics of peace led, as one man reported it, to "open-minded dealing with business customers." Harold was uncompromising, "supporting a clear ethical position has been part of my life." Amos "walked away from a $40,000 per year job in sales management in 1963 because of seeing corruption in the higher ranks which I spoke out against."

"In running the business," Bernard explained, "I tried to treat my employees fairly, hired all races . . . and women. I was ahead of Affirmative Action . . . . I tried to give the customers their money's worth."

There is little doubt that CPS strengthened our convictions and shaped our later years. What impact our testimony had on the world around us is a little more obscure. As individuals we made our convictions felt in diverse and subtle ways.

Career Choice

Ex-CPSers were occupied is a wide range of trades, crafts, professions, and businesses.

The following pages contain a representative cross-section of individual cases in a tremendous range of occupation .   But occupation is only part of the story. These men devoted their energies to an endless array of avocational endeavors in their quest for a better life. You will see that many men deliberately chose to limit their search for material reward to help "level out" some built-in injustices.   They sought no rewards, they demanded no recognition; they did what they were compelled to do.   As with the person who jumps into a raging stream to save a drowning child, they did not see themselves as heroes or as self-sacrificing "do-gooders".   The task was its own reward.   Most of these people would be embarrassed if someone tried to pin a medal on them, but their lives left a mark nevertheless.

Education

Education was a natural attraction for people convinced that distorted perceptions were fueling military systems, and only education could divert the world from disaster. Whether or not we chose educational careers, we saw the importance in spreading word about the power and wisdom of nonviolence.

The stimulating ferment of CPS had a major impact on decisions to become teachers and school administrators. One man said that "teaching had my name written on it." Albert chose education "to avoid a career in business that might be related more directly to the military."

"My CPS experience at Cheltenham, a juvenile delinquency institution for Black kids from the slums of Baltimore," Roland said, "led me to seek teaching in an interracial environment after CPS."

Kenneth spent his career with the underprivileged: "My decision to spend my teaching years on mostly Indian reservations . . . was influenced by my vision for a better life for the downtrodden of this earth. I spent . . . my summers visiting Indian homes contacting parents to try to get them to support the school by sending their children. . . . I felt that my testimony as a Christian influenced many of the children's parents in their decisions to at least give it a try."

Russell taught in public and parochial schools in a multi-ethnic community, but it took nineteen interviews to find someone willing to hire an ex-CO. His CPS experience pointed him toward teaching and to his later role as an ordained deacon.

Chester explained his teaching philosophy, "My prayer now is that I have been able to influence some key future leaders . . . to reflect the moral values, critical thinking, and Godly lifestyles."

A plaque given to Edward upon his retirement read, "In recognition of his thirty-five years of service to the University of Minnesota, Duluth, and of his deep concern for humanity. . . . "

Harlan was a teaching fellow in economics at Harvard when drafted. When he returned to Harvard after the war, "I sought an appointment, and the head of the department told me he was afraid of the reaction if he put a conchie in front of a class of returning veterans. . . . A year later I was recommended for a post at Brown where vets did not even ask my war role. I taught there while writing a dissertation to complete a Chicago PhD." Subsequently he taught principles of economics, international economics, and social philosophy, ending his career at the University of Minnesota.

Morris was a director and executive of the Council for Adult and Experimental Learning. He has led international student seminars, a metropolitan work camp, a younger diplomat seminar, and a peace mission to Germany.

Norman was "determined to force the State of Ohio to provide appropriate educational programs for . . . [the handicapped]. I was a pioneer in getting classes for the learning disabled child started. . . . We now have laws requiring each School District to provide AN APPROPRIATE EDUCATIONAL PROGRAM FOR EACH CHILD, after assessing the child's needs."

Duane taught at Colorado State University in Ft. Collins, Colorado, and was active in the International Center there. He was once introduced to a young Saudi student as a conscientious objector in World War II by a man who had been an Air Force pilot. After learning what it meant to be a conscientious objector, the Saudi student turned to the Air Force pilot, "He [pointing to Duane] is a much greater hero than you."

Wayne became a high school teacher. "At one time, the town where I taught invited me to join the local VFW!" When former students asked him to attend the twenty-five year reunion of their high school class, "I was asked to give a short resume of my life. I told of my service as a CO and, though many of them seemed surprised, they later came to me and asked questions about those years. Apparently, what they saw in me as a teacher and a friend was compatible with my stand during the war. Many of them were Korean or VietNam veterans."

Reed taught American government, foreign policy, peace studies, and international relations at a number of colleges, including Penn State, Baldwin-Wallace, University of Pennsylvania, and Wright State University in Dayton, Ohio. "I think my decision to go into social science in college (actually political science) was stimulated by CO and related concerns. . . . I'm always seeing things that should be changed, in whatever community or group I am in. Yet I do take responsible positions in organizations—keep minutes, do mailings, organize meetings, arrange speakers, make posters, attend or support vigils and demonstrations, write letters, lobby Congress, raise money, sell tickets."

David, a professor of philosophy, became a student of Gandhian nonviolence. He and his wife Gerry (who had been with David during CPS and regarded herself as a CPSer, too) inculcated the spirit of nonviolence in their children. One son spent a year in federal prison for refusing service during the Vietnam war. David was able to get the local school board to reject an ROTC unit for a local high school.

When Morris was principal of a two thousand student high school, he opposed bringing in an ROTC unit. The school superintendent, although a four-year military man, supported Morris' position; the proposal was rejected.

Robert taught history at a North Carolina college and helped in the ouster of a reactionary state political regime. In 1950 he moved to Switzerland and enjoyed a thirty year university teaching career where he founded the student United Nations Association that taught students how to simulate peaceful solutions to international conflicts. He also demonstrated some shrewd financial acumen, becoming quite wealthy through wise investments.

Leonard taught at Brooklyn College of the City of New York and authored more than forty books on issues of Quaker concern. He was the first director of UNESCO's division on education for international understanding and traveled extensively to over eighty countries.

Walter was a professor of Economics at New York University for 42 years and director of undergraduate studies. He also taught for a year at the University of Peshawar in Pakistan and at the Middle East Technical University in Turkey. He was administrator of Friends hospital in Kaimosi, Kenya. As a result of his interests in environmental issues, he constructed courses on the practical implications of pollution, destruction of resources, malnutrition, and population control.

Whitfield earned a PhD and taught college, switching from an early interest in physics and mathematics to statistics, "motivated by a greater interest in the social and psychological sciences." Speaking of his approach to war and nonviolence, he said, "I'm more inclined to make war itself seem stupid than to making nonviolence seem the moral solution. . . . I see the need for force in crime suppression, etc."

Several respondents were librarians. Delbert was a librarian in a Mennonite college for 38 years following two years in relief service in Europe after the war. Paul became librarian in a private school after teaching in public schools. Malcolm was a librarian following work for Church World Service. Ed was a university teacher and librarian at the University of Oregon.

Harold pursued his writing interests while making his living as a librarian. He has published eleven books of poetry and served as co-editor of *Blue Unicorn*, a national poetry magazine, and consulting editor of *Poet Lore*.

Health Care

Many careers in mental health originated with CPS mental hospital assignments. The National Mental Health Foundation, a public service association designed to improve care for the mentally ill, was founded by these ex-CPSers. Alex, one of the organizers of NMHF, said about his CPS experience, "It redirected my postwar career into working in behalf of the mentally ill." The book, *Turning Point* by Alex Sareyan published in 1993 tells the story of NMHF and of the CPS men who devoted their lives to the mental health profession.

"As a result of the opportunity to work in a mental hospital as an attendant", Floyd said, "I switched to medicine and became a psychiatrist. The . . . problem of how to help people without engendering hate was the conscious issue that drove me to psychiatry." Vincent had served at Norristown, Pennsylvania State Hospital, "I became interested and dedicated my life toward helping to improve the care and treatment of the mentally ill." Paul added, "My pacifist philosophy and CPS experiences . . . played a significant role in spending thirty-five years working as a clinical psychologist."

Bob explained that he became a therapist "to help others stand up and act on their beliefs—not as sheep. . . . We need to act on our beliefs."

Through their CPS experience, COs found that mental patients responded positively to even the slightest kindness. Amos' experience was typical of the struggle against outmoded and often brutal treatment of mental patients: "Mentally sick people . . . responded to love. They came to me and said, 'It is so much better here since you boys are here.'"

Following his work in a CPS state hospital unit, Walt spent thirty years in the California State Department of Mental Hygiene, eighteen years on the wards and as a supervisor and training officer and twelve years as administrator of training programs for the Department.

Arthur worked with the mentally ill for forty years. He assisted in establishing hospitals in Maryland and in Kansas, and he developed two major health care facilities in California. The King's View Center located in Reedley, California on a 43-acre rural site is a modern psychiatric facility that emphasizes individualized treatment by professional medical specialists. Arthur also served on numerous public boards and committees and consulted on a wide range of health issues.

Another fascinating aspect of Arthur's life was his encounter with the United States naturalization system. He was born in Canada, and his family emigrated to the United States when he was eight years old. During World War II he served four years in CPS. Since he had not obtained U.S. citizenship before the war, he petitioned the courts for citizenship in 1950. His petition was denied by a California Superior Court which contended that Mennonite teaching did not forbid service in the armed forces. Thus, he could not claim a right to CO status based on his religious training. That court's decision was affirmed by the California District Court of Appeals (117 Cal. App. 2d 469), and Arthur appealed to the United States Supreme Court seeking a reversal of these decisions. In this appeal, he was represented by former Secretary of State Dean Acheson. This was Acheson's first appearance before the Supreme Court after leaving the State department. The U. S. Department of Justice ultimately joined Acheson in asking the Supreme Court to reverse the lower court ruling, which it did. Dean Acheson's eloquent plea is worth quoting here: (Petition for a Writ of Certiorari,

Supreme Court of the United States, October Term, 1953, Arthur Jost, Petitioner v. United States of America.)

We live in a troubled time when wisdom is diluted by fear, when views slowly built by the experience and suffering of long ages are rent like a temple by an earthquake. And so a matter, inherently simple, has to be brought here for assurance that the perplexities of our generation shall not undo the solution which past generations have so painfully evolved for these very problems.

Medical doctors practiced in a great variety of locales, from foreign missions to Indian reservations, rural communities, and urban clinics, University hospital teaching and research, college and university health services, group practice, and private practice. John taught in a medical school, spent thirteen years in general practice, ten years in pathology, and ten years as director of a clinic at Riverside Hospital in Toledo, Ohio. Lloyd had a general practice in a small town before managing health clinics at two colleges in California.

Bob had a rural practice and also taught in state prisons. Even though he had served nearly three years in CPS, Selective Service attempted to call him up in the doctor draft during the Korean war. It took an appeal to reverse the draft board's action. Bob also entered politics and served as mayor of his small community; he was also a member of a community college board of trustees.

Bill returned to college fourteen years after CPS to obtain a medical degree. "During twenty-nine years in medicine I purposely refused to accumulate wealth, supported between twenty and thirty organizations financially, helped build a new clinic for our little town . . . spent a year in south Texas helping establish two clinics for migrant laborers and served as the only physician, volunteered my day off for over a year helping the multiply-handicapped children of Omaha in a new organization needing a physician, volunteered under AMA's Project USA to serve on two Indian Reservations in Barrow, Alaska, with the Eskimos."

Ministry

A number of men already in the ministry or in theological seminaries in 1941 when the United States entered the war refused to accept ministerial deferments and ended up in CPS. Others decided on the ministry during CPS. Over fifty of the thousand respondents in this study served in the ministry.

Edward's affliction with dyslexia, little understood in his youth, meant that his high school performance was not much above average. But CPS changed all that. "It was a good thing though that I was in a CO camp group, for it changed my entire life and way of thinking." The books he read, "put in me the desire for the ministry. . . . No matter what I was doing and no matter how hard the work from sun-up to sun-down, ideas for sermons came to me." Determined to go to college, in spite of rejection after rejection because of his poor high school grades, he simply wrote to one college and told them he was coming anyway. "I found out later that the officials said, 'he is either a fool or he means business; so we will try him for one year.' . . . I went, not knowing where I would live, where the money was coming from, but *with that inner push* . . . took a full load, graduating in three years from a four year course." He then went on to the seminary where his regimen included the care of an invalid wife. He eventually completed the seminary and entered the ministry. He summarized, "When I went to College, I was far from being college material. It is only by the grace of God that I really made it. . . . But without being a conscientious objector, I would not be where I am."

When war broke out, Calvin was preparing for the ministry and was deferred from the draft as a divinity student. He refused to accept a ministerial deferment and insisted that he be given the 4E conscientious objector classification. His persistence resulted in his being sent to a CPS Camp. This did not last long, for the seminary requested and obtained his discharge so that he could return to his pre-seminary training. At the urging of his fellow CPSers, he did leave CPS and return to college. Earlier in that year he had participated in some debates where he argued the pacifist position, and in the middle of the war this did not endear him to his fellow students when he returned to college—"I had a very cool reception."

When he completed his seminary work, Calvin took an associate pastorate at a downtown Chicago church. "There was strong feeling against pacifists on the part of the senior pastor and some others, and I was asked to promise that I would not use the pulpit as a sounding board for pacifism. . . . I had applied for positions in a number of churches in the middle west and was eliminated in several cases because I had been a conscientious objector." He finally obtained a position in the Presbyterian Church where he worked to obtain approval of a confession of faith (creed) for the denomination in 1967-68 which said that "reconciliation was a fundamental rubric for understanding the Christian life, and that it was appropriate to resist war even at the risk of national self-interests."

Karl graduated from a seminary after the war, "Guess where my first parish was—Cascade Locks, Oregon. [The closest town to the CPS camp described in the first chapter of this book.] . . . I'd had some misgivings, feeling there might be negative feelings in town because of the camp's former presence out at Wyeth (five miles from Cascade Locks). So I made it very clear to the folks (all in writing, never did meet face-to-face before hiring on) that I was a pacifist and former CPSer. But they took me on anyway, and my pacifism never proved to be either a hindrance or an embarrassment (although the Korean War began while we were there). It was a brief two year stint, but the happiest one of my career. You guys must have done a good job of public relations up there."

Howard, while already serving as a Congregational minister in 1940, had refused to register for the draft (even though he would have been deferred from the draft as a minister) unless the ministerial deferment was waived. General Hershey was willing to oblige; so Howard went to CPS. CPS interrupted Howard's pursuit of a doctorate in history, and his four-plus years in CPS, ". . . cost me my doctorate, for when I was finally released five months after Hiroshima/Nagasaki I simply <u>had</u> to get closer to 'the action' . . . . Instead of heading back to campus, I joined Andre Trocme, extraordinary leader of the French nonviolent resistance to Nazi racism and domination, in his Chambon-sur-Lignon center.

"The next thirteen years I devoted to the evolving tasks of relief, rehabilitation, reconstruction, and reconciliation required by the aftermath of World War II in the European area. I felt that CPS had seasoned me for more service rather than more degree-study, at the war's end. That seasoning was significant. . . . My very CO sort of concern . . . sensitized me to the hypocrisy of either ecumenical church or intergovernmental fraternization across frontiers if it turned a blind eye to the repressed dissenters in any society." Howard enjoyed a distinguished career in the ministry and public affairs. He was president of the Chicago Theological Seminary where he was also professor of church history, Executive Director for Specialized Ministries Overseas with the National Council of Churches, World Issues

Secretary for the United Church of Christ Board for World
Ministries, and visiting professor and writer in a great variety
of assignments throughout his life.

Social Service/Mission Work

Clifford combined the ministry with social service
work, receiving college degrees in both fields. He served for
five years as a pastor, four years in rehabilitative work for
emotionally disturbed boys, fourteen years as head of the
Department of Social Services in Illinois, and seven years as
executive director of a retirement community.

Stephen had a long career in social work, including a
position as executive director of family services in Duchess
County, New York. He was active in the Alternatives to
Violence Program (AVP) aimed at teaching the power of
nonviolence in the resolution of community conflicts and in
preparing prison inmates for return to civilian life. AVP has
worked with police departments, the Southern Christian
Leadership Conference, prison workshops, and a wide
variety of community organizations.

Bob worked for VISTA in the war on poverty program, in prison work with juveniles, in child protective
service, and in adult protective service. In his individual
therapy practice, he emphasized the importance of people
standing firmly for the things they believed and rejecting
demands from those who would have them compromise
their principles.

Walter was a graduate student in physics at Columbia
University before the war. After CPS he changed careers,
earning a graduate degree in Human Development from the
University of Chicago. Before completing his Chicago work,
he had taught physics at Fisk and at Harvard. Following
Chicago, he worked in a children's treatment center in
Minneapolis, served as a preschool consultant to families

with blind children, and became a community consultant
with the Wisconsin Division for Children and Youth. For
five years he worked with the Seneca Nation in their struggle
with the U.S. Corps of Engineers over the Corps' plan to
build a dam on Seneca land.

At midlife Walter moved to Canada where he worked
in a center for troubled children and youth and in various
Indian communities. He also managed to work in some
paralegal counseling for people with limited means. Speaking of the broader issues of peace and freedom, Walt
concludes: "I certainly struggle with 'an impossible ideal'. "
When I hear that my dream plan is totally impossible, I reply
that even were that true, it is also absolutely necessary."

Richard was a licensed clinical social worker with a
lifetime career in child welfare work. His busy life included
support to inner city youth against bullying police tactics, a
struggle for low income housing, a campaign for adequate
qualitative child support, and gaining recognition for the
plight of single parents.

John H. spent fifty years in professional social work,
including fourteen years as a professor in the social work
program founded at the University of Wyoming. His long
career included family counseling and management of a
family counseling service and psychiatric social work. He
volunteered his time to a number of organizations for the
elderly.

John S. participated in the work stoppage at the
Glendora, California, camp in May, 1946, where draftees
were demanding demobilization eight months after war's
end. Following their arrest for violation of the Selective
Service Act, the strikers endured a two-year- long trial after
which they were found guilty and sentenced to two years
probation and eight months suspended prison sentence. As
a result of this felony record, John was unable to obtain civil

service employment until a California Supreme Court decision restored his civil rights in 1965. After this, he became a probation officer with Los Angeles County.

Lawrence worked in overseas development and church missions following CPS. He was in agricultural development in Puerto Rico, and hospital and medical clinic administration. He was Latin American Director of the Mennonite Board of Missions.

Loyd worked as an agricultural missionary in Africa for the United Methodist Church. After retirement, he visited his former stations regularly to review the natives' progress and to introduce improvements.

Bob worked in family service agencies in Michigan and directed two such agencies in California. Later, as a college professor, he was instrumental in developing the social work curriculum in a California state college. He also was active in many political campaigns to elect officials who understood the importance of using government to improve the quality of life.

Agriculture

Continuing family traditions and in some cases operating businesses that had been in their families for several generations, many men went into farming and ranching after CPS.

Reuben used his farming experience to teach agriculture in Jamaica and in Sierra Leone in West Africa. His CPS service stimulated his interest in environmental issues; and with his agricultural background, he developed a number of improved agricultural practices.

Robert joined the faculty of Iowa State University in Ames in 1946, but two years later became embroiled in a campaign against a national program for universal military training in the United States. Pressure from the American

Legion resulted ultimately in his resignation from Ames. He went from Ames to the Oklahoma State University at a higher salary; but foreseeing the politicians' frenzy with loyalty oaths during the 1950's, he left Oklahoma for a career in farming. As most farmers will understand, he met with financial reverses. He told this story about the comradeship of his former CPS colleagues:

> In 1980 and 1982 we helped a son to buy his 100 acres by pledging 80 of ours as extra collateral. . . . The Federal Land Bank . . . made us co-signers of his entire debt. . . . In '85 and '86 with deflated farm values our son found himself owing more than he possessed. . . There seemed a high probability that the Land Bank would close out his real estate and as much of ours as necessary to meet 100% of what was owed them. . . . Our most recent [CPS] reunion was August, 1986. . . . In the course of the CPS reunion our likely imminent plight became known. On the last day . . . they made known that they had assembled pledges of some $85,000 to enable us to buy back as many acres as that would cover if we were indeed foreclosed!
>
> Of course we were overwhelmed with such a generous lending prospect. . . . These pledges (largest about $25,000 I think) represented a very substantial portion of the life saving of rather newly retired teachers and others. . . .Considerable risk was involved, and I think they knew and know it.
>
> I think this to be a nothing short of amazing tale of the *esprit de corps* engendered within a CPS group coming to fruition more than 40 years later.

<u>Business—Crafts/Trades/Construction</u>

John was an aircraft worker, radio repairman, electronics technician, jet propulsion researcher, and inventor. He developed, manufactured, and sold a vectorcardiograph machine for medical diagnosis.

Ernest combined an industrial career with teaching mathematics in a high school. He later worked in the central office of his church. For thirteen years he did refugee work in Jordan, Arab Jerusalem, and Zaire.

Paul was an architect and a consultant to developers and governmental agencies, concentrating on ecological issues. He put his architectural talents to work in community planning and urban development and took an active role in senior service activities and in the operation of soup kitchens.

Gordon, Gail, Rudy, Howard, and Gilbert organized a development and construction company in a central California city. They earned a reputation for square dealing and integrity in an industry that all too often is criticized for unethical practices. Their business philosophy can be stated quite directly: if we can't make a reasonable living by giving the home owner an honest deal, we'll get out of the business. With this philosophy they prospered and enjoyed an abundant life for over forty years. In their "off time" they participated in and sponsored a great variety of community and regional activities, joining in church, peace, and educational activities.

Norm organized and developed a residential construction business in the Northwest, fulfilling his lifelong aspiration of providing people with quality homes at reasonable prices. In later years Norm, in company with his son-in-law, produced and distributed a number of audio and video tapes explaining and promoting the peace movement and the peace message of conscientious objectors.

Bill expanded his cabinet-making talents to designing and building custom homes. His reputation for ethical and honest dealings resulted in his being appointed to a community advisory group which prepared county development policies. He supported and maintained a life-time interest in the service activities of his church.

Business—Commerce/Finance/Insurance

After working in accounting with a major industrial company, John went into banking. Banking became a very tangible way to help people, and he found that the high profile of a banker in a small community required strong stands on moral and ethical issues.

Herk was a petroleum distributor and accountant and spent the last years of his career as an insurance agent and broker. Convinced that peaceful means are possible in reaching amicable agreements among people, he developed community programs to teach peaceful relationships in the family, the neighborhood, and the community.

Alwin's profession included accounting, administration, personnel, and finance. Most of his working life was in nonprofit enterprises such as hospitals, colleges and universities, and refugee affairs. He kept his hand in many activities. "I doubt that there is any social issue that hasn't heard my voice or taken some of my time. . . . I've come to believe that it is not necessary to succeed, but it is necessary to stand for what you believe."

Business—Management/Entrepreneurship

Andrew was a jobber and salesman, a shop steward for his union, sought election to the state legislature, and worked in the production department of the New York Times and the Boston Globe where "I pricked the consciences of not only the writers but also the publisher."

Leonard combined careers in education administration (high school, six years; college, twenty-three years) and manufacturing management. Even in the conventional business world, he took strong stands on issues in which he believed; and even though in the minority most of the time, he never felt himself intimidated by the business climate. He said that his experience in a mental hospital during the war strengthened his courage to stand by his beliefs. He had observed there that administrators and supervisors warmed to the CPS men when they got beyond their "peculiar" beliefs and came to know them as individuals.

Charlie's formal training was in accounting, but most of his business life was in finance and general management. He was also appointed utilities commissioner by his state's governor. He was active in the American Civil Liberties Union where he worked to liberalize many state laws on civil rights. In retirement he served on numerous civic development and improvement projects.

Douglas was founder and chief executive of an electronics instruments manufacturing company which became listed in the book, *The 100 Best Companies to Work for in America*. Doug's community and national public service activities were far-reaching. He was Chairman of the Board of Pacific University and a board member of the Oregon Medical School Foundation and was active in the affairs of Reed, Lewis and Clark, and Marylhurst Colleges. He was national President of the Instrument Society of America and was named Portland "Philanthropist of the Year" in 1991. Doug summarized his years of service: "I believe that we largely create our own conditions in society rather than having them thrust upon us. To be effective in this endeavor, I believe we must work out for ourselves a set of principles we believe in and then be guided by them even when they are not in the mainstream of the views and motivations of the general public."

Before leaving the discussion of business, it would be interesting to separate the business world from the world of business. By the former is meant those occupations that make, sell, and service some product or service. When one looks at the broader community in modern nations, every occupation and all human endeavors have certain business aspects to them, and this is what is meant by the world of business. I hold no particular brief for these particular categories; it is merely a way of discussing two different ways of looking at business. This book, of course, is not a textbook on business economy.

Business world enterprises are established to bring products and services to people and can include production, sale, or service. It is a noble endeavor, bringing necessities of life to people when and where they need them. The men who talked about their business careers took pride in delivering products and services of full value, and they obviously saw their businesses as servants of their communities. They also wanted their enterprises to be satisfying places to work. In short, the aim was to serve not only the customers but the employees as well.

The other facet of business is what I have chosen to call the world of business. In every enterprise of gainful occupation and in the everyday exchanges that make up so much of life there is an element of commerce, a trade of money or commodities. Everyone who visits a grocery store or employs a neighbor boy to cut the lawn engages in business exchange. From these men's comments about their daily lives, it is apparent that they were seriously concerned about the fairness and equity in these everyday business matters. Thus, while teachers, doctors, or journalists were not directly engaged in what I have called the world of business, they did comment on their efforts to maintain fairness and openness in everyday commercial exchange.

Law/Politics

Tony had intended to use his law training for probation work. When he returned from CPS, however, he thought a career in public office was closed to him. He then joined his father in private practice and continued as a sole practitioner after his father's death ten years later. He said he lost some clients when they learned he was a CO, but "for the most part clients could care less if they thought I was representing them adequately. I am sure that practicing in Los Angeles made it simpler as such matters get 'lost' in the big city. . . . There is one fundamental principle that . . . continues to be confirmed by my experience in living—and that is that the end never justifies the means, but that means always determines the end results."

Leonard practiced law and taught in a law school. He also operated a real estate business where he refused to accept restrictive covenants, the "gentlemen's agreements" that excluded nonwhites from certain neighborhoods. He insisted on enforcing California fair housing laws in spite of bitter opposition from fellow realtors. Contrary to what he had expected, his business actually increased as a result of these stands. In his community service work, he was active in Teens Kick-Off, a teens-helping-teens program for breaking drug addiction.

Philip was a teacher of agriculture and a senior officer in the Food and Agriculture Organization of the United Nations in Italy. When he retired from overseas work and settled in a rural Tennessee community, he became active in peace and justice activities and was elected mayor of the city of Pleasant Hill. This did not inhibit his continuing interest and support to the American Civil Liberties Union, the American Friends Service Committee, the Friends Committee on National Legislation, and the Central Committee for Conscientious Objectors. Reporting on his acceptance by the community, Philip said, "I have made no effort to hide my experience, but in fact it never arose as an issue in the political campaign, and I received twice as many votes as my only opponent."

After retirement from teaching, Jesse entered politics, was elected to the Kansas state legislature, and was re-elected several times. He took a strong public position against the death penalty, without being rejected by the voters. He advocated strict environmental regulation and aid to the poor and homeless.

Writing/Journalism

Arthur was a journalist all his life, including college and prep school teaching, radio and TV broadcasting, and operation of the New England bureau of a travel agent magazine. Still working 60 to 70 hours a week at his profession in his 60's, Arthur worked on civil rights and environmental protection.

Except for some teaching and political campaigning, Wilbur has been a freelance writer. He writes on positive topics (avoiding crime and disaster): art, culture, economics, politics, and science. He was also a trustee of the Wayne County Public Library (Ohio).

Ray was office editor of his church's papers and later taught English and art in a church college. He also served as a church deacon and helped develop church programs, including sponsorship of refugee families. Ray's experience is typical of many who came from conservative backgrounds: "I suspect that my CPS years made me more liberal on political issues. I came from a background of general political noninvolvement; and if there were preferences, they would have been for the more conservative Republican postures. I have seldom if ever voted that ticket. Perhaps it is significant that at the present time I am registered as an

Independent, choosing not to cast my lot with either of the major parties."

Richard chose a career in church-related editorial activities where he served on the editorial staff of the Mennonite Weekly Review, an inter-Mennonite newspaper published at Newton, Kansas. He worked on housing projects for the needy and on church school programs.

Jack was writer-editor for the National Mental Health Foundation, the National Mental Health Association (successor to the NMHF), and the Mental Health Materials Center. Jack, like so many others, got his impetus for mental health work from his CPS mental hospital experience.

Jesse was a Washington correspondent for a number of newspapers and radio stations and later a business journalist for the McGraw-Hill Book Company. Jesse was a peace activist, planning and participating in numerous demonstrations and vigils. He took an active stand against the hysteria-creating civil defense programs of the 1950's and taught draft counseling during the Vietnam War. He helped establish a dispute settlement center in his local community to help defuse violence in inter-personal relations.

As a players' representative in a symphony orchestra union, Warren was able to improve the union's relations with management while establishing better working conditions. He left the orchestra in 1971 to return to college and obtain a journalism degree, after which he wrote for a daily public affairs research/environmental radio program. In his writing he emphasized the growing scientific cooperation between Soviet and American scientists.

Science/Environment

When seeking employment in the 1950's, Bob sought out an employer that would not assign him to any defense work. His ultimate employer—the Xerox Corporation—

respected that request. A physicist, Bob is the holder of 137 patents resulting from his work with Xerox. He participated actively in Vietnam War protests and marches, political campaigns, civil rights causes, and environmental protection activities. He has been involved in the Sanctuary movement and took part in conferences on science and society in Russia and China. From his scientific background, he is sensitive to the "mischief our technologies make available to self-centered maniacs. It is a sad truth that terrorists can justify destroying innocent people. . . ."

In his work for a rehabilitation hospital, Worden designed and fabricated electromechanical devices to aid adults and children afflicted with neuromuscular disabilities. He was a professor of biomedical engineering with special emphasis on rehabilitation engineering. He supported causes that furthered his pro-human, pro-individual beliefs.

Before CPS, Norman had intended to go into the ministry, but he was denied admission to his church's seminary because of his CO position. His CPS assignment to a hospital laboratory eventually led him into biochemistry. He operated his own private clinical laboratory performing biochemical services for the public. In spite of earlier disillusionment with his church, he served as Sunday school teacher, superintendent, church council member, and organist. He led a movement in the state of Ohio to provide state programs for the learning disabled. The consequence is that Ohio now has laws requiring all school districts to provide an appropriate educational program for every child in the district, according to each one's particular needs.

Jarrott operated a geological consulting and exploration service in the state of Texas. He was active in local peace groups and often spoke on conscientious objection to church groups. He participated in sit-ins with Blacks in civil rights demonstrations—no easy thing to do in Texas when one's name is associated with the business which provides one's living. He viewed conscientious objection as part of a long history of people who stand firmly for peace and freedom, and he sees that tradition continuing with those who volunteered for service in Central America during the 1980's in opposition to U.S. State Department policies.

Arthur's highly unusual CPS assignment with the National Park Service in Hawaii led to a career in forestry management and erosion control. He worked as a Forestry and Erosion Control advisor in Korea, Watershed Management advisor in Jamaica, and Soil Conservation Specialist and Forestry Officer in watershed management in Australia. Immediately after the war he went to China as an agricultural specialist with the Brethren Service Committee and with UNRRA. His concern for human life, he says, extends to the life of the planet.

Planned Communities

During the war some men talked about forming "intentional communities" of pacifist members. The Amish, the Amana, and the Shaker communities had survived and prospered for many years; could a group of conscientious objectors achieve the same type of results? A few men in this thousand had joined such community experiments after the war, some of them in the Hutterian Bruderhof communities which predated World War II. The Macedonia Co-op Community in Georgia was one of the major pacifist efforts at planned community, and it survived for a number of years. It is not the purpose of this study to evaluate the significance of these communities; but those who participated in such endeavors as the Hutterian Bruderhof, for example, were enthusiastic about the lifestyles offered in such experiments.

Religious Agencies/Foundations

Bob spent his career in Friends service, including the American Friends Service Committee and the Friends World Committee for Consultation. The latter agency took him to many parts of the world, including Cuba, China, Japan, USSR, East Africa, Nicaragua, Mexico, Australia, and New Zealand. His work with the service committees brought him into close working relations with many United Nations programs, including UNESCO. He was active in the Southern California ACLU chapter and successfully challenged a California state law requiring loyalty oaths of public employees. A court decision ultimately overthrew that law.

After a teaching career at the University of Maryland College of Agriculture and the University Extension Service, Harold directed the On Earth Peace program of the Brethren Church at New Windsor, Maryland. His years in a Brethren CPS camp led to his participation in many local district and national church programs.

Dorsa was personnel director of a mission board, a pastor, and overseas relief worker for the Mennonite church. CPS had led him to change his vocation from teaching to the ministry. His aim: if people in one country can be made to understand the social situation in other countries, peace would be possible.

In addition to ten years with church service organizations and a variety of other public projects, Richard headed a private foundation, was state chairman of a committee of the U.S. Civil Rights Commission, and was a White House consultant on race matters.

Peace Foundations

A number of colleges and universities across the United States have established peace studies programs, offering special courses for the study of peace. Centers have been established in over one hundred colleges and universities, including such institutions as Antioch University in Yellow Springs, Ohio, Boston College, several California State University and University of California campuses, Catholic University of America (Washington, D.C.), Colgate University, Columbia University, Cornell University, Dartmouth College, Georgetown University, Harvard University, M.I.T., Princeton University, Rutgers University, Stanford University, Syracuse University, University of Colorado, University of Michigan, University of Minnesota, University of Pittsburgh, and Wellesley College.

Two former CPS men contributed dramatically to the expansion of these programs. Peter D. Watson of Greensboro, Vermont, funded the *Peter D. Watson Center for International Peace and Cooperation* with an initial endowment of $1,000,000 at the University of Rochester in New York. The center was to be funded in the amount of $10,000,000, with the additional $9,000,000 to be obtained by the university from other sources. The Center will provide funds for professor's salaries, research, and an international symposium on world peace to which world leaders will be invited. In describing his aim for the Center, Peter said, "We would attract new thinking to the field, drawing from the best of the young scholars, and enticing them to commit their talents to the study of international peace and cooperation. . . . We would create a highly-visible lectureship series, bringing in several prominent scholars and/or decision-makers in the area of international peace and cooperation, for university-wide talks."

The family of William B. Lloyd created a similar program at Antioch College, Yellow Springs, Ohio, in 1989. The Lloyd family gift of $1,300,000 established the Lloyd Chair in Peace Studies and World Law. "The program will aim to prepare students first, as responsible citizens of the world and second, as possible future scholars or practitioners in peace studies. Students will gain an understanding of conflict and violence in international, intercultural, and intergroup relationships, as well as develop significant intellectual and practical skills. They will study in areas such as conflict analysis; intercultural dialogue; negotiation and mediation; organizational alternatives to destructive conflict; and personal intercession and constructive symbolic behavior."

SOCIAL AND POLITICAL ISSUES

We entered CPS convinced that war was both morally and socially wrong. We were, however, troubled by the gulf between us and our fellow citizens. We knew that our responsibility to society went beyond mere resistance; and when we returned to our communities after the war, we poured ourselves into all manner of social, political, and economic endeavors. In the postwar world, we were determined to see that the principles of peace and brotherhood would be better understood.

CPS deepened our interest in a broad range of subjects. We had generous opportunities to expand our knowledge about the arts, literature, wilderness and nature, religion and philosophy, politics and government, social institutions, economics, psychology and human behavior, communications, geography, and world affairs. Many of us developed a lifelong involvement with these subjects; a wanderlust for world travel; an abiding love of the outdoors, the mountains, and the plains; a broad participation in religious organizations; and an interest in public affairs. The issues which concerned ex-CPSers would fill several pages, ranging from abortion and capital punishment to racial discrimination and welfare.

Many spoke about how their lives in CPS camps stimulated a lifetime interest in ecological matters. We saw the issue of conservation in two dimensions: first, preserving the world's physical resources as a means of sustaining human life on the planet; and second, maintaining a balance of nature and protecting all living things for their own essential value and as a way of enhancing the quality of all life.

We saw a broader purpose of life in the conservation movement. "My appreciation of our environment," Paul observed, "I think is related to my type of 'faith'." George concurred, "It HAS increased an awareness of the importance of integrating all aspects of life into a whole that is in harmony with the Earth."

Wilbur saw the earth's contamination as a form of warfare, "I have come to see pollution of the environment as a form of violence—and capital punishment."

The organizations to which we gave our money and volunteered our time are a virtual encyclopedia of human endeavor. Here are a few of them: American Civil Liberties Union, American Friends Service Committee, Amnesty International, American Wildlife Federation, Bread for the World, Brethren Service Center, Bridges For Peace, Canadian Peace Alliance, Cancer Society, CARE, Catholic Peace Fellowship, Center for Race and Social Justice, Central Committee for Conscientious Objectors, Clergy and Laity Concerned, Educators for Social Responsibility, Farmers For Peace, Federation of American Scientists, Fellowship of Reconciliation, Food Bank, Food Pantry, Friends Committee for National Legislation, Friends World College, Goodwill Industries, Habitat For Humanity, Heifers For Relief, Interfaith Center for Corporate Responsibility, International Physicians for the Prevention of Nuclear War, Kiwanis, League of Women Voters, MADD, Mennonite Disaster Service, Model United Nations, Natural Resources Commission, Nature Conservancy, Peace Academy, Peace Corps, Peace Task Force (American Baptist Church), People to People, Physicians for Social Responsibility, Project Plowshares, Population Reference Bureau, Relocation Committee for Japanese Americans, Rotary, Scouting, Sierra Club, Society for the Blind, Southern Poverty Law Center, Teens Kick-Off, Unitarian-Universalist Service Committee, War Resisters League, Wider Quaker Fellowship, World Federalists, Zero Population Growth.

The world makes elaborate declarations of human rights and civil liberties, but it has barely gotten beyond lip service to these ideas. We have been working to put force into those declarations. Ernest is very clear about it: "Injustice in the world is a cause of unrest leading to violence. If one would be a peacemaker, one must confront injustice."

COs, a minority among minorities, Dale points out, "become sensitized to the numerous ways in which people are abused and discriminated against and the need to do something constructive." "In all social issues," Wellington observed, "it is not 'second nature' but 'first nature' for me to be very strongly on the side of the needy and weak."

In our youth we may have thought that substantial change would be easy to come by if it "made sense". Why would anyone continue in destructive ways when a better way is so easy to see? Many of us who participated in relief activities after World War II, however, came to appreciate the intractability of long-standing animosities and ethnic rivalries. After Leonard had visited the scenes of European horror in 1946, he declared: "I still maintain my pacifist position, but with a much greater sense of humility." A lifetime of "working in the vineyards" enable us to understand the tremendous inertia to change. So, we have a greater appreciation for the problem of making changes; but we have not wavered from our beliefs nor in our commitment to them. The goal is the same, but the timetable has changed.

The obstacles to change are not difficult to find, for they are in the minds and hearts of people and in their institutions. There must be some purpose to the law of inertia in preserving what mankind has achieved, and that undoubtedly is in the great schemes of things. But when institutions and practices that may have served a purpose some time in the past become a cancer, self-preservation then dictates that those practices be cut away. It was on those cancerous bodies that we took our aim in our occupations and avocations.

We were easily aroused by injustice, and we took every opportunity to rebuke a racial slur, to speak up for those on the short end of things. We had "been there", and we knew what it meant to stand against a tide. We realized the necessity of standing against employment and social discriminations. While the CO population was a fairly representative cross-section of the population, there was a relatively high percentage of people—greater than the general population—who came from middle income America. The realization of this probably made us even more sensitive to those are permanently deprived; ours had been a comparatively short-term disadvantage.

Above all, the CO saw that his stand against war was but one facet of a concern for peace in all aspects of life. There was a commitment to that goal, but no one claimed to have found the way of making that dream come true. As they appraised their life's journey, there was much left undone; but there was satisfaction in knowing that they had tried. They may have left a few traces of their convictions, but they never lost faith in their cherished conviction in one human family and in the abiding belief that every life counts for something. Whatever physical monuments we may have left behind would ultimately turn to dust, but the message passed to the next generation would live: life is sacred, human destiny is still unfolding, and the greatest splendor is yet to come.

Bill explained our faith in the ultimate triumph of human decency: "Love is not a luxury. . . . The human race has a sense of justice, compassion, kindness in its consciousness because we are going to need it in order to survive."

11
Peace
is
the Aim

It took us time to realize that it was no curse to be "out of step". Richard discovered that "being different is both possible and (often) welcome." We were not willing to accept what "they" say; rather we sought our own answers based on our own standards.

We lived by the prompting of conscience, hoping to achieve "inner direction and outer tranquility." But we did not know how things would turn out. "One never knows how an act of conscience is going to fly," observed Richard. "If you are worried about that matter, it may not be an act of conscience."

Following the years of our "exile", we tended to "draw in our horns" and avoid conversations about our pacifist beliefs. At the same time, we knew we had a story to tell, and "we needed to be visible". Ben explained, "I have found that openness in sharing my convictions and my history with those I come in contact with . . . has tended to make for more authentic, and often deeper relationships; and has often stimulated them to share some of their beliefs, histories, and dreams; and once in a while seems to lead some of them to consider seriously viewpoints different from those long-held."

Why should it be difficult for people to see the stupidity of mindless slaughter of children, women, and men? Why should an objective discussion of war arouse so much heat? We never did get a satisfactory answer to that question, but we never gave up trying.

Tony had a way of cooling the fire, "Reconciled to being considered a 'crackpot', I am freer to disregard the normal pressures of society to conform." We could go along with most things; but when fundamental principles were violated, we dissented.

Ultimately, we learned not to shy away from peaceful confrontations, and we came to welcome the chances for constructive interchange. Wilbert was open and frank, "I needed to give verbal reasons for my convictions. I always enjoyed doing this. . . ." John agreed, "I have appreciated opportunities to further propagate my views in society."

We were not inclined to call for a brass band, but at the same time we wanted the world to hear. Most COs could not be considered "pushy", but we learned not to withdraw, either. "In interpersonal relations," Wilbur reported, "when the situation seems appropriate, I always testify to my beliefs and my stand during W.W. II." Gordon did not shrink from getting his point across, "I have never hesitated in speaking my mind on opposition to militarism, nationalism, or war." Donald added, "I still express my peace position every opportunity I get."

We were not usually aggressive, but we did not intend to "hide our light under a bushel" either. Duane explained: "The role of the CO is to raise the consciousness of his fellow human beings, by raising issues that others don't want to be raised . . . ." Bill was direct: "I have worked all my life to discredit the military postures of the USA and other countries. . . . I am a militant pacifist and shoot off my mouth. . . . I like to travel (88 countries), and I take my 'liberal' views with me. . . . Lately there seems to be some swing against militarism in the world, and I push this every chance I get."

Considering the rampant patriotism during and immediately after World War II, this openness was not without its perils. In later years, however, the reaction mellowed. During the Vietnam war, for instance, World War II COs were often sought out by young people seeking to understand the pacifist point of view.

The act of taking the CO position did bolster our confidence. It helped Louis "to speak out in public in a number of different contexts—political, religious, human rights." Howard agreed, "CPS tended to strengthen my willingness to stand up and be counted." Robert was prepared for disagreement; "It is profitable to share your convictions in other areas of life with those who disagree with you, rather than remaining silent."

Some of us are comfortable with outspoken methods, but others use a quiet approach. "I take stands on political, racial, and religious issues contrary to the prevailing majority," Whitfield stressed. "But . . . [I am not] a street radical." Lon's manner was subdued, "I was not intended to be a proselytizer. . . . Hopefully, my pacifist attitude during routine work had positive social effects." Louis explained, "I am not an activist . . . I do not publicize my views. I think I set an example by my behavior and my stated views."

"There are no guarantees with pacifist action," Don reminds us. "I take pacifist action because I believe it is <u>right</u>, not because I think it is <u>effective</u>, though I certainly <u>hope</u> that it will prove to be so." Jacob knew his influence was unpredictable, but his action "should not be based solely on the kind of power I might exert. . . . "

Darwin looked for steady change: "I have become more sure of myself, but am without expectations of rapid change. . . . However, it is not something I, alone, can influence. Nor can the agreement with a like-minded minority do the job. I must influence those who have a different view in the direction of seeing the futility, destructiveness, and the contradiction of basic moralities that war and the war system represent. . . . The appeal must be to the basic morality of people and to the imperative to extend that morality beyond the artificial fences of kin, tribe, nation, religion, and race."

"I want to be an 'overcomer', especially in <u>all</u> areas of sin and evil," Floyd said. "I want to be 'a shining light for Jesus' and a good witness and ambassador for Christ in <u>everything</u>. The Lord wants the world to be a <u>better place</u> because of the way I live, think, talk, and act." Leroy underscores this point: "To help people to come to know Jesus Christ as Lord and Savior and to find His help in working through the problems common in life is yet the best solution to all peoples' needs."

While we preferred the quiet approach to change, we knew we were "disturbers of the peace". We wanted to see some basic changes. One man described himself as an "undercover agent for peace".

Instead of standing on the outside looking in, Harold thought it was important to be at least partly inside. "I try to conform as much as I can, so as to give myself 'social space' in which to 'object' on the important issues."

There are plenty of potholes to fill, whether we are looking for them or not. Bruce could not escape, "While I don't look for fights on issues, they do have a way of coming to my doorstep; and I can't sit idly by and not take up the challenge."

The obstacles to change are not difficult to find. They are in the minds and hearts of people and in their institutions. Is there really enough time to reform the human heart? Even those of us who are willing to face ostracism rather than kill know that our hearts, too, are not pure. A human mutation could solve the problem, but does mankind have the million years that would take? The world knows the impure in heart can learn to change their <u>behavior</u>. This is certainly no "roll over" task, but it is less remote than purification of the soul. Lee has faith, "I can see a good social order suppressing the greed of human nature."

In spite of it all, Fred is optimistic, "Many look on the betterment of society as mostly unattainable. I believe we have a far more optimistic outlook. . . . We can see in our daily activities and relationships how firm and positive approaches to problems and situations are accepted by others. . . . There <u>are</u> attainable levels worth working for."

We have "toiled in the vineyards", seeking ways to empower individuals—in daily living, in occupational pursuits, in family life, and in community affairs. We have organized meetings, arranged community programs, raised money, sold tickets, made posters, participated in vigils and demonstrations, written letters, and lobbied legislators. We have worked in our homes, on our jobs, in our churches, and in all manner of civic endeavors. We learned how to accept—and even to revel in—the tremendous differences among us. Differences became the bridges for building understanding and consensus.

NONVIOLENCE

Organized nonviolent action is a new phenomenon in human history, but it has demonstrated enormous power for peaceful change. In wartime, particularly with the viciousness of a Nazi regime, nonviolent resistance can be costly. Against enormous odds, however, there was a widespread underground movement throughout Nazi occupied Europe in World War II. It would be impossible to determine the ratio of lives lost in nonviolent resistance to those lost in violent action. The nonviolent resisters who lost their lives, however, took no other lives and destroyed no one's home. Nonviolent actions accomplished their ends in many ways. One of the most intriguing episodes followed the Nazi order that all Jews in Denmark were to wear a Star of David. The day the order was to take effect, King Christian X appeared with the Jewish star, as did all his citizens. The infuriated Nazis were powerless to do anything about it.

During that war when the Pope called upon the world to restrain violence, Stalin asked, "How many divisions does the Pope have?" It was not always so, but modern Popes have no military forces. They have a few Swiss guards, but these are not for battle. Whatever power the Pope has comes from the power of moral suasion. So how has this largest and longest-lived human enterprise survived and prospered? Could it be that the Pope retains his considerable influence <u>because</u> he gave up military power? Could it be that the ultimate demise of Stalin's Soviet Union resulted from an obsessive reliance on military power? And what lessons are to be taken from the prosperity of Japan and Germany after turning their backs on militarism following World War II?

Gandhi's nonviolent marches in South Africa and India galvanized his people against a colonial empire as nothing else had ever done. By drawing the world's attention to Indian independence, he changed the course not only of India's history but of Great Britain's as well.

The idea of peaceful nonviolent resistance has caught the imagination of people in all parts of the world. Martin Luther King, Jr. drew upon Gandhi's example in his nonviolent campaigns in the United States. Mother Teresa brought it to the care of destitute Indian children. Yeltsin received the acclaim of people everywhere for facing down his opponents without a shot being fired during an attempted coup in Moscow in August, 1991. The world was mesmerized as he stood atop tanks of the Soviet Army and turned away the soldiers that had been sent to arrest him. Praise for this courageous act of nonviolence was in dramatic contrast to the criticism for his shelling the Russian legislature's White House two years later.

One of the most fascinating turns of modern nonviolence again came in the Soviet Union. A popular uprising in Hungary was ruthlessly crushed by the Red Army of the Soviet Union in 1956, as was a similar movement in Czechoslovakia in 1968. But by the late 1980's Hungary, Czechoslovakia, and other Eastern European countries, dominated by the Soviet Union since World War II, were breaking free without a shot being fired. And the breakup of the Soviet Union itself after 1991 resulted in one the world's most remarkable political divisions as republic after republic peacefully established its independence. Considering the enormous complexity of these realignments, the amount of violence was minimal. While some of the former Soviet states squabbled over ethnic and territorial divisions, most of the differences were settled without bloodshed.

The violent breakup of Yugoslavia was such a gross exception to this peaceful process that it brought anxious pleas for sanity from every part of the world. During the same time, the division of Czechoslovakia into the Czech Republic and Slovakia was totally peaceful.

In 1989 the world had witnessed a similar confrontation between 100,000 Chinese protestors and the Chinese army at Tiananmen Square in Beijing. The picture of a single Chinese student standing alone against a military tank dramatized once again the power of nonviolent confrontation. That act did not end the violence, but its raw courage captivated people everywhere. As in the later Moscow stand-off, the local Chinese troops refused to fire upon the massed demonstrators. It was only after the Chinese leadership brought in troops from outer provinces that the crowd was fired upon and the demonstration collapsed. This barbaric attack was condemned around the world, just as was the Soviet Union's earlier cruelty against Hungary and Czechoslovakia. The brutality in Tiananmen Square was only the first round, just as were the Eastern European oppressions in 1956 and 1968. Meanwhile, the nonviolent movement in China continued to grow.

Nelson Mandela's courageous campaign for racial equality in South Africa illustrated the power of nonviolence in a unique way. As a young man Mandela had campaigned against Apartheid with nonviolent campaigns and demonstrations. Frustrated with the results of those efforts, he turned to violence, ending in a twenty-seven year imprisonment. Released in 1990, he began again his nonviolent program to dismantle Apartheid, having renounced violence during his long years in prison. This culminated in the free democratic elections of 1994 and the overwhelming victory of Mandela's reconciliation government for South Africa.

That quite remarkable election was not only a tribute to Mandela the man, but a bold expression of the people's confidence in the "old man's" nonviolent strategies. In spite of violent provocations by right-wing extremists, the people assembled peacefully for their first-ever election, standing in three-mile-long lines for hours to cast their votes.

While the pacifist has confidence in the possibilities of conciliation, we have no illusion that a few days of talk will wash away the hatreds and animosities of centuries. Instead of crying "fire" in a crowded theater, however, we prefer to concentrate on preventing the fire from breaking out in the first place. Part of that strategy is to post "early warning signals" about actions that lead to disaster. We want to see governmental leaders trained in the techniques of conflict resolution, not in shooting from the hip. Our objective is quite simple: *those people who represent their citizens in negotiations across national borders must understand that they no longer have the option of sending soldiers out to kill other soldiers because they fail to settle differences peacefully.*

Peaceful international relations will ultimately be maintained in the same manner that domestic peace is maintained; namely, by the formulation and enforcement of laws that protect the public order. When reconciliation replaces confrontation, the **force of law** will replace the **law of force.**

A Marshall Plan for Europe after World War I would have kept Hitler painting houses instead of trying to rule the world. The price of a Europe rebuilt after World War I would have been nothing compared to the devastation of World War II. After signing the Versailles Treaty, Marshall Foch of France is reputed to have said, "Somewhere I hear babies crying—Oh, God, it is the class of 1940."

Violence is a *consequence* of something else. Its eradication thus requires locating and attacking the guilty virus. If violence is to be prevented, the problems that "justify" violence must be addressed. The irony in all this is that practically all of the conflicts between individuals are resolved in nonviolent ways. Peaceful resolution of conflict is not some supremely demanding and impractical discipline. It is an everyday occurrence in the home, the workplace, the city council, the legislature, and the athletic field.

The major difference between day-to-day domestic affairs and international affairs is that in the former case, nonviolence is demanded and in the latter case it is not. In short, nonviolent solutions have not failed; they are used constantly. Indeed, during the so-called Communist threat after World War II, the United States government was obsessed with those who advocated the <u>violent</u> overthrow of government. Even in domestic affairs, nonviolence may not always "work" the first time, but it is always right; and a range of sanctions is available to assure that it is used.

For a world accustomed to settling squabbles with the sword, nonviolence is awkward. Mohandas Gandhi's nonviolent campaigns in India taught him that resolve can waver, just as it can on the battlefields of war. When he felt the people were unprepared, he would cancel a demonstration. In the CPS years we too learned the importance of personal discipline. "We need to have peace with ourselves," Wilbert explained, "before bringing lasting peace to others." Joe described how he conditioned himself for the discipline of nonviolence, "I feel committed to doing and being the best I can without reacting with violent thought toward those of other opinions."

There can, of course, be perils in "turning the other cheek". Elmo added, "Just being against violence is not enough. If one does not also follow a positive and constructive lifestyle in which nonviolence as a paramount value is convincingly demonstrated, then nonviolence itself becomes a form of violence."

Robert observed, "My adult life has not been restricted to just my opposition to war. I have practiced nonviolence as a family man, as a social worker, as an educator, etc. My total life philosophy is one of caring and helping." Ernest elaborated, "Pacifism is not something to be implemented in a crisis when all else has failed. It must be a constant way of life to avoid crises of the kind that lead to violence."

"My nonviolence," Harold says, "[leads me] toward figuring out what makes the other one tick and away from figuring out how to erase or eliminate the other one. If the other one is nonviolent, then this changes . . . from escape to attempts to comprehend and cooperate."

Since COs refuse to take part in violence, they feel a special obligation to demonstrate their faith in nonviolence. For Allen, this "laid on me a responsibility to live and to create the conditions for peace and to develop the skills of nonviolent resolution of conflicts to the best of my limited ability. . . . I have never felt that refusal to participate in war is sufficient in itself. . . . You have to validate a refusal of anything by positive demonstration of your position,"

There are, of course, two ways to settle disputes. In the day-to-day routines of life, civilized society expects the citizen to rise above fisticuffs and abide by "the rule of law". This simply means that individual rights are protected by a judicial system made up of law enforcement officers and courts. For the past few hundred years the world has been gradually evolving a rule of law for nations just as individual nations had done for individual citizens. In the early part of the seventeenth century Hugo Grotius began codifying International Law, and it continues to evolve just as does domestic law.

As transportation and communication technologies collapsed the distances between nations, the people of the world are now literally crowded into the same room. Nation-to-nation conflicts are being seen in the same light as person-to-person conflicts. The United Nations is attempting to apply a rule of law to nations that individual nations apply to citizens, but it still remains for the individual nations to abandon warfare.

The pace of international peacekeeping has expanded enormously since World War II. The Hague Conventions of 1907 spelled out the concept of formal international peace-keeping programs, and numerous other declarations have followed: the League of Nations articles, the 1945 United Nations Charter, the 1949 Geneva Convention, and the 1977 Geneva Protocols. The Foreign Service Institute of the United States Department of State reports frequently on the remark-able achievements of U.N. missions: Internal pacification missions such as the Yemen Observer Mission in 1963-1964 (UNYOM) and Dutch West New Guinea in 1962-1963 (UNSF); the border dispute between India and Pakistan by the Military Observer Group (UNMOGIP); supervision of the truce in the Arab-Israeli war in 1948 (UNTSO); and monitor-ing of Soviet troop withdrawal from Afghanistan in 1988 (UNGOMAP)

The existence of international peacekeeping forces does not assure the elimination of violence in the world any more than domestic police forces eliminate domestic violence. International policing agencies will face the same issue that national police agencies face: shall the law be enforced nonviolently or violently? In domestic affairs the emphasis is upon nonviolent law enforcement, some jurisdictions even forbidding their officers from carrying lethal weapons. The law enforcement process is difficult, and some people on either side of the controversy could resort to violence. Notice the public outcry, however, when a police officer is killed in the line of duty or when a police officer kills a suspect. Such violence goes beyond the range of reasonable conduct.

While human lives may be lost when laws are en-forced, that is not the <u>purpose</u> of police agencies. People's lives are lost while traveling in a motor vehicle, too; but, again, that is not why people drive cars. Peace officers are prepared to deal with violence, but their aim is to keep the peace by negotiation, arbitration, and conciliation. International peacekeeping is much more complicated than domestic peacekeeping, of course; but the aim in both cases is to resolve conflict peacefully.

In the case of war, on the other hand, killing is the purpose. In warfare you shoot first and ask questions later. The history of human warfare makes one lesson clear: wars breed wars by planting seeds of bitterness, animosity, and hatred. It makes no sense to take it out on people three or four generations after an original conflict, but that is what happens in trouble spots all around the globe. The hatred of the past feeds the animosities of today. The pacifist simply says, enough is enough!

12
Folly
or
Prophecy

The first ten chapters described what American conscientious objectors did during World War II, how they saw their wartime experience, and what happened to them after the War. Throughout the book COs talked about their beliefs on war and pacifism and the reasons for those beliefs. This chapter explains the idea of conscientious objection as a personal testimony against war and as a strategy for peace.

Why would a patriotic citizen reject one of mankind's most enduring "rites of citizenship"? Each objector had his own answer to this question; but in this chapter I will present what I believe is an authentic description of the CO faith, its beliefs, its rationale, and its enduring qualities. No single person—including the author—will totally agree with everything said. The ideas, however, are taken from the extensive comments of the COs themselves. I believe them to be a fair representation of what these COs believe about war and peace.

The CO, not unlike most people, looks at the human being as a marvel of life, a creature with capabilities for magnificent physical achievement, with abilities for fertile expression, and with capacities for joy, happiness, and love. We are awed by the indomitability of the human spirit and peoples' ability to "pick up and go ahead" in the face of devastating calamities. The catastrophes of nature—floods, volcanoes, fires, storms, earthquakes, and pestilence—are bad enough. But mankind has added its own roster of miseries. While exhibiting marvelously creative talents, people can also plunder and destroy what others have built; visit agony and desolation on their fellows; and despoil a magnificent physical world. In short, human history is the chronicle of an insatiable will to build and a powerful lust to destroy.

One committed to the principles of nonviolence is faced with a number of bewildering questions: In such a beautiful world, why is there so much mindless destruction? Why does mankind squander its precious resources in military weaponry and pour out the blood of its finest youth in the madness of battle? Even more to the point, why are human beings willing—yes, eager—to take up arms and kill total strangers?

People everywhere are as dumbfounded as we are by these questions. They are eager to see an end to war. The CO claims no priority in the yearning for peace. Our primary difference seems to be our perception of the conditions that bring about war and the actions necessary to stop it. We allege no great purity of heart and no special wisdom of mind. We do, however, part company with our non-CO brothers in our firm, resolute, and unequivocal refusal to take part in legalized murder. We believe that the history of human behavior has proved beyond any rational doubt that what people do determines the result they get. To put it another way, the means that are used will determine the type of end that results. When peaceful means are used, peaceful ends will result. When a nation prepares for war and engages in war, it breeds more war.

A number of years ago the Encyclopaedia Britannica codified a list of Great Ideas for its Great Books of the Western World. This monumental work included what its editors thought were the greatest books produced in the Western world. From the writings of 78 great minds and two collections of American state papers, they compiled a list of one hundred and two Great Ideas. In this brilliant array of thought, the compilers concluded that Peace was not itself a Great Idea. Instead Peace was coupled with War and given second billing in the "Great Idea" of *War and Peace*. More important than Peace were these other ideas: Aristocracy, Definition, Hypothesis, Mathematics, Monarchy, One and Many, Punishment, Same and Other, Slavery, Tyranny, and Wealth.

Conscience did not make it into the ranking of great ideas either; but Emotion, Mind, and Soul did. So perhaps conscience is wrapped up somewhere in these other ideas. Whether conscience is or is not a great idea, civilized society could not exist without it. Without the operation of individual human conscience—that is, human beings acting on the knowledge of right and wrong, good and evil—human society would collapse. All the enforcing authorities of parents, teachers, police, and courts are useless without it. How many police would it take to watch every individual all day every day, and who would watch the police? Indeed, the epidemic of lawlessness and terrorism in the latter half of the twentieth century can in large measure be traced to the decapitation of human conscience. When the individual conscience is subordinated to the will of the state and when individuals are molded to conform to the dictates of authority, the force of human conscience is annihilated.

THE EXERCISE OF CONSCIENCE

Civilized society is still searching for a reasonable balance between the rights of individual conscience and the needs of society. Or, to put it another way, how far can the rights of one individual impinge upon the rights of another? The issue is complicated because social conditions constantly change the range and limits of acceptable behavior. What may be reasonable conduct in a primitive society on sparsely settled land may be completely unreasonable in a heavily populated city. Modern states attempt to protect individuals from the encroachments of their neighbors, but it is also necessary to protect the people from the threat of state tyranny. The last word certainly has not been written on this matter.

Societies' recognition of individual conscience has advanced beyond Thomas Hobbes' seventeenth century notion that if one feels compelled to follow one's individual conscience against the state's demands, one should be prepared to suffer the consequences and look to heaven for reward. Very few people would claim that a person has an absolute right to say anything, do anything, or refrain from doing anything regardless of the consequences. When the State attempts to place itself between individuals and their conscience, however, the stabilizing force of conscience begins to break down. When the demands of individual conscience conflict with general social behavior, Western societies at least make an effort to accommodate the demands of conscience.

There are many issues on which society acknowledges the prior claim of individual conscience:

■In the court system, individuals may <u>affirm</u> rather than <u>swear</u> to an oath.

■Vegetarian meals are provided at public gatherings for individuals who oppose the killing of animals. Students so disposed are excused from the animal dissecting sessions of biology classes.

■People generally will refrain from certain types of conduct in the presence of those who object: drinking alcoholic beverages, smoking, gambling.

■The practices of religious groups are accommodated: not working on the sabbath, religious rituals, and the like.

■A student's objection to the Pledge of Allegiance is generally respected.

■A student with an aversion to violent forms of P.E. such as boxing will normally be excused from those sports.

■Peoples' living styles or forms of dress based upon religious considerations are accepted.

These are relatively noncontroversial issues, but there are many other examples where society assumes that individuals will be "governed by their consciences". The system of commerce rests on the assumption that people will pay their honest debts and meet their contractual commitments. Drivers on roads and highways trust other drivers to comply with the rules of the road. The people expect their government officials not to enrich themselves at the cost of the citizens.

Not every person abides by the dictates of conscience all the time; so we have laws to deal with transgressors. There is no way, however, that overseers could catch every deviant act. The entire social fabric would unravel if citizens could not expect their fellow citizens to abide by the dictates of their consciences most of the time.

The conscience of the CO is enriched by <u>faith</u>, a faith in people and in an order of things. For some of us this is a faith in God while for others it is belief in the ultimate sanity of the human mind. For both it is a belief in the sanctity of human life. While there is no single set of beliefs to which all COs subscribe, it is probably safe to say we agree that human life is sacred, that all people have worth, and that there is an inherent goodness in every person. The Friends have a beautiful way of saying this: "There is that of God in everyone".

We certainly do not disagree with our nonpacifist brethren that human beings are capable of both good and evil. People do not all grow up to be kindly and understanding, and the world must deal with evil and corruption. Indeed, it may be necessary to swat a few flies from time to time, but that does not translate into lining up groups of innocent young people to shoot at each other. The CO does not part company with the non-COs in the <u>need</u> to deal with those who would threaten, deceive, coerce, or enslave others; but we probably do disagree on the <u>way</u> to deal with them.

For those COs who express their beliefs in conventional religious terms, conscientious objection is based upon allegiance to a higher authority than the State. They see themselves as living in two kingdoms, the earthly kingdom and the kingdom of God. When the demands of those two kingdoms clash, the CO's ultimate loyalty is to God's kingdom. To put it another way, we have a dual loyalty: to Heaven (God) and to Earth (Man).

Christian COs come to their beliefs from their understanding of the Biblical teaching. Followers of other religions find their commitments in the sacred books of their religions. The serious practice of religion is a high and difficult calling, but all the great religions recognize that there is one human family. To the serious believer these teachings are not themes for posters or slogans for club mottoes; rather, they are rules for the morning, afternoon, and evening of life. As one man expressed it, "We grew up with these teachings in our homes along with country sausage and home baked bread."

For the Christian believer, pacifism is a personal religious conviction and does not derive from a "peace movement". The consideration of others' beliefs is important in placing those views in perspective. We are not, however, inclined to adjust our doctrine on the basis of "what others will think". We value our beliefs above social approval and are willing to take the slings and arrows of opposing views. But that does not mean we enjoy it.

We yearn for a world in which national pride and patriotism are augmented by loyalty to the whole human family. Affection for one's city or nation does not prevent the open acceptance of other lands and other peoples. There is no place in the modern world for the type of nationalism that demands rejection of those who live across the border or across the world. National borders are convenient ways of identifying geographical territories, but there are no human boundaries. There are no foreigners in the human race.

Beliefs About War

It has been said so often that it is now an axiom: *there will always be wars and rumors of wars!* **The CO absolutely and completely rejects this assumption.** We do not minimize the snares and pitfalls; but since human beings are capable of behaving in creative and productive ways—particularly when it is in their best interests to do so—there is no sensible reason for deliberately choosing destructive rather than constructive behavior.

COs and non-COs alike agree that war is the ultimate obscenity. Certainly the people who know say it is "hell". While there may be some agreement as to what war is, there are tense disagreements on what to do about it.

First, the CO disagrees with the flip-flop thinking which says: "peace is desirable, but sometimes you have to put your principles on hold and *do what has to be done.*" "If there is a rabid dog loose in the neighborhood, you simply have to stop it. Any other course is impractical, unrealistic, and does not work." Destroying a rabid dog is thus equated with "saturation bombing" of civilian targets. This leap of reason from destroying a mad dog to mass killing of human beings baffles the CO. So, on this point, we simply will not put our beliefs "on hold" or to "do what has to be done" in the name of mass destruction.

Second, the CO believes that if a standard of conduct is accepted as morally right, it is right under all circumstances. Again, we do not differ from our fellow citizens in <u>most</u> things: honesty in business, fidelity in marriage, protection of children and aged, and the like. The difference is that we see no reason to make an exception in the case of war. There are two sides to most arguments, but war is the exception. The commandment, "Thou Shalt Not Kill" is a compelling standard for behavior under any and all conditions.

There are many instances in the day-to-day routines of life where strict compliance with established standards, rules, and practices is demanded, even when such rigid enforcement does not appear to make good sense. For instance, if a person posts a letter without the proper postage, that letter is returned to the sender for the correct amount. At first glance this appears to be a foolish thing for the post office to do because it doubles their handling time. When the full implication of this process is understood, however, such a practice is necessary to assure that senders affix the correct amount of postage.

Third, warfare—in addition to destroying people and property—leaves a society morally degraded. War masks the real issues and aggravates legitimate grievances. War, instead of overcoming hatred, deepens animosities and plants the seed for yet more conflict. It is a short-term treatment without a long-term vision. As COs we believe there is no military path to permanent peace. We believe that you stop the next war by avoiding this one.

Society suffers permanent scars from war and so, too, do individual soldiers. Soldiers are taught that the taking of another's life is acceptable *when the circumstances are right*. It is not unusual for a returning soldier, following his country's teaching, to decide for himself when the circumstances are right for killing again. The soldier can be told that killing is acceptable only when a government orders it; but the glorification of war, by denying the sanctity of human life, distorts normal thinking.

Fourth, in war the innocent pay for the mistakes of the guilty. The soldiers who die in wars do not start the fight. U.S. soldiers in Vietnam were placed in double jeopardy. They were first asked to risk their lives on the battlefield and then were reviled by their fellow citizens when they returned. This chapter of American history disgraces a nation that conditioned people to the glory of war and then condemned soldiers for doing what society asked of them. Instead of condemning the institution that created the atrocities of Vietnam, the public scorned the men who did what society asked of them. The CO sees some hypocrisy in this. Is this not what is meant by killing the messenger who brings ill tidings?

One is reminded of the cartoon where the young boy asks his father, "Dad, how do soldiers killing each other solve the world's problems?" The bewildered and hopeless expression on his father's face leaves the boy to muse, "I think grownups just *act* like they know what they're doing."

Fifth, we are incensed by the military's euphemisms which obscure the true character of war. Like the false fronts of the motion picture sets, the sanitizing terms conceal the truth: *hostile/friendly fire, surgical strike, precision bombing, collateral damage* (usually referring to dead civilians), *carpet bombing, re-entry vehicle* (bomb), *taking out.* The vicious business is cleaned up to divert the public's mind from killing, maiming, and destruction.

Sixth, we are appalled by the claim that "God is on our side". When each side trumpets God's blessing, are we to assume that God is confused, or did the message get mixed up? How does God choose which ones shall go to perdition? How does He select those who are to do the killing; is God using agents to take over the job because He cannot get around to it? Would He really need people to do that for Him? And why would he want to kill His own creatures anyway? And what makes the human race feel it is so important in the first place? We believe we know blasphemy when we see it.

The taking of a human life is a sin against the Creator of all life. But it is also a sin against humanity, a senseless squandering of both human and physical resources. The creation and nurturing of human life entails an enormous investment of time and energy by the family and by the community. The child suckled at the mother's breast, clothed and housed through a dependent childhood, educated and inspired by society is a treasure for all the world. That child is an asset that could ultimately enrich the lives of all. The deliberate and calculating destruction of this treasure is nothing short of madness.

The human toll is the most ghastly consequence of war, but that is not all. War also destroys the creative and loving work by generations of people in the buildings, the art, the literature, the farms, and other physical treasures of civilization. If a commercial enterprise wasted its assets this way, stockholders, consumers, and governments would invade with investigators, grand juries, and prosecutors.

The creations of the human spirit deserve protection and preservation. What one person has created no one else has the right to destroy or plunder. What the world knows of former civilizations and what future civilizations will know of this one are the creations of human hands, minds, and souls in the objects left behind, whether they be buildings, art, literature, drama, science, or technology. These creations transcend the temporary glories of great nations, for in the end only these works of individual humans remain.

These are some of the disagreements that CO's have with the war system. So what are the alternatives? Well, it is not as though people spend all their time killing each other. The world does have inspiring religions, great cities, vast industrial and productive facilities, and magnificent educational institutions, and vast works of art, literature, and architecture. That is where most human energy is expended. So the alternatives are already there in our daily lives: rising each morning to earn our daily bread, building and maintaining the sources of our sustenance, loving and being loved, worshiping to our Gods, sharing the creativity of our minds and hearts, and leaving something of ourselves for those who come after us. With these enormous resources, there is no doubt that war could be brought to an end in a single generation. It is not that mankind does not know <u>how</u> to end it; it is that there is not the <u>will</u> to do it.

Beliefs About Conscientious Objection
There are as many ways of arriving at conscientious objection as there are individual COs. For purposes of this discussion I have classified conscientious objection into three

parts. The beliefs of one group is referred to as "philosophical"; but in a more precise meaning of that term, all three groups are philosophical objectors. The division I use here simply makes it more convenient to present the different points of view.

First are the people who base their objection on religious principles. In United States draft laws, one is deferred from military service as a Conscientious Objector if one's "religious training and belief" prevents one from participating in war. The courts, as we have seen, have given the term "religious" a very broad interpretation. Even with liberal interpretations, however, the legal definition of conscientious objection does not cover the full range of CO belief about war.

Many COs—and perhaps most, when "religious" is broadly interpreted—do base their objection to war on religious grounds. For some religion is a matter of personal salvation and obedience to the word of God; for others, religion is a guideline for moral and ethical conduct. Many people's beliefs probably encompass both ends; that is, they see their religion as a means of personal salvation and also as a guide for daily living. Above all, war objectors hold that killing other human beings violates the order of life.

For religious believers, their faith unites them with the total human family. In Christian and non-Christian faiths alike, loyalty is to a higher order. As one CO expressed it, "we say yes to life and no to war." Conscientious objection is "a fruit of the spirit," in the words of another.

The second group of conscientious objectors rely on philosophical principles. In these cases, while they may have religious beliefs, convictions also relate to nonreligious matters. War is seen as an evil act that violates the right of all people to enjoy the creative miracle of human life. There is boundless potential for good even in the face of evil; and in this view of life, one person has no right to decide that another person shall die.

Philosophical pacifists are often confronted with the argument that war is nature's way of playing out the process of evolution. There is a constant struggle for life and only the fittest survive. War plays a part in weeding out weaker creatures. There are two flaws in this reasoning. First, the notion of species survival explains how one species "takes out" another species; it is not lions killing off lions or gorillas killing off gorillas. The struggle is between species, not within one species. Only humans, and a few other excessively savage beasts, have that distinction. Second, the higher principle of mutual aid governs life within a species. Peter Kropotkin in his delightful book *Mutual Aid* explains how members of the animal kingdom cooperate with each other to protect and preserve life. The CO embraces the rule of mutual aid and rejects violence not only because it is counter-productive but because it is a gross perversion of man's purpose.

The human spirit transcends individual lives and links people in a universal chain of life. When the state demands that people destroy these ties, the conscientious objector says "No!" Wars disconnect people from their common humanity. This severing of common bonds breeds social chaos.

The third group of COs base their opposition to war on social, political, and economic issues. War perpetuates human misery and prevents order and decency. The cost is exorbitant and the consequences wretched. It is an insane act with no redeeming virtues, promulgated by people who seek social, political, or economic advantage for themselves. It is the world's most deadly confidence game.

These COs are often thought of, by themselves and others, as "non-religious" objectors. (As pointed out above, however, the term "religious" is interpreted to include this classification of objectors.) These types of objections, however, create genuine alarm; for they strike at the heart of entrenched economic and political power. A society may be willing to accommodate a few religious radicals since they just make trouble in the military with their religious preaching and hunger strikes. But to exempt people because they object to war on political or economic grounds would open the floodgates to all sorts of dissension. If a nation's—or an industry's—interests in oil, minerals, or territory are in jeopardy, the refusal of citizens to protect those interests could destabilize the world order. Individual citizens are not really capable of understanding the fine nuances of international finance, and a weak military response would undermine the world's economic system.

While these three types of conscientious objectors have different bases for their beliefs and express themselves in different ways, the common belief is that war is the ultimate enemy. The fires of today's war come from the embers of the last disaster. As a war ends, grievances that brought it about may be smothered, but they are rarely eliminated.

THE RATIONALE FOR
CONSCIENTIOUS OBJECTION

Conscientious objection is rooted in faith and confirmed by human experience.

First, we recognize that human beings are self-seeking creatures capable of deceit, deception, and double dealing. While we have faith in the capability of people to do what is necessary to survive, our belief does not assume that angels inhabit the earth. At the same time, however, we know that people are capable of love, compassion, and joy.

Second, we believe that some common-sense standards of behavior are necessary to keep people out of each other's way, including such routine day-to-day matters as agreeing to drive motor vehicles on the same side of the road or honoring commitments to pay for goods delivered by the store. Further, it means that people's relations with each other must be subjected to the rules of fair play. Those who insist on violating the rules need to be corralled and stopped. In short, arbiters (law enforcement personnel, if you prefer) are needed to enforce the rules. In a totally communitarian society where every citizen abides by the Golden Rule, enforcers would be unnecessary. But until that day arrives, the pacifist is willing to settle for a little enforcement in order to eliminate the mass killing.

Third, we believe the world is now mature enough—perhaps desperate enough—for nations to live by the types of rules that apply to individuals in community living. The world is now ready for the enforcement of international laws, just as national police enforce national laws.

The lust for power and deep-seated ethnic, national, and religious rivalries are probably inevitable. Ancient enmities are easily inflamed by a Hitler, a Napoleon, an Alexander, or such lesser tyrants as Franco, Idi Amin, or Saddam Hussein. If ordinary citizens were left alone to resolve their differences without the inflammatory rhetoric of self-serving leaders, within a generation or two most of the world's animosities would dissolve. The hatred between Jews and Arabs, Serbs and Croats, Chinese and Tibetans, Russians and Armenians, and the scores of family and cultural feuds are rooted in their respective heritages and usually have little to do with the current generations who face each other across man-made boundaries. Two farmers arguing over property held by their respective ancestors for

six generations could resolve their feud in a single generation. The Serb living inside Bosnia, the Zulu in South Africa,
the French in Canadian Quebec, or the Basque in Spain
would find ways to live at peace with their neighbors.

Fourth, we believe that individual nations—or seg-
ments of nations—have no right to "protect" themselves by
military aggression or "police actions" against their neighbors. In the world of day-to-day living, one can find plenty
of occasions to disagree with one's neighbors. There are
tinderboxes all over the world capable of exploding any time,
and there is always someone somewhere willing to strike the
match.

Accepting the world for what it is while at the same
time seeing what it is capable of being, the rationale for the
CO position has three dimensions: first, social responsibility;
second, the political forces in war; third, claims for the
"good" war.

Social Responsibility

When one acts on a matter of conscience against the
popular will, one is saying, "This is where I stand, and these
are my compatriots." One acting on conscience does not
"put a finger into the wind" to test the popularity of an act.
The morality of an act is sufficient unto itself. If others
disagree, prudence says, did you overlook something? But
when all the evidence is reviewed and the demand of
conscience still leaves one standing alone, that is simply the
price to pay.

For a world in the habit of solving problems by force
and violence, the pacifist is a nuisance. Indeed, some critics
say it is only because others are willing to fight that COs
enjoy the "luxury" of refusing. Such an argument belies the
fact that pacifism existed before draft laws exempted COs

from military service. A person is a CO because of conviction, not because it is recognized by some law.

Americans often point to their own Revolution as evidence that war advances the cause of freedom. Whose freedom was advanced? Certainly not the Black slaves. Indeed, their enslavement was confirmed and enforced by that war. Even the great protectors of freedom, the U.S. Constitution and a government of balanced powers, failed black America.

Wars, including the American Revolution, have spread a virus of military adventurism through all reaches of American society. The poison of the American Civil War still festers and eats away at America's social fabric.

The French and Russian Revolutions did the same thing in their countries. The violence of the French Revolution made possible the Reign of Terror and the subsequent restoration of a despotic monarchy. The Russian Revolution introduced the world to a tyranny as ruthless as any ever seen. The Spanish Civil War of the 1930's established a pattern of state oppression which lasted until Franco's death. The civil wars in Latin America vested governments with dictatorial controls during most of the nineteenth and twentieth centuries.

In the face of overwhelming evidence to the contrary, the world still believes that disputes are settled by fighting about them. The Allies may have crushed Hitler's dreams in World War II, but the commitment to military power generated by that war spawned a series of hot and cold wars throughout the twentieth century. The world has yet to understand that war is a short-range adventure with long-range calamities while peace is a long-range dream made possible only by short-range rejection of war.

Everything that science knows about human life confirms that there is only one human race. Civilized societies recognize each person's inherent right to life, and this belief is so deeply imbedded that murder is universally condemned. Yet the same world that penalizes individual murder sanctions mass murder. In short, private murder is a crime, but mass murder is approved. In whatever way the murder occurs, the taking of a human life divides the human family. And war is the greatest of all dividers.

In the normal events of everyday life, human beings are drawn together in a natural human bond. Without a thought to personal safety, people will spontaneously jump into a stream to rescue a drowning child, administer first aid to an injured stranger, help the handicapped across a street. People inherently know that the one in distress is connected to them. Nonviolence nourishes this bond and enriches this relationship; war severs the bond and debases the participants. Indeed, the aim of warfare is to break the social strands that bind human beings together.

The CO will yield to no one in love of country and defense of its honor. The CO's patriotism is based on pride in one's people and in their accomplishments, the love of freedom, the right to speak freely, the right to one's own religion, and personal attainments and accomplishments. The CO is passionate about individual freedom and justice. But we believe that national well-being does not depend on "national security"; it is found rather in the well-being of all citizens. It is not in killing the young soldier from some other part of the world; it is in saving and nourishing human life wherever it happens to be.

The Political Forces in War

"The best way to prevent war is to be prepared for it." War is thus akin to a physical malady for which one must be inoculated. The CO rejects this premise, contending instead that wars occur because of the way nations relate to one another, not because one country has more or less armaments than another. War is prevented by changing the way countries conduct their affairs, not by piling up mountains of armaments.

Human conflict is inevitable, but war is not. Two people cannot occupy the same space at the same time. If one covets what someone else has and is determined to have it at the expense of its current owner, conflict results. The issue is not in how to eliminate conflict; it is, rather, how to prevent conflict from ending in violence.

There are many <u>conditions</u> that bring wars about, including the aspirations of one nation to obtain the resources of another. In the final analysis, however, wars are made possible because individual citizens relinquish to governments the power to commit them to fight. All that remains is for the nation's leaders to give the call and citizens will march off to battle. When the order comes to march, the citizen is conditioned to ask, *Where?* not, *Why?* Thus, *War is made possible when political operatives have armies readily available to enforce their schemes or to cover up their mistakes.*

It is the CO's contention that government officials escape accountability for their scheming or their blunders because they can call on others to get them out of their predicaments. In day-to-day personal relations, people who use guns to get rid of opponents are criminals; in international affairs, the gun is the ultimate tool of diplomacy. When diplomats come to understand that soldiers will no longer kill and die for their power ploys, the provocations will stop. It is simply not acceptable for innocent citizens to pay the price.

But it is not as simple as that, you say. The world is a wide and dangerous place filled with desperadoes and modern-day tyrants seeking to steal from their neighbors and oppress their people. An imbalance of military power will entice the aggressor. Let's take a look at that possibility. There may be some disagreement as to whether Hitler was the world's worst tyrant, but he is at least a modern example. So how could the world have dealt with him?

The history of Europe after World War I is a classic case for the seeding of war. European and United States policies paved the road for Hitler. Germany's Weimer Republic was shackled; and when Chancellor Heinrich Bruening in 1931 asked for help to diffuse Hitler's frenzied demand for German rearmament, the pleas were ignored. We now know that the rearming of Germany was made possible by financial backing from outside Germany; indeed, there is considerable evidence that <u>even after World War II started,</u> the United States and other nations kept Hitler's supply lines full. So how many people were killed with the hardware paid for by money from their own countries?

It is this type of hypocritical international dealings that COs find so appalling. But it did not stop with World War II. Arms-exporting nations all over the world sell arms to terrorists; and in the 1991 Persian Gulf War, American soldiers were attacked on the deserts of Iraq with weapons produced by American technology. International arms dealers know no boundaries; the guns are available to all.

Well, it is said, the world may be culpable in the rise of tyrants; but does that mean they can be left to overrun their neighbors? Can you simply ignore their marauding ways? The best way to avoid a fire, of course, is to prevent it from happening. If Hitler's trading partners had been less greedy for the profit in arms, that regime would have collapsed overnight. That assumes, of course, that those same partners would have been as willing to help rebuild the German economy as they had been to rebuild the German military machine.

Ultimately the world chose war, the alternative that Hitler was allowed to dictate. But even when war breaks out, there are still two alternatives. The first is the conventional all-out war. Army is met by army, each aiming to inflict the maximum damage upon the other until one side exhausts itself and retires (surrenders). This is how wars are traditionally fought with "honor" and patriotic defense of the homeland. In the modern world, the entire nation is absorbed in launching the maximum possible force against the enemy. The carnage is not restricted to the battlefield, and civilians suffer along with the soldiers.

There is, however, a second violent scenario. Let it be clear that the following alternative is not a pacifist proposal. Taking military strategists at their word that the objective of war is to defeat the enemy in the shortest time with the least damage and loss of life, the process described below is the most logical course.

This alternative is rarely practiced and is spoken of only in the most hushed whispers. For optimum results, however, it is far superior to the first method. It is infinitely simple: the individual or individuals fomenting the problem are "eliminated" by any means possible. If the Kaiser, Hitler, Tojo, or Hussein is the cause of the problem, you take the battle to the source. Instead of massing thousands of troops and mounds of killing machines, a team of agents is dispatched to find the leaders fomenting the trouble. In short, the culprits are eliminated, and the innocent are relieved of playing the bloody game.

This second option undoubtedly leaves the world aghast. It terrifies the pacifist even to speak about it. One can imagine the anguished cries: barbaric, inhuman, contrary to the codes of war! Removing the leaders would de-stabilize the situation and create chaos! While it is usually swept under the rug as a dirty little secret, when economic or political considerations are powerful enough, governments do not hesitate to employ covert operations in overthrowing uncooperative regimes. While the perpetrators have tried to lock the deeds away, United States governments either employed or encouraged such methods to destabilize governments all over Latin American. If these methods are acceptable methods for helping the rich and powerful, why can they not be done to prevent innocent citizens from killing each other? Of course, it would be said, if their leaders are attacked, the people would rally with even more ferocity. But such an argument assumes that the people of a nation are as ready for the war as the leaders. This is doubtful—that is, if they are left free to make their own judgements without the help of propaganda. Further, every war ultimately comes to an end with one side laying down its arms to the great relief and rejoicing of both sides. In this exercise, the inevitable end result simply occurs sooner. But even more to the point, it would put adventurers on notice that they would be the first casualties of war. If proponents of war are unwilling to face the unvarnished consequences of their own folly, they have no right to ask others to bear the brunt of it. Does anyone doubt that this would stop a war before it got started?

These, then, are the choices when nations confront each other with guns drawn. But what happens after the crisis passes and the world returns to peace? The aftermath of World War II gives us a range of answers to that question; some good and some not so good. That war literally destroyed the war-making capability of Germany and Japan, a blessing that the world came to see in a brilliant industrial burst. Stripped of their military power, these two industrious peoples were compelled to invest their energies in peaceful development. As a consequence, both nations achieved a level of economic prosperity that could never have been achieved by military adventure.

There are two engrossing episodes here. First was the assistance given by the victorious Allies in rebuilding Germany and Japan. Instead of the vindictiveness that followed World War I, the Marshall Plan in Europe and the reconstruction program in Japan enabled these two vanquished countries to attain levels of prosperity that had eluded them in their military adventures.

There is a second part to the story. While Germany and Japan were being helped to rebuild, the Soviet Union was dealt out of the Marshall Plan. Instead, the United States and the Soviet Union became intractable adversaries in a forty year "Cold War". The Soviet Union eventually collapsed in upon itself, and the United States dangerously crippled its economy by a frenzied military buildup.

In the years since World War II many nations have poured out their substance in crushing military expenditures and costly military adventures. The United States ventured into Vietnam as did the French before them, the Soviet Union into Afghanistan, China into Tibet; and scores of nations in Europe, Asia, Africa, and Latin America tore themselves apart in bloody civil wars. Clearly, the expansion of militarism in the twentieth century has extracted an enormous price in loss of life, destruction of property, and human suffering.

This leads to one of the most troubling issues in consideration of war; namely, the "Good War".

The "Good" War
When the words Good and War are combined in one phrase, it deserves some explanation. In Studs Terkel's 1984 Pulitzer prize-winning book of that title, he commented on the absurdity of using those two words together. To suggest

that there are such things as good wars does seem incompatible with sound reason. It is one of those unique mental processes by which the mind conceals the madness of behavior.

In modern times World War II was the quintessential "good" war, a war that rid the world of evil and assured lasting peace. To the CO, on the other hand, it is a classic case of accelerating the pace of violence. Fifty years later there were more wars around the world than at any time in the human history.

We think we are at least entitled to an accountability from those who make claims for "good" wars.

When kings ruled by "Divine Right", they did not find it necessary to justify war; they simply ordered the troops to shoot. But that divine charade did not hold up; so rulers had to give their citizens <u>reasons</u> for killing strangers. Thus arose a series of rationalizations for violence and justifications of "good" wars.

The string of reasoning goes something like this: Human conflict is in the nature of things, violence is the natural outcome of conflict, and since violence between individuals is inevitable, violence between nations—war—is also inevitable. So, since wars can not be abolished, they should be "civilized". There are two ways to do this. First, some types of war are outlawed and some are sanctioned. Second, once a war is under way, certain conduct—"rules of war"— must be adhered to. In short, some wars and some methods of war are all right, provided that all parties agree to abide by the same rules.

The energy expended in learning how to live with war is not unlike a person whistling by the cemetery; if one makes cheerful sounds, there is nothing to fear from dark and frightening places. There is a considerable body of literature to help in the whistling. The United States Library of Congress Catalog, for example, has a special designation for the subject: Just War Doctrine. As of 1994, there were sixty-five volumes listed in this entry. The On Line Computer Library Center (OCLC) which catalogs books from even more sources, listed two hundred and sixty five titles. It was a relief to learn that some of these books criticize the notion of the "good" war, and at least one of them (Marian Maury, *The Good War*) describes a truly good war; namely, the UN's worldwide fight against poverty, disease, and ignorance.

Apologists for the "good" war divide the subject into a number of topics: first, just causes; second, right intention; and third, right conduct.

Just Causes

The "good" war must be authorized by a legitimate governing authority. But what is a legitimate authority? In the United States that question is answered in the Constitution which gives Congress the authority to "declare war". As commander-in-chief, however, presidents have ordered armed forces into potential war zones on their own initiative, claiming "U.S. security interests" or "police actions". These infringements on its prerogatives caused the Congress to pass the War Powers Act requiring consultation with Congress for certain types of troop deployment.

In any event, whatever a country's charters happen to be, a war is presumed to be legitimate when a government's officials act in accordance with those charters. This process defines the parties to the conflict, identifies the war zones, safeguards the interests of neutrals, and places the world on notice that a state of war exists. Neutral parties are thus able to stay out of the way.

After deciding that there will be a war, the next question is, who is going to fight it? Herein lies one of the dilemmas—indeed, hypocrisies—of the system. A number of years ago the famed Christian clergyman, Harry Emerson Fosdick, proposed that the first persons to vote for a declaration of war should be the first soldiers on the battlefield. It is disturbing to the rational mind when the people who dispatch others to the front stand above the fray. The Athenian, Euripides, as early as the fifth century B.C., was troubled by this same question. He argued that those who vote on the question of war should be required to consider the possibility of their own death. If they had seen death before their own eyes, there would have been no desire for battle. If Napoleon and Genghis Khan could ride at the front of their troops, why not the solons who declare war?

If politicians and statesmen are to be exempt, why not others? Thomas Aquinas, writing in the thirteenth century, thought there should be others. He claimed that warlike pursuits were simply not compatible with the duties of the clergy. War duties were full of unrest and hindered sacred contemplation and the praise to God. It was "unbecoming" for holy men to shed blood. They must remain on the sideline and offer spiritual help to those who do fight.

But what is "becoming" about a farm boy running a bayonet through the body of another farm boy? Are clergymen the only Men of God? If it is unseemly for an agent of Christ to kill, does not the Church teach that all members are agents of Christ? Is battle consistent with the occupations of farming, shoemaking, or engineering?

Aquinas' distinction between clergymen and laymen found its way into the United States draft law in World War II. Some might see hypocrisy in the exclusion, but it does at least recognize that Christian teaching and warfare are incompatible. As was described above, during World War II a number of churchmen and seminary students refused their exemptions on the basis that it was no more wrong for them to kill than for anyone else.

The "good" war doctrine says that when soldiers, acting in obedience to command, kill persons in opposing armies, they are absolved of violating the commandment, Thou Shalt Not Kill. After Constantine embraced Christianity in the fourth century, their three hundred years of pacifism would ultimately bring Christians into conflict with the Empire. St Augustine in his famous work, *The City of God*, helped the Roman cause along by releasing Christians from their duty not to kill under two conditions: first, when the soldier/killer is carrying out a delegated duty and thus is not personally responsible for what is done; second, when the person to be killed is guilty of wrongdoing. Aristotle had laid the foundation for this latter notion in his dictum that it is permissible to wage war against those who are destined to be governed and enslaved.

In the Middle Ages, when church and state were one, defense of the state was seen as defense of the faith. Since it was the church/state's job to control sin, war became a religious mission. The Christian crusades were the ultimate glory.

Next comes the question of defensive versus offensive war. If a nation had a chance to avoid a war but "voluntarily" initiated it, defense against that attack would constitute a "good" war. This is referred to as Volunteerism. Does this mean it would be unjust to resist an attack when the attacker accidentally crossed a border on its way back from some other war? Why it is necessary to determine that an aggressor could have avoided the incursion is not clear. This raises the issue of the preemptive strike, the "anticipatory retaliation". This rule says that aggression against another state is justified when it is known that the other is planning an attack. Thus, there is justice in a preventive war. The question of how one country determines that another is preparing to attack is left unanswered. The preemptive strike was flatly rejected in the Nuremberg declaration that no aggressive war is justifiable.

Just causes also include wars fought to protect a way of life, to resolve moral issues, or to avenge a wrong. If a state is obligated to protect its citizens from enemies within, it has an equal duty to ward off enemies from without. If a violent and marauding neighbor is disturbing the serenity of the region, that neighbor may be dealt with as one would a wild and savage beast. No society is secure with a barbarian on the loose.

In all these contentions and justifications, some bothersome questions remain: Who decides that a wrong has been perpetrated? When is an action determined to be aggression? Against whom was the aggression directed? Who is paying the price for the war? Is the war "good" for those who killed and for those who died? Who has the right to say that it is "good" for another to kill or die?

Are any wars so pure as to have only "just" causes? How does one distinguish the just from the unjust, and who decides? How does one separate the motives for personal revenge, unscrupulous ambition, thirst for military glory, and material gain?

Right Intention

In the "good" war soldiers must have clear-cut and cleanly definable ends. There must be a clearly defined purpose, and the war must be fought for that purpose only. This idea might have had some relevance in more innocent times, but who in the latter half of the twentieth century now believe that a war would "make the world safe for democracy," "destroy communism," or "avenge ruthless aggression." The true purposes of war are masked in slogans and obscured by passion.

The value of a victory must outweigh the evil of war; in other words, the good attained must be worth the losses. This is the doctrine of <u>proportionality</u>. It is akin to the idea that punishment must fit the crime. War is to continue only until its purpose is achieved. Crushing an enemy for the sake of revenge is ruled out. Again, this dogma raises more questions than it answers: who makes these judgments, who pays the price for those judgments, and who defines the benefits.

Charity to the vanquished is the next precept. Some ancient versions of charity are startling to the modern world. During the Crusades, for instance, imprisonment and torture were employed to save the souls of the nonbeliever. This was done out of "love" for the heretic. If this sounds strange to the modern mind, how will future generations view the claim of saving lives by delivering two atomic bombs?

Rightful Conduct

Closely related to the idea of Right Intention is Rightful Conduct, which apparently means conforming to the "Rules of War".

In 1625 Hugo Grotius sought for the first time to define the rules of war. Since then the world has evolved a variety of mandates, including: (1) conduct of armies in enemy territory; (2) spoils of war; (3) safe conduct; (4) prisoners of war; (5) implements of war; (6) the use of only those means that are absolutely necessary; (7) discrimination of targets; and (8) peace treaties.

The Hague Convention of 1907 and the Geneva Conventions of 1949 and 1977 prescribed a number of rules for the conduct of war. There are three primary elements in rightful conduct:

First, <u>Proportionality</u>: the military means must be proportionate to the goals, and the total "good" to be realized by the war must at least balance its evils.

Second, <u>Discrimination</u>: direct and intentional strikes at noncombatant and nonmilitary targets are prohibited.

Third, <u>Means</u>: crimes against humanity (Genocide) are forbidden.   Prohibited are weapons whose ills heavily outweigh their merits: those that "uselessly aggravate suffering of the disabled", chemical warfare, and biological warfare.

It seems to the pacifist that these articles, however well-intentioned and honestly formulated, can never inject morality into an institution that is irredeemably evil. Even when all these articles are scrupulously followed, the uncertainties lead to absurd results: who judges good and evil goals, who defines noncombatant, and who decides the ills and merits of particular weapons.

The reality is that once a war is started, the methods of warfare become technical questions to be determined by the military officials on the ground. Once war starts it makes no sense to take account of justice or injustice, mercy or cruelty. The goal is to win the war with a minimum of cost in the least possible time. These choices lead inevitably to such military expediences as the Bataan Death March, the bombing of Coventry and Dresden, the My Lai Massacre, and the horrors of Hiroshima and Nagasaki.

The effort to "clean up" war by outlawing certain methods of warfare has been a dismal failure. The battlefield is not a community debate. When one generation of weapons is outlawed—poison gas, for instance—a new generation becomes more horrifying than the last. While little has been done to reduce these atrocities, the effort to place boundaries around military conflict does represent a deep yearning to eliminate the monstrous affair. The pacifist's question is simple: why not just outlaw the whole thing?

The effort to define acceptable weapon systems puts the world on a slippery slope. The weapons of tomorrow have yet to be developed, and prohibiting yesterday's weapons does nothing about tomorrow's technology. Thucydides in his history of the Peloponnesian War probably best expressed our sentiment, "We bless your simplicity but do not envy your folly."

Summary
Everyone, including the most fervent apologist, understands that war is hell. The honesty or sincerity of its perpetrators does not eliminate the misery and destruction. At war's end tangible losses can be calculated: human beings killed, physical property destroyed, and money expended. However, how can one ever measure the human pain and agony, the anguish of a parent at the death a child, the loss of priceless physical treasures, and the hatreds that grow and magnify with each succeeding generation?

Pacifists depart from their war-apologist friends, not because they judge physical conflict in some pious or sanctimonious way. We simply interpret historical events differently, and we see different causes and solutions. Wars begin long before the shooting starts, fed by a number of concealed conditions: (1) the way commerce and trade are conducted; (3) the way military forces are trained, equipped, and mobilized; (4) the way a vanquished people are treated at the end of a war; (5) the way one people are kept indentured to another; (6) the way one country covets the wealth of its neighbors. In short, war results from a series of overt and covert conditions, no one of which may be enough to light the fuse. The ultimate <u>causes</u> of war probably reside in the flaws of human character, and not much can be done

about that.   Something, however, can be done about the
<u>conditions</u> which make war possible because these arise out
of human behavior.

The pacifist's second major contention is that national
leaders, assuming the military option is always an ultimate
choice, engage in practices that create the conditions for war.
Wars will end when the rulers of nations understand their
citizens are not at their beck and call. Some pacifists believe
that humans are destined to live in sin until God imposes his
order upon the world. Still others see that wars will cease
only when leaders no longer gain political and economic
advantages from military adventures.   And there are yet
others who spurn worldly concerns and focus their attention
on personal salvation. But from whatever perspective they
see the world, pacifists know that the human destiny lies in
peace and brotherhood, not in violence and division.

ACTING ON BELIEFS

Pacifism is an *ideal*, just as democracy, freedom, and
equality are ideals. It is a goal, a dream. It was dreams that
flooded American shores with immigrants, that created the
Declaration of Independence and the Constitution of the
United States, that led Martin Luther to post his 95 Theses at
Wittenberg, that ended slavery in the Emancipation Procla-
mation, that developed the Salk polio vaccine, and that
produced Adam Smith's *Wealth of Nations.*

Idealists (dreamers) do not ignore the real; they simply
seek ways to make their ideals real. If humans had been
meant to fly, it was said, they would have been given wings.
But the Wright brothers had a different idea. To the French-
man who invented the fork, people said that God gave

people hands so they could eat. And what does the believer in democracy say when told that it makes no sense to vote: one vote cannot make any difference. And what about the ideal of universal education? If there ever was a dream, that was it; how absurd to want everyone to read, or to add up a column of numbers, or to understand the principles of democracy!

Differences can divide people or unite them, bring them to blows or bring them together. Differences in skin, color, shape, and body size irritate, agitate, and confound the people of the world. Likewise, people divide themselves according to where they live, the languages they speak, and the songs they sing. Yet it is these varieties that enrich and enliven all our lives. There is nothing in nature's plan which makes "strangers" out of people on the other side of the river. The conditions that unite people are <u>universal</u>; the differences that distinguish people—color, shape, and size—are <u>superficial</u>; and geographical boundaries are <u>fabrications</u> of the human mind. The superficial is irrelevant and the fabrication is immaterial.

The pacifist's <u>vision</u> is not so different from other people; people everywhere want a world without war. The pacifist perceives that peace will be found in the diversity of the human family and in the richness of human differences. As was described in Chapter 10, COs returning from World War II embraced that diversity, pursuing their individual interests in a great range of endeavors. As religious leaders, they inspired their parishioners to apply their faith in their daily lives. As educators, they taught nonviolence and commitment to the peaceful resolution of conflict. As civil rights workers, they helped elevate the quality of life for people everywhere. As missionaries, they brought new technological methods and social practices to remote regions of the world. As farmers, craftsmen, and tradesmen, they produced products of value and enjoyment. As nurses and physicians, they ministered to the sick and needy. As elected officials, they contributed to the public service of their fellow citizens.   As business people, they provided goods and services to their communities. As social workers, they served people caught in economic and social deprivation. As social activists, they marched, they demonstrated, they spoke, and they wrote about the dream of a world without fear, poverty, deprivation, or war. Above all, they attempted to practice nonviolence in their daily lives and to live in peace and harmony.

CONCLUSION

If war is ever to be abolished, citizens must lead the way.   Those with a vested interest in preserving their power—the "leaders"— will never do it so long as they can conscript others to enforce their will.   Citizens are learning that they cannot leave even local school board or city council matters totally in the hands of officials.   If people that close to home must be watched, how much more important it is to keep tabs on those who handle international affairs.   The ideal state of affairs is for governmental officials to know, "the people back home just won't put up with that."

The pacifist speaks softly and carries a wand of hope. We are wanderers in a fragile world, perhaps with more hope than good sense warrants, but with a profound faith that love will triumph because only love will make us whole. We do not know if it is written in the stars, but we cling to the belief that there is order and purpose to human existence.

Epilogue

Conscientious objectors are often asked why they believe all wars are wrong. A comprehensive answer to that question would require a volume of its own. What follows is not a complete discourse on the subject. It does, however, cover the main elements in the pacifist interpretation of war, its conditions, its causes, and its cures. While some of the issues discussed below have been touched on in the previous chapters of this book, this chapter will attempt to clarify some of those ideas.

APOLOGY FOR WAR

Humankind has developed some truly abominable customs: cannibalism, human sacrifice, torture, serfdom, witchcraft, slavery, and war. It is testimony to the potential wisdom of the human race that of all these curses, war alone retains an accepted place in human affairs. This is not to say that the other sins no longer exist; but only war is still openly taught, prepared for, and routinely practiced in "respectable" company. Those who would have us believe that warfare is here to stay offer a number of explanations. First, the "inevitability" of war; second, the "benefits" of war; and third, the ends of war.

"Inevitability" of War

There is a seductive attraction in the solemn pronouncement that war is ordained by the nature of things. Human history certainly gives that proposition a ring of truth. It has commanded the attention of people everywhere and has devoured enormous quantities of the people's material substance.   It has been seen as a "necessity of existence".

War is inevitable, it is said, because of: first, human nature; second, the nature of society; third, economic interests; and fourth, population pressure.

Human Nature

The *human nature* explanation says war is unavoidable because people's competing interests lead to conflict. Just as individuals have conflicts with other individuals, communities have conflicts with other communities. By this unique leap of reason, individual proclivity for conflict explains organized mass killing. Domestic legal structures and social customs compel individuals to resolve differences peacefully, but differences between nations have traditionally been expected to result in war.

The war-is-inevitable reasoning says that if two people or two nations claim the same property which they cannot enjoy together, they become enemies.   There is ample evidence that some people enjoy a good fight, but there is also evidence that most people work out their differences peacefully.   There is no compelling reason to believe that fighting is better than reason, nor is there any proof that two people inevitability become enemies simply because they both want the same thing. Some may, but most will not.

The *human nature* explanation of war does not really explain how "mad-at-nobody" young soldiers can be made to fight. The regular army soldier is not there because of some inherent lust to kill. Indeed, it is the rare soldier who carries any deep hatred against an opposing soldier. Certainly, in preparation for battle, the soldier is conditioned to see the opposing solider as a monster because "he will kill me if I don't kill him first." However, left to their own devices, those with the greatest exposure to danger have no reason to hate their opponents before the fight begins. It is a rare soldier who is looking for opportunities to shoot people down. When armies employ mercenaries or when modern armies recruit "mad dog" killers, such soldiers are motivated by their own personal desires or warped personality, not by any normal human behavior.

The other side of this story is that the normal soldier does not lust to kill and destroy. They are simply "doing a job," taking pride in their disciplined ability to "follow orders and serve my country." The savagery of modern warfare results from a system gone wild, not from individuals driven by their lusts. Indeed, the front line soldier is the first to tell you that the battlefield is no glorious display of natural human traits.

The *human nature* argument also includes the right of self-defense. The right of people to defend themselves is found in the social codes of civilized societies everywhere. People are entitled to safety within their space, within their "aura". Individual self-defense is accepted as a natural consequence of living in civilized society. To compare personal self-defense with the methods of modern warfare, however, breaches sound reason. Self- defense is one thing; but the bombing of cities, the launching of rockets from sea, and the "neutralizing" of power plants with mortar fire is something else again.

The war-is-inevitable argument points to such human traits as hate, greed, lust, and avarice. It says the world will never rid itself of war because these base emotions will always cause people to fight. But if these emotions were uncontrollable, no civil society could exist. The fact is that civilization is made possible by the restraint of base emotions, not by their repeal. Communities found that two things were necessary: first, appealing to peoples' better instincts and making it safe to live by those instincts; second, defining unacceptable behavior and prescribing sanctions for such unsocial behavior. The world has very little chance of eliminating violations (crimes). But most people most of the time do not take out their frustrations on other people. When they do, however, they are penalized by the community.

Nature of Society

Anthropologists and sociologists explain that human communities usually pass through a nomadic period. Nomadic people were unconquerable and unassailable because they had nothing that anyone else wanted. Nomads carried their dwellings with them; so there was no plunder for an enemy to carry away. They were occasionally taken as slaves; but as moving targets they were quite invulnerable. While such an existence may seem idyllic in an age of military horror, it seems unlikely that mankind will escape war by returning to nomadic life.

When people organized themselves into communities, they did not assume they could eliminate personal conflict. But civil order did require some system for resolving conflicts. And almost universally, communities recognized peoples' rights to defend themselves. But self-defense did not embrace aggression, and strict limits were placed on what constituted self-defense: how much force was reasonable, how far it could be carried, and to what limits it could be carried.

As a collection of individuals, the nation inherits the individuals' right of self-defense. To put it another way, the prerogatives of the individual are "delegated" to the nation. An attack against a nation is an attack against its residents; so, by repulsing attack, the people are defending not only their nation but their individual rights.

There are some troubling issues, however, in this transfer of individual rights to the state. For instance, how does one identify the offending party? If one country sends an army into another country, who is the offending party? Is it the soldier? The officer directing that soldier? Or the commander of that officer? These questions pose their own dilemmas because the soldiers on the ground probably have no way of knowing the broader purposes of the conflict; they are there merely to follow orders.

There is another dilemma in comparing a state's right of self-defense to that of an individual. The two forms of space and the two forms of invasion are quite different. An individual's space moves with the person and cannot be occupied by two people at the same time. Both the space and the person exist or cease to exist at the same time. Geographical territory, on the other hand, does not disappear; it merely becomes occupied by people. The territory may fall into another's hands as a result of war, but it continues to exist.

As communities grew, "national security" led to all manner of defensive devices: walls, barricades, moats, and the like to keep the enemy at bay. While such defenses may seem quaint in the modern world, it was not very long ago—between the two world wars in the twentieth century—when Germany's Siegfried Line and France's Maginot Line were seen as impregnable defenses. The aim was to have sufficient power—or to be seen as having sufficient power—to discourage potential aggressors. World War II, of course, demonstrated the folly not only of those types of fortifications but of the premise that military power brings security. Indeed, every war has shown that the effective defenses of the last war are useless in the current one.

A state is entitled to defend itself, protect its sovereignty, and preserve its peace and tranquility. If the best defense is an offense and if there is reason to believe that another state is preparing an attack, it is possible to justify a first strike. What about an attack provoked by a series of inciting acts? Who is the aggressor in these cases? The Pearl Harbor attack on December 7, 1941, we were told, will "live in infamy." It was a brutal act by an imperialist power. But historical perspective has raised a number of questions about United States culpability. Provocation does not justify acts of terror, but it does cloud the issue of accountability. Did the Japanese military see it as a preemptive strike against a nation that had initiated the war?

When a nation bases its security on military power, it is easy to believe that offense is the best defense. Self-preservation might require a "first strike" when a nation believes that its neighbor is preparing to move. The "preemptive" attack becomes the first line of defense. Thucydides' comment about the Peloponnesian Wars in the fifth century BCE has a modern ring, "It is necessary to punish an enemy not only for what he does, but also beforehand for what he intends to do . . . the first to relax precaution would . . . . be also the first to suffer."

While the preemptive strike was a prudent and wise strategy in the ancient world, the modern world universally condemns it. It has not totally vanished, of course, but the international community exacts a high price from the nation that attacks first. At the end of the twentieth century the world is still living with China's brutal invasion of Tibet. The Soviet Union was unable to submerge the cultures of Moldavia or Estonia when it absorbed them after World War I. Whether the Chinese are able to subjugate the Tibetan people remains to be seen, but Tibet has survived centuries of oppression before. This harsh and forbidding environment was quite inhospitable to the Chinese who emigrated there. And the world community will not let China forget the barbarity of its invasion. The Nobel Prize committee focused the world's attention on the issue when it gave its Peace Prize to the Dalai Lama in 1989.

Another rationalization for initiating war is the intransigence of opponents. Again we find an object lesson in the ancient world struggle between Athens and Sparta. The irony is that the ultimate triumph of Sparta cut short what might have been another great period in Greek history, while the victorious Spartans, obsessed with military prowess, left the world no significant culture.

The preoccupation with "military superiority" lives on. Apologists for this doctrine point to the Cold War era of the twentieth century as proof for the wisdom of their idea. In the military frenzy that followed World War II, the greater might of one "Super Power" brought the other to its knees and ended the Cold War. Whatever sense of security came to the world after the Cold War, however, came because of the <u>reduction</u> in military forces. When the military forces were at their most formidable levels, the world was most insecure. The lessons of history are clear: a state which relies on the sword must forever be prepared to defend itself by the sword. Both Gibbon in his monumental work, *The Decline and Fall of the Roman Empire*, and Arnold Toynbee in his meticulous multi-volume, *A Study of History*, showed how reliance on military power destroys every nation seduced by its lure. It is when people turn their creative energies to social, cultural, and technological achievement that great civilizations arise.

What did the two "super powers" prove in their Cold War? The United States in Vietnam and the Soviet Union in Afghanistan learned that overwhelming military power can not break the will of a people determined to maintain their independence. In addition, in the modern world, sanctions of the international community have a power of their own to turn the spotlight of world attention on brutal treatment of native populations.

Economic Interests

Nations are attracted by abundance in their neighbors' resources: verdant pastures, rivers and lakes, commercial access to the sea, mineral deposits, manufacturing plants, and other industrial treasures. With attractive assets nearby, it is easy for a nation to convince itself of the "unfairness" in someone else having so much while "we have so little." Perhaps the neighbor also has a surplus of productive people who would make excellent craftsmen—or soldiers.

Military adventures for economic gain can be found on every page of human history. One may doubt that economic motivations are at the root of all wars; but there is no question that economics and politics are closely related. The Russian empire sought for centuries to obtain ice-free ports; France and Germany quarreled over Alsace-Lorraine; and Japan longed for the resources of Northern Manchuria. And how many wars have been fought over oil and banana plantations! In the modern world it can be mighty hazardous to possess oil resources while living next door to a reckless marauder.

The craving for land and physical treasures drove the European colonial powers to wars of conquest throughout the Western Hemisphere, and the booty that flowed from the new world burdened the hold of many a ship. In the modern world, there are rich advantages in gaining control over markets, technologies, or natural resources.

While the drive for economic gain has fueled many a military adventure, this does not mean that economic benefits always flow from war. Indeed, in modern warfare whatever potential advantage may be gained from military victory is lost in the disruption of commerce and the destruction of economic resources. Further, there is ample evidence that commercial advantage may just as easily go to the defeated. The cases of Japan and Germany after World War II are well known.

The victor in modern military conflict may suffer more economic distress than gain; although it may not be apparent at war's end. The tremendous industrial production of World War II in the United States, for example, was purchased at the cost of governmental regulation and control. Governmental regulation was accepted then as necessary to assure fair value during the war. However, excessive government intervention became a hindrance to business efficiency in the postwar years, particularly in the so-called defense industries where government bureaucrats literally invaded corporate management.

There was another more crippling dimension to American industrial might that had its origin in World War II. The extravagant prosperity of American business during and immediately after the war deluded the titans of industry. They began to believe that United States industry was impregnable and that the American economy was invincible. Industrialists from throughout the world came to learn about the U. S. miracle. As it turns out, they learned all too well.

In the unbounded prosperity of World War II and its aftermath, a "quick buck" psychology resulted in long-term decisions based on short-term premises. Business leaders, acting as though U.S. preeminence was permanent, relaxed their standards; and products from other countries took over market after market all around the world, including markets within the United States itself.

If one assumes that the United States' economic interests made its participation in World War II inevitable, does that also mean that war assured its world economic superiority? Some industrialists acted as though this were the case. The only inevitability in this process is that war disrupts economic security. In the case of the United States, economic gain from the war ultimately overwhelmed sound business judgments. World War II demonstrated that war is the great economic destabilizer. The disruption of shipping lanes, the destruction of plants and docks, and damage to factories and products are but the visible price of war. The fact is that modern warfare denies commercial advantage to any side. War in the modern world is nothing short of economic calamity.

Population Pressure

It is one of the myths in history that wars are caused by over-population. Thomas Hobbes in his classic work *Leviathan*, called upon war to eliminate the problem, "When all the world is overcharged with inhabitants, then the last remedy of all is war, which provideth for every man, by victory or death." War will rid the world of excess mouths to feed. There have been periods of mass starvation in human history, but there is little evidence that nations have consciously chosen war as a way of reducing their populations.

In his 1968 book, *The Population Bomb*, Paul Ehrlich startled the world by dire warnings that overpopulation was a ticking bomb waiting to destroy civilized life. People who study such matters had been talking about the perils of over-population for decades, but Ehrlich's predictions caught the public's attention as nothing had before. The story of population explosion goes something like this: when there are more people than the resources of the world can support, mass famine and desperate human migrations occur. When some have less than enough to eat while others have more, the have-nots will attempt to even out the rations. Ultimately, this could lead to wars of mass annihilation, even genocide.

There is no doubt that excess population—that is, more people than the world's resources can support—contributes to social distress and conflict. There are, however, several questionable issues in the proposition that population pressure makes war inevitable. In the first place, those who suffer from the deprivations of overpopulation do not have the energy or resources to wage war against anyone. A country's leaders could use its citizens' misery to divert their attention to outside issues, thereby keeping them from probing too deeply into why conditions are so bad in their own country. Distracted from their domestic agonies, citizens could "take it out" on a neighbor. But it is not the citizens suffering malnutrition who rise up in arms, nor are they the ones to benefit. It is the power-seeking leader who uses the peoples' plight to justify their aggression.

An imbalance of population may very well make mass starvation inevitable, as the world saw in Africa in the 1980's and 1990's. But these are not the elements that make war inevitable. Who could claim, for instance, that those migrating masses of starving men, women, and children on the African plains posed a military threat to anyone?

Common sense dictates that population should be kept in balance with the earth's capability of sustaining life. Overpopulation will indeed affect the quality—or perhaps even the survival—of human life. It is folly to ignore the problem or to assume that it will work itself out. At the same time, however, the pressures of excess population do not explain the origins of war.

Summary
If war were really so inevitable, why does it take such elaborate argument to persuade people to fight? War's true intention is papered over with glossy fantasies. People are told that war will "protect and defend freedom" or "make the world safe for democracy" when the real aim is to gain commercial advantage; "repulse an invader" when the goal is to capture an oil field; or "protect ethnic minorities" when the reason is ancient religious animosity.

Wars, of course, have had a dreadful impact on human life; but the attention given to them in the telling of human history is grossly overbalanced. The overwhelming preponderance of human time and energy has been spent in peaceful pursuits, while war has captured an inordinate portion of both human and material resources. Civilizations are enriched not by the glories of war but by the inspirations of a Taj Mahal, a Mona Lisa, a symphony, a sailing vessel, a university campus, or a cathedral.

A thin veneer of civilization barely conceals the sinister forces that threaten it, but that veneer is all the world has. Mankind's ultimate challenge remains the harnessing of creative talents in a human brotherhood envisioned by the prophets and foretold by the universal human spirit.

"Benefits" of War
Human imagination has fabricated quite an array of benefits for this monstrous enterprise. The claimed virtues of warfare are of two types: first, benefits to the participant; and second, benefits to society.

<u>Personal "Benefits"</u>

Although in the modern age there is much less talk about the glory of war, it occasionally creeps into patriotic orations. Ancient civilizations trumpeted the heroic qualities of the warrior, and in the modern world military men parade their gold braided uniforms. In Homer's *Iliad* the Greek warrior Sarpedon relished his elevated status, "The choicest portions are served us and our cups are kept brimming, and . . . men look up to us as though we are gods."

War was sprightly and full of adventure. It purged one of slothful and wicked ways, offering an escape from the dull and sleepy times of peace. Indeed, prolonged peace would degrade the character of the nation by breeding self-interest, cowardice, and effeminacy. War would bring out the manly qualities of courage, bravery, and heroism.

War was the ultimate in camaraderie, where the common shedding of blood in battle fashioned a true brotherhood. It was an antidote for idleness, a place "to evaporate the too vehement heat of youth." There was a "sublime" quality in this contest of heart and spirit. It drew strength from the soul.

The heroic qualities of superior strength and courage may have seemed plausible in the Middle Ages, but they have a hollow ring to the modern ear. While modern war still generates an intense brotherhood among soldiers, the trauma of seeing the men on either side of you blown apart sears the soul in everlasting agony. Hear this soldier who fought in one of the bloody battles in Vietnam: "If people have never walked a battlefield of dead and decaying bodies, they should not talk about the glories of war. There is none."

There is bravery and self-sacrifice in battle, but that is the result of human qualities, not the qualities of war. Selfless acts of courage occur in calamities everywhere—the rescue of people trapped in a smashed automobile, a child clinging to log in a flooded river, or a person trapped inside an earthquake-collapsed house. As heroic as it is to save the life of another human being, one would certainly not glorify the calamity because it brought out compassion in the rescuer. Courageous people who place themselves in harm's way to protect another are not searching for personal glory.

Social "Benefits"

If war brings glory to the soldier, it must also bring glory to his country. But who deserves the glory, the attacked or the attacker? Certainly not the attacker, you say. But aggressors also claim they are fighting for freedom for the oppressed people of another land. Who is the judge—the victor or the vanquished?

In his master work, *The Decline and Fall of the Roman Empire* Edward Gibbon describes the Crusades. These were "wars of liberation", a term not unfamiliar to the modern ear.

> *The two hundred years of the crusades . . . appear to me to have checked rather than forwarded the maturity of Europe. The lives and labours of millions which were buried in the East would have been more profitably employed in the improvement of their native country: the accumulated stock of industry and wealth would have overflowed in navigation and trade; and the Latins would have been enriched and enlightened by a pure and friendly correspondence with the climates of the East.*

Another claim is that war stimulates creativity and spurs innovation and productivity. The supreme commitment of war brings out the noblest qualities of human nature and leads to exceptional attainment. War is an incentive for new invention and new technology. To be sure, scientific advances have occurred in wartime; but the effort devoted to designing and producing instruments of destruction makes no contribution to civil society. Some discoveries may turn out to have civilian application, but how much more could have been accomplished if the total effort were devoted to civilian purposes!

War is said to have a purifying quality. In the same way that winds blowing across the ocean purify the waters, so war purges society of the stultification bred of perpetual peace. War checks unrest at home and offers exciting adventures abroad. As the farmer prunes his trees to improve the fruit, war clears the community of too many bodies. Society is enriched by eliminating the "useless" members. How nice for the ones left! Who decides which ones are useless?

In the anticommunist hysteria of the mid-twentieth century, the cry was, "I would rather be dead than red." Presumably, this meant that life would not be worth living in a communist state and that the clash of ideologies must ultimately be settled on the battlefield. But the centralized tyrannies of communism in the Soviet Union and Eastern Europe ultimately collapsed from their own internal failures in the 1980's, not from any test on the battlefield. Before the downfall of those regimes, there were many signs of disaffection dating back to the uprisings in Czechoslovakia in 1968 and in Hungary in 1956. It is legitimate to speculate that the communist regimes of Eastern Europe would have collapsed earlier if the Soviets had been unable to point to a hostile world on the other side of the communist curtain.

As it turned out, the attempts to "defeat communism" with military force—in Korea and Vietnam—served only to consolidate the power of those regimes and extend the sway of their rulers against outside "imperialists."

The cleansing qualities of warfare are presumed to prepare the way for the rule of law. The victor in a noble cause will establish a principled regime. This presumes that victory goes to the just, a claim that would be difficult to prove. One wonders how Attila the Hun or Ivan the Terrible would fit this scenario. The French saw the Reign of Terror and a counter-revolution followed by the disastrous Napoleonic wars and restoration of the monarchy. The Russian Revolution was followed by a devastating civil war and the ultimate rise of a communist dictatorship. Franco in Spain had also been seen as a savior. South America's history is a painful chronicle of one tyrant overthrowing another, and the people remained as oppressed under one as the other.

Proponents of the arms buildup in the United States after World War II contended that the Soviet Union threatened world domination and that United States military supremacy was necessary to preserve freedom. There are valid doubts about these contentions.

First, Soviet buildup was fueled by fear of Western motivations. The Soviets were well aware that many people in the West were advocating destruction of the Soviet Union. The withholding of reconstruction aid created further animosities and deepened suspicions. Soviet fear was further compounded by the postwar strategy to surround the Soviet Union with military bases. On those occasions when Soviet troops occupied other countries—as in Hungary and Czechoslovakia—they saw these nations as buffers against potential European threats.

This is not an apology for Soviet strategy or a justification of its foreign policy but rather a reminder that the treatment of the Soviet Union by the Western powers after World War II was not unlike the treatment of Germany after World War I. They had their own agenda, and it turned out to be unfriendly to the West; but what would have happened if they had not been frozen out of the European recovery plan?

Second, a Soviet Union devastated by long years of war had pitifully few resources—and certainly no will—to threaten anyone. In later years when Stalin drained the Soviet economy to build an enormous military machine, the country was left economically crippled and probably unable to sustain major military expeditions. Certainly its Afghanistan adventure did not show its ability to execute a successful military campaign. Some scholars have observed that, except for the technology of its military, the Soviets had a "third world" domestic economy. The cumbersome and ineffective—and, as the world later learned, corrupt—governmental system would inevitably collapse of its own weight.

Did any war ever bring a truly better life? There may have been times when some people were better off after a war than before. But what price was paid for it, and why would war be given the credit? What about the people killed, the lands ravaged, the building ruined, the arts and treasures destroyed? Why are those who survive always willing to say the world is better off? Perhaps because they cannot ask all those who died or all those whose minds were destroyed by the horror of battle.

To question the positive consequences of war is not to say that tyrants are to be suffered lightly. But the rubble of war is fertile ground for the birth of tyranny. The United States, in the name of national security, has cooperated with dictators all over the world: Franco in Spain, Lon Nol in Cambodia, Somoza in Nicaragua, Pinochet in Chile. All through Latin America the United States supported military coups that simply replaced one dictator with another, and the landless peasant in whose names the revolutions were fought remained mostly landless.

While not much is said about it in the modern world, military adventures were once deemed essential to maintaining the virility of a nation. By going to war, leaders would prove their power abroad and secure their power at home by sapping the energy of their own people.

Pericles, speaking to the Athenians in the midst of the Peloponnesian Wars, reminded them that their country had the greatest name in the world because it had never retreated from the threat of attack and showed great valor in war. If the city sank into inaction, it would decay. As history knows, this advice led the Athenians against the even more committed warriors of Sparta whose searing passion for battle crushed the Athenians. The lesson is written in bold letters across the pages of history: those who live by the sword perish by the sword.

Putting aside all the sound and glory of war, let's give Aristotle the final word,

> It must appear very strange that the statesman should be always considering how he can dominate and tyrannize over others, whether they will it or not. How can that which is not even lawful be the business of the statesman or the legislator? Unlawful it certainly is to rule without regard to justice, for *there may be might where there is no right* . . . . What men affirm to be unjust and inexpedient in their own case they are not ashamed of practicing toward others; they demand just rule for themselves, but where other men are concerned they care nothing about it. (*Politics*)

Ends of War

War was expected to bring honor and glory to the nation. The Macedonians, to stimulate warlike qualities, honored only those soldiers who had killed an enemy. The Romans, it is said, were greedy for praise, prodigal of wealth, desirous of great glory, and content with a moderate fortune; but, of these, glory was the most ardently loved. By his valor, the soldier brought honor to his land—assuming that he also returned with some booty. In the hour of victory, the wealth of nations became the rewards of war. The tradition of spoils persists, and fighting men have always brought home trophies.

If the end of war is conquest, Machiavelli (in *The Prince*) has some advice for the conqueror: if the conquered are accustomed to the rule of a prince, you will have an easy time of it; but if they have enjoyed liberty, they will never allow the memory of their former freedom to rest. You must either destroy them or keep an eye on them by residing there.

Abraham Lincoln had intended for the Southern states to be brought back into the Union without recrimination. But such was not to be. Lincoln's ends were noble, but the seeds of hate sown by that conflict continued to sprout in every part of the land. Over one hundred years later they were still sprouting.

The mischief done in the name of war is explained by Montesquieu:

What good might not the Spaniards have done to the Mexicans. They had a mild religion to impart to them; but they filled their heads with frantic superstition. They might have set slaves at liberty; they made freemen slaves. They might have undeceived them with regard to the abuse of human sacrifices; instead of that they destroyed them.

The noblest treaty of peace ever mentioned in history is, in my opinion, that which Gelon made with the Carthaginians. He insisted upon their abolishing the custom of sacrificing their children. After having defeated three hundred thousand Carthaginians, he required a condition that was advantageous only to themselves, or rather he stipulated in favor of human nature. (*The Spirit of Laws*)

War came to be seen as the only recourse when states could not settle their differences with talk. When it is said that nations disagree, however, what this really means is that the <u>leaders</u> cannot agree. Certainly the farmer of one country would usually have little reason to be angry at the farmer of another. When individuals have differences with other individuals, there are expected to settle them peacefully; yet statesmen see the military strike as the ultimate tool of diplomacy. The United States Secretary of State in the Reagan administration, for example, often advocated military strikes to enforce policies that could not be achieved through diplomacy. The irony here was that the Defense Department, grown cautious about open-ended military engagements, resisted calls for "diplomatic military strikes."

War has also been seen as a means for personal redemption. During the Crusades, for example, Christians saw it as their duty to retrieve lands from the infidel and restore Christian control. God had bestowed the land upon them, and they demanded their inheritance.

When it is claimed that the aim of war is to restore the peace, for whom is the peace? The vanquished? The victors? The dead? It is the ultimate mockery to say that war has brought peace. What right does one person have to ask another to die so the living can have peace? What kind of a peace is it? Nations honor those who die in war, but did they ask to die so they could be honored? In the celebrations that honor the commanders who send soldiers into battle, what peace is there for the parents whose children lie dead?

Conclusion

These, then, are some of the issues that trouble the pacifist about the inevitability, the benefits, and the ends of war. While this sketches some elements of pacifist belief, more complete discussions will be found in the books listed in the Bibliography.

The pacifist view of war is deeply personal, but it is also social.

Human life is sacred, and one person has no right to take the life of another.

War is an abomination whose presumed benefits are overshadowed by the evil consequences.

War will cease when the people demand that political leaders resolve international differences peacefully and when they refuse to be drafted for war.

Appendix A

Civilian Public Service
Religious Denominations
(Number of Members in CPS)

Advent Christian	3
African Methodist Episcopal	1
Ambassadors of Christ	1
Antinsky Church	1
Apostolic	2
Apolostic Christian Church	3
Apolostic Faith Movement	2
Assemblies of God	32
Assembly of Christians	1
Assembly of Jesus Christ	1
Associated Bible Students	36
Baptist, Northern	178
Baptist, Southern	45
Berean Church	1
Bible Students School	1
Body of Christ	1
Brethren Assembly	1
Broadway Tabernacle	1
Buddhist	1
Calvary Gospel Tabernacle	1
Catholic, Roman	149
Christadelphians	127
Christian Brethren	1
Christian Catholic Apostolic	1

Christian Convention	1
Christian Jew	1
Christian & Missionary Alliance	5
Christian Missionary Society	1
Christian Scientist	14
Christ's Church	1
Christ's Church of the Golden Rule	3
Christ's Followers	1
Christ's Sanctified Holy Church	2
Church (The)	1
Church of the Brethren	1353
Church of Christ	199
Church of Christ Holiness	1
Church of Christian Fellowship	1
Church of England	1
Church of the First Born	11
Church of the Four Leaf Clover	1
Church of the Full Gospel, Inc.	1
Church of God of Abrahamic Faith	13
Church of God of Apostolic Faith	4
Church of God Assembly	1
Church of God in Christ	12
Church of God, Guthrie, Okla.	5
Church of God, Holiness	6
Church of God, Indiana	43
Church of God & Saints of Christ	12
Church of God, Sardis	1
Church of God, Seventh Day	21
Church of God, Tennessee (2 bodies)	7
Church of God (several bodies)	33
Church of the Gospel	1
Church of Jesus Christ	1
Church of Jesus Christ, Sullivan, Indiana	15
Church of Light	1
Church of the Living God	2
Church of the Lord Jesus Christ	1
Church of the Open Door	1
Church of the People	1
Church of Radiant Life	1

Church of Truth (New Thought)   1
Circle Mission (Father Divine)   10
Community Churches   12
Congregational Christian   209
Defenders   1
Disciples Assembly of Christians   1
Disciples of Christ   78
Dunkard Brethren   30
Doukhobor (Peaceful Progressive Society)   3
Elim Covenant Church   1
Emmissaries of Divine Light   1
Episcopal   88
Essenes   5
Ethical Culture, Society of   3
Evangelical   50
Evangelical-Congregational   2
Evangelical Mission Convent (Swedish)   11
Evangelical & Reformed   101
Evangelistic Mission   3
Faith Tabernacle   18
Federated Church   1
Filipino Full Gospel   1
Fire Baptized Holiness   3
First Apolostic   1
First Century Gospel   28
First Divine Assn. in America, Inc.   16
First Missionary Church   2
Followers of Jesus Christ   4
Four Square Gospel   2
Free Holiness   3
Free Methodist   6
Free Pentecostal Church of God   4
Free Will Baptist   2
Friends, Society of [Quakers]   951
Full Gospel Conference of the World, Inc.   4
Full Gospel Mission   3
Full Salvation Union   1
Galilean Mission   1
German Baptist Brethren   157

German Baptist Convention of N.A.	4
Glory Tabernacle	2
God's Bible School	1
Gospel Century	1
Gospel Chapel	2
Gospel Hall	1
Gospel Meeting Assembly	1
Gospel Mission	2
Gospel Tabernacle	2
Gospel Temple	1
Grace Chapel	1
Grace Truth Assembly	1
Gracelawn Assembly	1
Greek Apostolic	1
Greek Catholic	1
Greek Orthodox	1
Hepzibah Faith	6
Hindu Universal	1
Holiness Baptist	1
Holiness General Assembly	1
House of David	2
House of Prayer	1
Humanist Society of Friends	2
Immanuel Missionary Association	13
Independent Assembly of God	2
Independent Church	2
Institute of Religious Society & Philosophy	1
Interdenominational	16
International Missionary Society	2
Jehovah's Witnesses	409
Jennings Chapel	9
Jewish	60
Kingdom of God	1
Kingdom Missionaries	1
Latin American Council of Christian Churches	1
Lemurian Fellowship	9
Lord our Righteousness	1
Lutheran (nine synods)	108
Lutheran Brethren	2

Mazdaznam	1
Megiddo Mission	1
Mennonites	4,665
Methodist	673
Missionary Church Association	8
Moody Bible Institute	2
Mormons (Church of Jesus Christ of Latter Day Saints)	10
Moravian	2
Moslem	1
Multnomah School of the Bible	2
National Baptist Convention, U.S.A., Inc.	5
National Church of Positive Christianity	5
Nazarene, Church of the	23
New Age Church	3
Norwegian Evangelical Free Church	2
Old German Baptist	7
Open Bible Standard	1
Orthodox Parsee Z.	2
Overcoming Faith Tabernacle	1
Oxford Movement	1
Pentecostal Assemblies of Jesus Christ	1
Pentecostal Assemblies of the World	3
Pentecostal Assembly	2
Pentecostal Church, Inc.	2
Pentecostal Evangelical	1
Pentecostal Holiness	6
People's Christian Church	1
People's Church	3
Pilgrim Holiness	3
Pillar of Fire	1
Pillar and Ground of the Truth	1
Placabel Council of Latin Am. Churches	1
Plymouth Brethren	12
Plymouth Christian	1
Presbyterian, U.S.	5
Presbyterian, U.S.A.	192
Primitive Advent	2
Progressive Brethren	1

Quakertown Church	1
Reading Road Temple	1
Reformed Church of America (Dutch)	15
Reformed Mission of the Redeemer	1
Rogerine Quakers (Pentecostal Friends)	3
Rosicrusian	1
Russian Molokan (Christian Spiritual Jumpers)	76
Russian Old Testament Church	1
Saint's Mission	1
Salvation Army	1
Sanctified Church of Christ	1
Scandinavian Evangelical	1
Schwenkfelders (Apostolic Christian Church, Inc.)	1
School of the Bible	1
Serbian Orthodox	1
Seventh Day Adventist	17
Seventh Day Adventist, Reformed	1
Seventh Day Baptist	3
Shiloh Tabernacle	1
Spanish Church of Jesus Christ	1
Spiritual Mission	1
Spiritualist	1
Swedenborg	1
Taoist	1
Theosophists	14
Trinity Tabernacle	1
Triumph the Church & Kingdom of God in Christ	1
Triumph Church of the New Age	1
True Followers of Christ	1
Truelight Church of Christ	1
Twentieth Century Bible School	5
Unitarians	44
Union Church (Berea, Ky.)	4
Union Mission	1
United Baptist	1
United Brethren	27

United Christian Church	2
United Holiness Church, Inc.	1
United Holy Christian Church of Am.	2
United International Young People's Assembly	2
United Lodge of Theosophists	2
United Pentecostal Council of the Assemblies of God in America	1
United Presbyterian	12
Unity	3
Universal Brotherhood	1
Universalist	2
War Resister's League	46
Wesleyan Methodist	8
World Student Federation	2
Young Men's Christian Association [YMCA]	2
Zoroastrian	2
Total affiliated with denominations:	10,838
Non-affiliated	449
Denominations unidentified	709
Grand Total:	11,996

Appendix B

Civilian Public Service
Project Units

I. BASE CAMPS

A. U. S. Forest Service (30 units)
**

1.	Manistee (Copemish), Michigan (BSC)
2.	San Dimas (Glendora), California (AFSC)
8.	Marietta, Ohio (BSC-MCC)
9.	Petersham, Massachusetts (AFSC)
10.	Royalston, Massachusetts (AFSC)
11.	Ashburnham, Massachusetts (AFSC)
12.	Cooperstown, New York (AFSC)
13.	Bluffton, Indiana (MCC)
15.	Stoddard, New Hampshire (ACCO)
16.	Kane, Pennsylvania (BSC)
17.	Manistee (Stronach), Michigan (BSC)
21.	Cascade Locks, Oregon (BSC)
28.	Medaryville (Jasper-Pulaski), Indiana (MCC)
30.	Walhalla, Michigan (BSC)
31.	Camino (Placerville), California (MCC)
32.	West Campton, New Hampshire (AFSC)
35.	North Fork, California (MCC)
36.	Santa Barbara, California (BSC)
37.	Coleville, California (AFSC)
42.	Wellston, Michigan (BSC)
48.	Marienville, Pennsylvania (BSC)

53. Gorham, New Hampshire (AFSC)
54. Warner, New Hampshire (ACCO)
56. Waldport, Oregon (BSC)
76. Glendora, California (AFSC) and (SSS)
89. Oakland, Maryland (AFSC)
103. Missoula (Huson), Montana (MCC)
134. Belden, California (BSC)
148. Minersville, California (SSS)
149. Various Locations - U.S. Forest Service Res.(AFSC), (BSC),(SSS)

B. Soil Conservation Service
(19 Units)
4. Grottoes, Virginia (MCC)
5. Colorado Springs, Colorado (MCC)
6. Lagro, Indiana (BSC)
7. Magnolia, Arkansas (BSC)
14. Merom, Indiana (AFSC)
18. Denison, Iowa (MCC)
20. Wells Tannery (Sliding Hill), Pennsylvania (MCC)
22. Henry, Illinois (MCC)
23. Coshocton, Ohio (AFSC)
24. Hagerstown, Maryland (MCC)
    Williamsport, Maryland (BSC)
    Boonsboro, Maryland (MCC)
    Clearspring, Maryland (MCC)
    New Windsor, Maryland (BSC)
25. Weeping Waters, Nebraska (MCC)
33. Fort Collins, Colorado (MCC)
40. Howard, Pennsylvania (MCC)
46. Big Flats, New York (AFSC), (SSS)
52. Powellsville, Maryland (AFSC), (MCC)
64. Terry, Montana (MCC) *
67. Downey, Idaho (MCC)
94. Trenton, North Dakota (AFSC) *
138. Lincoln, Nebraska (MCC)
    * Joint Sponsorship with Farm Security Administration

C. National Park Service (9 Units)

3.   Patapsco (Elkridge), Maryland (AFSC)
19. Buck Creek (Marion), North Carolina (AFSC)
29. Lyndhurst, Virginia (BSC)
39. Galax, Virginia (MCC)
45. Luray, Virginia (MCC)
55. Belton, Montana (MCC)
107. Three Rivers, California (MCC)
108. Gatlinburg, Tennessee (AFSC), (SSS)
121. Bedford, Virginia (BSC)

Hawaii (SSS)

D. Bureau of Reclamation (4 Units)

57. Hill City, South Dakota (MCC)
60. Lapine, Oregon (MCC)
111. Mancos, Colorado (SSS)
128. Lapine, Oregon (SSS)

E. Farm Security Administration (2 Units)
* See Soil Conservation Service above

F. Fish and Wildlife Service (2 Units)

34. Bowie (Patuxent), Maryland (BSC), (SSS)
135. Germfask, Michigan (SSS)

G. General Land Office (1 Unit)

59. Elkton, Oregon (AFSC)

II. SPECIAL PROJECTS

A. State Mental Hospitals (40 Units)

41. Williamsburg, Virginia (AFSC), (SSS)
44. Staunton, Virginia (MCC)
47. Sykesville, Maryland (BSC)
49. Philadelphia, Pennsylvania (AFSC),
       (SSS)
51. Fort Steilacoom, Washington (BSC)
58. Farmhurst, Delaware (MCC)

63. Marlboro, New Jersey (MCC)
66. Norristown, Pennsylvania (MCC)
68. Norwich, Connecticut (BSC)
69. Cleveland, Ohio (AFSC), (MCC)
70. Dayton, Ohio (BSC)
71. Lima, Ohio (MCC)
72. Macedonia, Ohio (MCC)
73. Columbus, Ohio (BSC)
74. Cambridge, Maryland (BSC), (ABHMS)
75. Medical Lake, Washington (AFSC)
77. Greystone Park, New Jersey (MCC)
78. Denver, Colorado (MCC)
79. Provo, Utah (MCC)
81. Middletown, Connecticut (AFSC), (SSS)
82. Newton, Connecticut (BSC)
83. Warren, Pennsylvania (AFSC), (SSS)
84. Concord, New Hampshire (AFSC), (SSS)
85. Howard, Rhode Island (MCC)
86. Mt. Pleasant, Iowa (MCC)
87. Battleboro, Vermont (AFSC), (SSS)
88. Augusta, Maine (BSC)
90. Ypsilanti, Michigan (MCC)
93. Harrisburg, Pennsylvania (MCC)
109. Marion, Virginia (BSC)
110. Allentown, Pennsylvania (MCC)
118. Wernersville, Pennsylvania (MCC)
120. Kalamazoo, Michigan (MCC)
122. Winnebego, Wisconsin (MCC)
131. Cherokee, Iowa (MWPC)
136. Skillman, New Jersey (ABHMS)
137. Independence, Iowa (EARC)
139. Logansport, Indiana (DOC)
143. Catonsville, Maryland (MCC)
144. Poughkeepsie, New York (MCC)

B. General Hospitals (3 Units)
26. Chicago, Illinois (ACCO)
50. New York, New York (AFSC)
61. Durham, North Carolina (MWPC)

C. Veterans' Administration Hospitals (3 Units)
80. Lyons, New Jersey (BSC)
150. Livermore, California (MCC)
151. Roseberg, Oregon (MCC)

D. State Training Schools (16 Units)
62. Cheltenham, Maryland (AFSC)
91. Mansfield Depot, Connecticut (BSC)
92. Vineland, New Jersey (MCC)
95. Buckley, Washington (BSC)
102. Owings Mills, Maryland (ACCO
105. Lynchburg, Virginia (BSC)
117. Lafayette, Rhode Island (MCC)
119. New Lisbon, New Jersey (AFSC), (SSS)
123. Union Grove, Wisconsin (MCC)
124. Stockley, Delaware (AFSC), (SSS)
127. American Fork, Utah (MCC)
129. Spring Grove (Pennhurst), Pennsylvania (AFSC),
        (SSS)
130. Pownal, Maine (AFSC), (SSS)
132. Laurel, Maryland (AFSC), (SSS)
142. Woodbine, New Jersey (MCC)
147. Tiffin, Ohio (MCC)

E. Public Health Service (2 Units)
27. Tallahassee, Florida (BSC)
       Mulberry, Florida (MCC)
       Orlando, Florida (AFSC)
       Gainesville, Florida (BSC)
141. Gulfport, Mississippi (MCC)

F. Puerto Rico Reconstruction Administration (1 Unit)
43. Castaner Project, Adjuntas (BSC)

Aibonita (MCC) Zalduondo (AFSC)

St. Thomas, Virgin Islands (BSC)

G. *Office of Scientific Research and Development (32 Projects)*
115.   District of Columbia and Various Other Places
            (OSRD)
        1.   .Malaria, California Institute of Technology, Pasadena,
              California
        2.   Altitude Pressure, University of Southern California, Los
              Angeles, California
        3.   Altitude Pressure, Welfare Island Hospital, Welfare
              Island, New York
        4.   Life Raft Ration, Welfare Island Hospital, Welfare
Island,   New York
        5.   High Altitude, Welfare Island Hospital, Welfare Island,
              New York
        6.   Frost Bite, Metropolitan Hospital, Welfare Island, New
              York.
        7.   Psycho-Acoustic, Harvard University, Cambridge,
              Massachusetts
        8.   Poison Gas, New York University, New York City, New
              York
        9.   Malaria, Stanford University, Stanford, California
       10.   Sea Water, Massachusetts General Hospital, Boston,
              Massachusetts
       11.   Malaria, Massachusetts General Hospital, Boston,
              Massachusetts
       12.   Weather, University of Michigan, Ann Arbor, Michigan
       13.   Sensory Device, Haskins Laboratories, New York City,
              New York
       14.   Cold Weather, University of Rochester, Rochester, New
              York
       15.   Climatology, Indiana University, Bloomington, Indiana
       16.   Physiological Hygiene, University of Michigan, Ann
              Arbor, Michigan
       17.   Starvation, University of Minnesota, Minneapolis,
              Minnesota

18. <u>Thiamine</u>, University of Minnesota, Minneapolis, Minn.
19. <u>Malaria</u>, Massachusetts Institute of Technology, Cam bridge, Massachusetts
20. <u>Physiology</u>, Ohio State University, Columbus, Ohio
21. <u>Physiology</u>, University of Rochester, Rochester, New York
22. <u>Malaria</u>, Goldwater Memorial Hospital, Rochester, New York
23. <u>Malaria</u>, University of Chicago, Chicago, Illinois
24. <u>Malaria</u>, Massachusetts General Hospital, Boston, Massachusetts
25. <u>Malaria</u>, Columbia University, New York City, New York
26. <u>Bed Rest</u>, New York Hospital, New York City, New York
27. <u>Bed Rest</u>, Cornell University, Ithaca, New York
28. <u>Cold Weather</u>, University of Illinois, Chicago, Illinois
29. <u>High Altitude</u>, University of Chicago, Chicago, Illinois
30. <u>Heat</u>, University of Illinois, Urbana, Illinois
31. <u>Diet-Altitude</u>, Northwestern University Medical School, Chicago, Illinois
32. <u>Aero Medical</u>, Mayo Clinic, Rochester, Minnesota

H. Office of the Surgeon General (9 Units)

140. Various Locations
 1. <u>Atypical Pneumonia</u>, Pinehurst, North Carolina
 2. <u>Jaundice</u>, Philadelphia, Pennsylvania
 3. <u>Neurotropic Virus</u>, New Haven, Connecticut
 4. <u>Life Raft Ration</u>, Welfare Island, New York
 5. <u>Frost Bite</u>, New York City, New York
 6. <u>Physiological Hygiene</u>, Ann Arbor, Michigan
 7. <u>Starvation</u>, Minneapolis, Minnesota
 8. <u>Nutrition</u>, Chicago, Illinois
 9. <u>Physiology</u>, Chicago, Illinois

I. Agriculture Experiment Station (9 Units)
- 104. Ames, Iowa (AFSC), (SSS)
- 106. Lincoln, Nebraska (MCC)
- 112. East Lansing, Michigan (BSC)
- 113. Waseca, Minnesota (BSC)
- 116. College Park, Maryland (BSC)
- 125. Orono, Maine (MCC)
- 126. Beltsville, Maryland (MCC)
- 133. Wooster, Ohio (AFSC), (SSS)
- 146. Ithaca, New York (MCC)

J. Dairy Farms (34 Units)
- 97. **Various Locations**
    1. San Joaquin County, California (MCC)
    2. El Paso County, Colorado (MCC)
    3. Hartford County, Connecticut (AFSC)
    4. McHenry County, Illinois (BSC)
    5. Worcester County, Massachusetts (MCC)
    6. Cecil County, Maryland (BSC)
    7. Harford County, Maryland (BSC)
    8. Montgomery County, Maryland (AFSC), (BSC)
    9. Queen Anne County, Maryland (MCC)
    10. Genessee County, Michigan (MCC)
    11. Lenawee County, Michigan (MCC)
    12. Hillsboro County, New Hampshire (MCC)
    13. Sussex County, New Jersey (BSC)
    14. Chenango County, New York (BSC)
    15. Delaware County, New York (BSC)
    16. Madison County, New York (BSC)
    17. Orange County, New York (BSC)
    18. St. Lawrence County, New York (BSC)
    19. Cuyahoga County, Ohio (MCC)
    20. Lorain County, Ohio (MCC)
    21. Summit County, Ohio (MCC)
    22. Wayne County, Ohio (MCC)
    23. Coos Bay, Oregon (BSC)
    24. Tillamook County, Oregon (MCC)
    25. Allegheny County, Pennsylvania (AFSC)(MCC)
    26. Lancaster County, Pennsylvania (MCC)

27. Susquehanna County, Pennsylvania (BSC)
28. York County, Pennsylvania (MCC)
29. King County, Washington (BSC), (MCC)
30. Dane County, Wisconsin (MCC)
31. Dodge County, Wisconsin (MCC)
32. Fond du Lac County, Wisconsin (MCC)
33. Green County, Wisconsin (MCC)
34. Outagamie County, Wisconsin (MCC)

K. Dairy Herd Testing (14 Units)
    100. Various Locations
      1. Connecticut (AFSC)
      2. Delaware (AFSC)
      3. Georgia (AFSC)
      4. Illinois (BSC)
      5. Iowa (MCC)
      6. Maine (MCC)
      7. Maryland (BSC)
      8. Michigan (MCC)
      9. New Jersey (BSC)
    10. New York (BSC)
    11. Pennsylvania (MCC)
    12. Virginia (BSC)
    13. Vermont (AFSC)
    14. West Virginia (BSC)

L. *Coast and Geodetic Survey*
    98. Various Locations (SSS)

M. *Weather Bureau*
    114. Mount Weather, Bluemont, Virginia (BSC)

Appendix B

KEY

Sponsoring Agencies

ACCO	Association of Catholic Conscientious Objectors
ABHMS	American Baptist Home Mission Society
AFSC	American Friends Service Committee
BSC	Brethren Service Committee
DOC	Disciples of Christ
EARC	Commission on Christian Social Action of the Evangelical and Reformed Church
MCC	Mennonite Central Committee
MWPC	Methodist World Peace Commission
SSS	Selective Service System

** Civilian Public Service Unit Number. Unit numbers were assigned as each unit was established, not necessarily in the order in which they were opened. Unit No. 3 In Patapsco, Maryland, was the first unit opened in May, 1941. The following units were suspended before opening: 38, Salem, Oregon; 65, Utica, New York; 96, Rochester, Minnesota; 99, Chungking, China; 101, Philadelphia, Pennsylvania; 145, Wassaic, New York.

Appendix C

C. P. S. Survey
Questionnaire

1. Did your CPS experience change or confirm the beliefs and attitudes you had when you entered camp? How?

2. Do you think that, in having been a CO, you see the conditions in society differently from others? In what ways?

3. Do you think the approach of the CO (that is, the refusal to participate in war, the willingness to stand with unpopular minorities, the radical commitment to nonviolence) contributes to alleviating the stresses of modern life? How?

4. Did you find the "stubborn conviction" entailed in being a CO showing up in other facets of your life?

   — Did it lead you to take strong stands on other issues? In what ways?

5. What types of work, activities, or social services have you undertaken that were stimulated by your CO position?

   — What have been your occupations or occupation since World War II?

6. Do you share a feeling of close kinship with others who went through the CPS experience? If so, to what do you attribute this kinship? (Do you think it was the similarity of beliefs, faith, or values; was it the close and confining group life; or was it some thing else?)

7. In reviewing your life, how do you rate the CPS experience? (Positive, Negative, Significant, etc.)

8. Other beliefs or activities which were affected by your CO position?

9. How long were you in CPS? (years, months)

10. To what camps/facilities/projects were you assigned?

Signature, Address

Date

The answers to these questions covered the following range of subjects:

I. IMPACT OF CPS

A. *On Individual Beliefs*
   1. Confirmed
   2. Changed
   3. Not Changed/Unaffected
   4. Little Change/Effect
   5. Strengthened, Broadened, Enriched, Solidified, Reinforced, Intensified, Matured, Deepened, Clarified, Expanded, Wid-

ened, Elaborarted, Sharpened, Mellowed, Verified

   6. Increased Understanding/Social Justice/Sensitivity/of: Religious Principles/Tolerance/Nonviolence/Appreciation/Other People
   7. Tested/Challenged Conventional Views

B. On Individual Life
1. Significant/Personal Improvement. "Standing Up"
2. Positive
3. Positive and Negative
4. Inadequate/Insufficient/Insignificant
5. No Impact/Nothing Positive
6. "Ground Down"
7. Time for maturing/Growth/Social Awareness
8. Intellectual Stimulation/Educational/Learning Experience
9. Incentive to Continue Education
10. Stimulation of Other Interests
11. Learning to Live With/Accept Others
12. Learning to Live With Little Money
13. Learning Conflict Resolution
14. Hindsight Regrets

C. On Solidarity with Other COs
1. Kinship/Comradeship/Bonding/Belonging/Harmony/Socializing/Support
2. Limited Solidarity/Some Kinship/Not Much Kinship
3. Absence, Weakness of Beliefs/Shared Beliefs, Values, Faith
4. "I was not alone"/Something in Common
5. Solidarity/Kinship Not Unique to CPS

D. Reactions to/Relations with Other Assignees
1. Types of People
2. Broad Range of Beliefs, Interests
3. Unconventional/Unfamiliar Ideas
4. Differences in Viewpoint
5. Friendships
6. Continuing Association

7. Little Continuing Association
8. Negative Reactions/Experiences

E. On Peace Movement/Religious Organizations

F. Administrative, Political Considerations
1. Positive
2. Negative
3. Neutral

G. *On Public*

1. Positive
2. Negative

H. *"Work of National Importance"*
1. Acceptance/Positive
2. Grudging Acceptance
3. Positive, Negative
4. Work Not As Significant As Other Matters
5. Criticism/Negative
6. Government/Public Recognition

I. *On Work Skills/Occupational Practices*
1. Acquisition of/Exposure to: Occupational Skills, Experience, Knowledge

II. IMPACT OF CO BELIEFS

A. *On CO's Individual Lives*
1. Inner Calmness/Fulfillment/Satisfaction/Clear Conscience, Contentment/Maturity/Self-Reliance/Sense of Self Worth
2. Enhanced/Benefitted Life
3. Values Became Part of Personality/Beliefs Strengthened Over Time
4. Personal Commitment: Way of Life/Search for Truth
5. Holding Firmly to Beliefs and Values/Rejecting Social Conformity
6. Gives Strength to Deal With Daily Life

Appendix C

7. Strength From Solidarity With Others Of Similar Beliefs
8. Acceptance of, Patience With, Tolerance of, Respect for, Empathy for Others
9. Religious Affiliation/ Church Activity/Religious Interest/Religious Experience
10. Fulfilling the Expectations of Others
11. Reacting to the Uncertainties, the Unknown, the Hostility of Others
12. Little Impact on Later Life
13. Acceptance by Others/Acceptance of Others
14. Separation from Others
15. Ostracism/Discrimination/Rejection/Isolation/ Persecution/Punishment/Alienation
16. Eases/Relieves/Reduces/Resolves: Tensions, Stress, Strain
17. Creates/Increases/Causes: Tensions, Stress, Strain
18. Has No Affect On/Does Not Relieve: Tensions, Stress, Strain
19. Both Reduces and Increases: Tensions, Stress, Strain
20. Should Not Reduce Stresses and Strains

B. On CO's Occupation/Avocation/Career
1. Selection of Occupation
2. Application In Occupation
3. Not Crucial/Relevant/Material
4. Detriment to Occupation
5. Not a Detriment to Occupation

C. On CO's Social Perceptions
1. Broadened/Intensified/Strengthened/Influenced/ Deepened: Awareness, Understanding, Evaluation of Social Needs
2. Taking Firm Positions On, Part In, Responsibility For: Other Issues, Activities
3. Sensitized Awareness of Being a Minority
4. Gained:Appreciation/Understanding/Tolerance/ Feelings/Sympathy/Identify/Rapport for: Position of/Needs of: Others/Minorities/ Underdog/Oppressed/Forgotten/ Underprivileged

5. Appreciation of heritage
6. Efficacy of the Strategy of Nonviolence
7. Breadth of Anti-War Sentiment
8. Awareness of the Nature and Power of Militarism
9. Understanding the Nature and Causes of War
10. Awareness/Understanding the Nature and Breadth of Human/Social Problems
11. Rejection of Authoritarian Methods and System
12. Relations With/Attitude Toward: Government/Politics/Conscription
13. Relations With/Attitude Toward: Organized Religion
14. Awareness of Need for Changes in Social Systems/Structures/Mores
15. Need for Changes in/Social Systems/Structures/Mores
16. As a CO, See Things Differently
17. As a CO, See Things Differently, But Do Not Act Differently
18. Common Beliefs, Solidarity With Non-COs.
19. Acceptance of/Resignation to Society As It Is
20. Difficulty of Effecting Change
21. Skepticism/Inhibition to Act/Disillusion With Social Institutions

III. IMPACT OF CO BELIEFS

A. *On Society*
1. Some Impact
2. Little Impact
3. Impact Unknown
4. On Established Social Systems and Structures
5. Hope for Acceptance of CO Ideas
6. Barriers to Acceptance of CO Ideas
7. Eases/Relieves/Reduces/Resolves: Conflict, Stress, Strain
8. Creates/Increases/Causes: Conflict, Stress, Strain
9. Has No Affect On/Does Not Relieve: Conflict, Stress, Strain
10. Should Not Reduce: Conflict, Stress, Strain

B. On Other People

1. Influence On/Changes In: Others' Beliefs/Perceptions
2. Acceptance of: Pacifist/CO Ideas
3. Rejection Of/ Reservation About: CO/Pacifist Ideas
4. Respect For COs
5. Eases/Relieves/Reduces/Resolves/ Relaxes: Conflict, Stress, Strain
6. Creates/Increases: Conflict, Stress, Strain

IV. APPLICATION OF CO IDEAS

A. Dealing With Individuals

1. Day-to-Day Affairs
2. Reinforcing Commitment to Nonviolence
3. Example in Personal Life
4. Psychotherapy
5. Support/Help To Others
6. Patience With/Understanding of Others
7. Allowance for Different Viewpoints
8. Sensitivity to One's Impact
9. Shortcoming in Applying Ideas

B. Dealing with Social, Political, and Economic Issues

1. Individual Testimony/Testifying to CO Ideas/Testifying Against The Military
2. Reconciliation/Overcoming Objections
3. Injustice/Human Rights/Human Dignity/Prejudice
4. Nonviolence, Peace Action
5. Environmental Protection
6. Resisting Peer Pressure/The Establishment/Social Norms
7. The Power of Belief in Change
8. Humility, Doubt About Knowing the Answers
9. Dissatisfaction With Extent of Personal Effort
10. Shortcomings of CO Presentation

C. Changing Social, Political, and Economic Systems and Structures
    1.   Concern About/Support For/Participation In: Social Causes, Issues
    2.   Strategies For Bringing About Change
    3.   Use of Nonviolence In Bringing About Change
    4.   Essential Conditions For/Elements Of Change
    5.   Barriers to Change
    6.   Limitations of the CO's Contribution/Participation
    7.   Skepticism About Future

V. STRENGTH/CONTRIBUTION OF CO IDEA

A. Stand for Belief
    1.   Preservation of Ideals, Principles
    2.   Keeps Positive and Negative Ways Alive
    3.   Can Make a Difference
    4.   Example of Alternative to War, Violence
    5.   Speaking, Acting Without Concern for Popular Acceptance

B. Opposing War, Violence
    1.   Alternatives to Violence/Power of Nonviolence
    2.   Absurdity/Cruelty/Horror/Evil of War
    3.   Results of Violence

C. Sources of Creative Relationships, Conciliation
    1.   Psychological Preparation/Conditioning for Reducing Tensions,
        Bringing About Change
    2.   Settlement of Differences, Resolution of Conflict

D. Individual Integrity
    1.   Power of the Individual
    2.   Impact on Others

VI. ORIGINS/SOURCES OF CO BELIEFS

A. *Personality/Psyche*
   1.   Underlying Impulse, Temperament

B. *Belief Systems*
   1.   Beliefs Derived From Compelling Ideas, Philosophies
   2.   Beliefs Originated with Religious Precepts
   3.   Family Heritage
   4.   Beliefs Evolved and Expanded

VII. LIMITATIONS OF CO IDEAS/POSITION

A. *Overcoming Injustice/Evil/War*
   1.   Basic Limitations/Weakness In the Pacifist Rationale
   2.   Difficulty In Practicing Nonviolence
   3.   Strength of Other Ideas/Actions
   4.   Danger of Self-Righteousness
   5.   Peace Movement
   6.   Lack of Force/Acceptance of CO Ideas/Position

B. *Self-Doubt*

VIII. MODERATION OF CO POSITION/IDEAS

IX. RATIONALE FOR CO POSITION

X. CREDO OF PACIFIST POSITION

XI. SOCIAL PERCEPTIONS OF THE CO

XII. ACCEPTANCE OF PACIFIST BELIEF

XIII. IMPACT OF SOCIETY ON COS

A. *Acceptance/Rejection*
B. *"Blunting" the Message/Testimony*

XIV. COMPARABILITY OF CO EXPERIENCE/MILITARY SERVICE

BIBLIOGRAPHY

CONSCIENTIOUS OBJECTION

American Friends Service Committee. *The Experience of the American Friends Service Committee in Civilian Public Service.* Philadelphia: American Friends Service Committee, 1945.

Babin, Robert L. *The Conscientious Objector: A Study in Legal Efficacy.* Evanston IL: Northwestern University, 1967. Doctoral Dissertation.

Bender, Urie A. *Soldiers of Compassion.* Scottdale, PA: Herald Press, 1969.

Brubaker, John W. *Old German Baptists in Civilian Public Service.* West Alexandria, OH: John W. Brubaker, 1989.

Cornell, Julien D. *The Conscientious Objector and the Law.* Englewood, NJ: Jerome S. Ozer, Publisher, Inc., 1972.

Dasenbrock. J. Henry. *To the Beat of a Different Drummer.* Winona, MN: Northland Press, 1989.

Dick, Robert T., ed. *Guinea Pigs for Peace. The Story of CPS 115-R (1943-1946).* Windsor, VT: Annex Press, nd.

Eisan, Leslie. *Pathways of Peace: A History of the Civilian Public Service Program Administered by the Brethren Service Committee.* Elgin, IL: Brethren Publishing House, 1948.

Eller, Cynthia. *Conscientious Objectors and the Second World War. Moral and Religious Arguments in Support of Pacifism.* Westport, CT: Praeger Publishers, 1991.

Ewing, E. Keith. *The Pacifist Movement in the Methodist Church During World War II: A Study of Civilian Public Service Men in a Non-pacifist Church.* Boca Ratan, FL: Florida Atlantic University, 1982. (M.A. Thesis)

Finn, James, ed. *A Conflict of Loyalties: The Case for Selective Conscientious Objection.* New York: Pegasus, 1968.

Gaylin, Willard. *In the Service of Their Country: War Resisters in Prison.* New York: Grosset and Dunlap, 1970.

Gengerich, Melvin. *Service for Peace A History of Mennonite Civilian Public Service.* Akron, PA: The Mennonite Central Committee, 1949.

Graham, John W. *Conscription and Conscience: A History 1916-1919.* New York: Augustus M. Kelley Publishers, 1969.

Hassler, R. Alfred. *Conscripts of Conscience.* New York: Fellowship of Reconciliation, 1942.

Horton, Robert F. , Ron Martin-Adkins, Editor. *Profiles of Conscience: Stories and Statements of War Objectors.* Washington, DC: NISBCO, 1990.

Keim, Albert N. *The CPS Story: An Illustrated History of Civilian Public Service.* Intercourse, PA: Good Books, 1990.

Keim, Albert N. and Grant M. Stoltzfus. *The Politics of Conscience.* Scottdale, PA: Herald Press, 1988.

Kohn, Stephen M. *American Political Prisoners. Persecutions under the Espionage and Sedition Acts.* New York: Praeger Publishers, 1994.

Kohn, Stephen M. *Jailed For Peace. The History of American Draft Law Violators, 1658-1985.* Westport, CT: Greenwood Press, 1986.

Lynd, Alice. *We Won't Go: Personal Accounts of War Objectors.* Boston: Beacon Press, 1968.

Mayer, Peter. *The Pacifist Conscience.* New York: Holt, Reinhart, and Winston, 1966.

McNeal, Patricia. "Catholic Conscientious Objection During World War II", *The Catholic Historical Review* 61 (April, 1975): 222-242.

Mitchell, Hobart. *We Would Not Kill.* Richmond, Indiana: Friends United Press, 1983.

Moskos, Charles C. and John Whiteclay Chambers, eds. *The New Conscientious Objectors, From Sacred to Secular Resistance.* New York: Oxford University Press, 1993.

Naeve, Lowell. *A Field of Broken Stones.* Glen Gardner, NJ: Libertarian Press, 1950. [Also Denver, CO: Alan Swallow,1959.]

Nunnally, Joe. *I Was A Conscientious Objector: In Camp - In Prison - On Parole.* Berkeley: Sooner Publishing Company, 1948.

Olmstead, Frank. *They Asked for a Hard Job: CO's at Work in Mental Hospitals.* New York: Plowshare Press, 1943.

Peck, James. *We Who Would Not Kill.* New York: Lyle Stuart, 1958.

Peterson, H. C. and Gilbert C. Fite. *Opponents of War, 1917-1918.* Madison: University of Wisconsin Press, 1957.

Reeves, George B. *Men Against the State.* Washington, DC: Human Events, Inc., 1946.

Robinson, Mitchell Lee. *Civilian Public Service During World II: The Dilemmas of Conscience and Conscription in a Free Society.* Ann Arbor, Michigan: U.M.I., 1990.

Rohr, John Anthony. *Prophets Without Honor: Public Policy and the Selective Conscientious Objector.* New York: Abingdon Press, 1971.

Schlissel, Lilian, ed. *Conscience in America: A Documentary History of Conscientious Objection in America, 1757-1967.* New York: E.P. Dutton, 1968.

Sibley, Mulford Q. and Philip E. Jacob. *Conscription of Conscience: The American State and the Conscientious Objector, 1940-1947.* Ithaca, NY: Cornell University Press, 1952.

Stafford, William, *Down In My Heart.* Elgin, IL: Brethren Publishing House, 1947.

Stucky, Solomon. *For Conscience' Sake.* Scottdale, PA: Herald Press, 1983.

Swalm, Ernest J. *Nonresistance Under Test: Conscientious Objectors in Two Wars.* Nappanee, IN: Evangel Press, 1949.

VanDyck, Harry R. *Exercise of Conscience. A WW II Objector Remembers.* Buffalo, NY: Prometheus Books, 1990.

Wagler, David and Roman Raber. *The Story of the Amish in Civilian Public Service.* North Newton, KS: Bethel Press, 1945.

Waring, Thomas. *Something for Peace.* Hanover, NH: Waring, 1989.

Wilhelm, Paul A. *Civilian Public Service. A Report on 210 World War Conscientious Objectors.* Washington, DC: NISBCO, 1990.

Wilson, Adrian. Edited and with Commentary by Joyce Lancaster Wilson. *Two Against The Tide.* Austin: W. Thomas Taylor, 1990.

Wright, Edward Needles. *Conscientious Objectors in the Civil War.* New York: A. Barnes & Co, Inc., 1931.

Zahn, Gordon C. *Another Part of the War.* Amherst, MA: The University of Massachusetts Press, 1979.

CONSEQUENCES OF WAR

Davidson, Bill. "Why Half Our Combat Soldiers Fail to Shoot", in *Colliers*. 130:16-18, November 8, 1952.

Hartigan, Richard Shelly. *The Forgotten Victim: A History of the Civilian*. Chicago: Precedent Pub., 1982.

Marshall, S.L.A.. *Men Against Fire: The Problem of Battle Command in Future War*. New York: Morrow, 1947.

Polenberg, Richard. *War and Society. The United States 1941-1945*. Philadelphia: J. P. Lippincott Company, 1972.

THE "GOOD WAR"

Berg, Sigval M., et. al. *Peace and the Just War Tradition: Luther Perspectives in the Nuclear Age*. St. Louis: Concordia Publishing House, 1986.

Jersild, Paul. "On the Viability of the Just War Theory", in *Peace and the Just War Tradition*. St. Louis: Concordia Publishing House, 1986.

Johnson, James Turner. *Can Modern War Be Just?* New Haven: Yale University Press, 1984.

Johnson, James Turner and John Kelsay, eds. *Cross, Crescent, and Sword: The Justification and Limitations of War in Western and Islamic Tradition*. New York: Greenwood Press, 1990.

Johnson, James Turner. *Just War Tradition and the Restraint of War. A Moral and Historical Inquiry*. Princeton: Princeton University Press, 1981.

Miller, Richard Brian. *Interpretations of Conflict: Ethics, Pacifism, and the Just War Tradition*. Chicago: University of Chicago Press, 1991.

O'Brien, William V. *The Conduct of Just and Limited War*. New York: Praeger Publishers, 1981.

Ramsey, Paul. *The Just War. Force and Political Responsibility*. New York: Charles Scribner's Sons, 1968.

310 Bibliography

Russell, Frederick H. *The Just War in the Middle Ages.* Cambridge, New York: Cambridge University Press, 1975.

Teichman, Jenny. *Pacifism and the Just War: A Study in Applied Philosophy.* New York: Basil Blackwell, Ltd., 1986.

Terkel, Studs. *"The Good War" An Oral History of World War Two.* New York: Pantheon Books, 1984.

Tucker, Robert W. *The Just War A Study in Contemporary American Doctrine.* Baltimore: The Johns Hopkins Press, 1960.

PACIFISM — PACIFIST BELIEF AND ACTION

Baskir, Lawrence M. and William A. Strauss. *Chance and Circumstance: The Draft, the War and the Vietnam Generation.* New York: Alfred A. Knopf, Inc., 1978.

Brock, Peter. *Pacifism in the United States—From the Colonial Era to the First World War.* Princeton: Princeton University Press, 1968.

Brock, Peter. *Twentieth-Century Pacifism.* New York: Van Nostrand Reinhold Company, 1970.

Cady, Duane L. *From Warism to Pacifism: A Moral Continuum.* Philadelphia: Temple University Press, 1989.

Carsten, F. L. *War Against War: British and German Radical Movements in the First World War.* Berkeley: University of California Press, 1982.

Crum, Richard H. *Rethinking History. The War-Myth from Pericles to Roosevelt with Other Historical Studies.* Ontario, Canada: Vesta Publications Ltd, 1991.

DeBenedetti, Charles and Charles Chatfield. *An American Ordeal: The Antiwar Movement of the Vietnam Era.* Syracuse, NY: Syracuse University Press, 1990.

DeConinck, Therese, ed. *Essays on Nonviolence.* New York, Fellowship of Reconciliation, 1985.

Dellinger, David. *From Yale to Jail The Life Story of a Moral Dissenter.* New York: Pantheon Books, 1993.

Delp, Paul S. *Path to Peace.* Orange, CA: A Chapman College Publication, 1986.

Duke of Bedford. *Straight Speaking from a Pacifist to a Militarist.* Brooklyn, NY: Revisionist Press, 1982.

Dyck, Peter and Elfrieda. *Up From The Rubble.* Scottdale, PA: Herald Press, 1991.

Fry, A. Ruth, Jenny Goodwin, eds. *Victories Without Violence.* Santa Fe, NM: Ocean Tree Books, 1986.

Gibbs, Christopher C. *The Great Silent Majority. Missouri's Resistance to World War I.* Columbia, MO: University of Missouri Press, 1988.

Gregg, Richard B. *The Power of Nonviolence.* Canton, ME: Greenleaf Books, 1984.

Harris, Ted. *Jeannette Rankin: Suffragist, First Woman Elected to Congress and Pacifist.* Salem, NH: Ayer Company Publishers, Inc.,

Heath, Louis G., ed. *Mutiny Does Not Happen Lightly: The Literature of the American Resistance to the Vietnam War.* Metuchen, NJ: Scarecrow Press, Inc., 1976

Kohn, Stephen M. *Jailed for Peace. The History of American Draft Law Violators,* 1658-1985. Westport, CT: Greenwood Press, 1986.

Lynd, Staughton, ed. *Nonviolence in America: A Documentary History.* New York: Bobbs, Merrill Company, Inc., 1966.

Mason, Rae. *The Inimitable George Mason.* Centralia, WN: Privately Published, 1991.

Muste, A. J. *Nonviolence in an Aggressive World.* New York: Harper, 1972.

Nelson, John K. *The Peace Prophets: American Pacifist Thought, 1919-1941.* Chapel Hill, NC: University of North Carolina Press, 1967.

Rings, Werner. *Life with the Enemy: Collaboration and Resistance in Hitler's Europe 1939-1945.* New York: Doubleday, 1982.

Robinson, Jo Ann. *A. J. Muste: Pacifist and Prophet.* Wallingford, PA: Pendle Hill Publications, 1981.

Rothfels, Hans. *The German Opposition to Hitler. An Appraisal.* Chicago: Henry Regnery Company, 1962.

Sareyan, Alex. *Turning Point.* Washington, DC: American Psychiatric Press, 1993.

Seeley, Robert A. *The Handbook of Nonviolence.* Westport, CT: Lawrence Hill & Company, 1986.

Sharp, Gene and Marina Finkelstein, eds. *The Politics of Nonviolent Action.* Boston: Porter Sargent Publishers, Inc., 1974.

Stiehm, Judith. *Nonviolent Power.* Lexington, MA: Heath, 1972.

Van der Dungen, Peter, ed. *West European Pacifism and the Strategy for Peace.* New York: Saint Martin's Press, 1985.

Vellscott, Jo. *Bertrand Russell and the Pacifists in the First World War.* New York: Saint Martin's Press, 1981.

Weber, David. *Civil Disobedience in America.* Ithaca, NY: Cornell University Press, 1978.

Wittner, Lawrence S. *Rebels Against War: The American Peace Movement, 1933-1983.* Philadelphia: Temple University Press, 1984.

Yoder, John H. *What Would You Do? A Serious Answer to a Standard Question.* Scottdale, PA: Herald Press, 1983.

Zahn, Gordon C. *In Solitary Witness: The Life and Death of Franz Jägerstätter.* Springfield, IL: Templegate Publishers, 1964.

Zahn, Gordon C. *German Catholics and Hitler's Wars. A Study in Social Control.* Notre Dame: University of Notre Dame Press, 1962.

PEACE, WAR, AND RELIGION

Bainton, Roland H. *Christian Attitudes Toward War and Peace. A Historical Survey and Critical Re-evaluation.* New York: Abingdon Press, 1960.

Bowman, Rufus D. *The Church of the Brethren and War.* New York: Garland, 1971.

Brown, Dale W. *Biblical Pacifism: A Peace Church Perspective.* Elgin, Ill.: Brethren Press, 1985.

Brown, Dale W. *Brethren and Pacifism.* Elgin, IL: Brethren Press, 1970.

Cadoux, C. J. *The Early Christian Attitude to War.* London: Headley Bros., Publishers, 1919.

Dyer, Gwynne. *War.* New York: Crown Publishers, Inc., 1985.

Forest, James H. *Catholics and the Conscientious Objector.* New York: Catholic Peace Fellowship, 1981.

Hirst, Margaret E. *The Quakers in Peace and War: An Account of Their Peace Principles and Practice.* Englewood, NJ: Jerome S. Ozer, Publisher, Inc., 1972.

Karp, Walter. *The Politics of War.* New York: Harper and Row, 1979.

Nathan, Otto and Heinz Norden. *Einstein on Peace.* New York: Avenal Books, 1960, 1981.

O'Gorman, Angie, ed. *The Universe Bends Toward Justice: A Reader on Christian Nonviolence in the U.S.* Philadelphia: New Society Publishers, 1990.

Orser, W. Edward. "World War II and the Pacifist Controversy in the Major Protestant Churches", *American Studies*. 14 (Fall, 1973): 5-24.

Hershberger, Guy. *The Mennonite Church in World War II*. Scottdale, PA: Mennonite Publishing House, 1951.

Hershberger, Guy. *War, Peace, and Nonresistance*. Scottdale, PA: Herald Press, 1953.

Horsch, John. *The Principle of Non-resistance as Held by the Mennonite Church*. Scottdale, PA: Mennonite Publishing House, 1940.

Marrin, Albert, ed. *War and the Christian Conscience: From Augustine to Martin Luther King, Jr.*, Chicago: Henry Regnery Company, 1971.

Nuttall, Geoffrey. *Christian Pacifism in History*. Berkeley: World Without War Council, 1971.

Roop, John D. and Daniel C. Moomaw, eds. *Christianity versus War*. Ashland, OH: Brethren Publishing Company, 1949.

Wells, R., ed. *The Wars of America: Christian Views*. Grand Rapids, MI: William R. Eerdmans, 1981.

Index